Introducing
CANADA

Content Backgrounders, Strategies, and Resources for Educators

edited by
William W. Joyce
and Richard Beach

Published by
National Council for the Social Studies
in association with
National Consortium for Teaching Canada

NCSS
Bulletin
94

Editorial staff on this publication: *Michael Simpson, Terri Ackerman, Melissa Spead, Rainey Tisdale*
Editorial services provided by *Lynn Page Whittaker, Charles River Press*
Art Director/Production Manager: *Gene Cowan*
Cover design: *George Sherman*

Library of Congress Catalog Card Number: 97-075637
ISBN 0-87986-075-8

Printed in the United States of America

10 9 8 7 6 5 4 3 2 1

Contents

Acknowledgments

We wish to acknowledge and thank Dr. Norman London, Chief Academic Relations Officer at the Canadian Embassy in Washington, D.C., who recently retired, for his longstanding support and encouragement of the National Consortium for Teaching Canada since its inception; and Lois Bouvier, senior secretary at the Center for the Study of Canada at the State University of New York, Plattsburgh, for her assistance over many months with the preparation of this book.

William W. Joyce
Richard Beach

Foreword

The National Consortium for Teaching Canada (NCTC) was founded in 1988 by a group of academics who believe wholeheartedly in the importance of a professional outreach organization dedicated to helping teachers gain an understanding of Canada. Today, the NCTC is comprised of thirteen college and university Canadian studies programs throughout the United States. The NCTC's mission is to capture the imagination and attention of K-12 teachers, students, media-resource specialists, businesspeople, and the general public by communicating to those audiences the most recent research, themes, and ideas about Canada and its place in the world.

Introducing Canada is made possible by the generous contributions of Bridgewater State College, Michigan State University, the State University of New York at Plattsburgh, the University of Maine, the University of Vermont, the University of Washington, and Western Washington University. Its precursor was the 1985 *Canada in the Classroom*, edited by William W. Joyce and published by National Council for the Social Studies. Because that publication is now dated, the NCTC decided to write a new book representing the latest insights and trends concerning Canada and that country's role and relations in the world. *Introducing Canada* also offers innovative suggestions about how to incorporate Canada into the social studies.

Since the publication of *Canada and the Classroom* in 1985 and the founding of the NCTC in 1988, our organization has maintained a close relationship with NCSS. That role has expanded to include regular participation by the NCTC in the annual NCSS conference and the creation of the NCSS Special Interest Group (SIG) on Teaching Canada.

The National Consortium for Teaching Canada, in cooperation with National Council for the Social Studies, takes great pleasure in making available *Introducing Canada*.

Michael S. Bittner
Past Chair, Board of Directors
National Consortium for
Teaching Canada

Introduction

William Joyce of Michigan State University and Richard Beach of SUNY Plattsburgh, coeditors of this publication, engaged a galaxy of excellent writers and skilled educators to bring their special insights to the large canvas of the Canadian entity. *Introducing Canada* lives up to its title: It is more than a textual update of the earlier basic and popular *Canada in the Classroom*. The authors bring clarity to Canada's present role in the new world order, its trade and economic dimensions, and the intricacies of its history and multicultural heritage. And at long last, the professional needs of teachers are turned to the social studies structures within which they work. There are chapters discussing modes of social studies instruction, resources for learning and teaching, and the use of films and videos, as well as new technologies, in the classroom. Finally, the inclusion of a section of well-designed student activities provides a reward and a springboard for teachers interested in sharing with students their knowledge of our neighbor to the north.

PART 1. CANADIAN ISSUES

In Chapter 1, Professor Victor Howard masterfully provides "a sketch of the major factors and features in the history of Canada" from the time of its earliest European settlers to the present day. There is considerable discussion about nationalism in Canada and, in particular, in the Province of Quebec. Although the major thrust of the chapter concerns the historical role of the French and British in the development of Canada, there is also reference to the country's ethnic diversity and multiculturalism.

Professor Michael J. Broadway, in Chapter 2, presents the geography of the second largest country in the world by region: Atlantic Canada, Great Lakes-St. Lawrence Lowlands, The Western Interior, British Columbia and the North. His thorough commentary on each region underscores both the physical and cultural aspects of Canada's geography, with detailed attention paid to such matters as landforms, climate, resources, industry and its peoples.

In his discussion of Canadian Government and Politics, George Sherman is mindful of the "important caveat that the Canadian confederation today...is very much a work in progress." In addition to tracing Canada's constitutional origins to present day realities, in Chapter 3 Sherman provides a clear and concise description of the country's political parties, its parliament and the role of the monarch.

In their examination of Canada's relationship to the world beyond its borders in Chapter 4, Professors Donald K. Alper and Matthew Sparke comment on multilateral cooperation and Canada's commitment to peace-keeping, and on the special relationship our northern neighbor has maintained with the U.S. Special attention is paid to Canada and the Pacific.

In Chapter 5 on The Canadian Economy, Anthony Cicerone and Mark Kasoff use a comparative approach in analyzing the similarities and differences of the Canadian and U.S. economies. They clearly illustrate the evolution of Canada's economy and pay significant attention to the country's international trade, the role of government, foreign investment and regional disparities.

William Metcalfe's chapter on Canadian Culture leads the reader through a thoughtful and thought-provoking discussion of Canada's "differentness" from the U.S. In creative prose, Professor Metcalfe helps us to appreciate the accomplishments of many Canadian artists, but more importantly, his chapter provides a fascinating perception of Canada's complex and diverse character.

Special attention is paid to Canada's only officially French-speaking province, Quebec, by Professor Richard Beach in Chapter 7, where he succinctly presents Quebec in modern times, from the political unrest which expressed itself during the Quiet Revolution of the 1960s to the special economic complexities facing the province today. Nor does he overlook the important questions of ethnic diversity, language, and education in this chapter dealing with the "unique character of Quebec."

PART 2. CURRICULAR AND INSTRUCTIONAL ISSUES

Particularly useful to the teacher is Professor William Joyce's chapter, "Canada Within the Social Studies," which discusses rationales for studying Canada, problems with textbooks and Canada's position in the curriculum. In a sense, Dr. Joyce illustrates how Canada has been neglected in the U.S. social studies curricula and he offers significant contributions about why this should be rectified. It is hoped that this publication, inspired by Professor Joyce, is part of the "how" Canada can be better known and understood in our country.

Useful suggestions abound in Chapter 9, "Instructional Activities," by Janet Alleman, who provides teachers with meaningful, stimulating and cost effective activities. Detailed activities for Chapters 1-7 "incorporate the 10 themes that serve as organizing strands for the social studies in the NCSS Curriculum Standards":

❶ CULTURE
❷ TIME, CONTINUITY AND CHANGE
❸ PEOPLE, PLACES AND ENVIRONMENTS
❹ INDIVIDUAL DEVELOPMENT AND IDENTITY
❺ INDIVIDUALS, GROUPS AND INSTITUTIONS
❻ POWER, AUTHORITY AND GOVERNANCE
❼ PRODUCTION, DISTRIBUTION AND CONSUMPTION
❽ SCIENCE, TECHNOLOGY AND SOCIETY
❾ GLOBAL CONNECTIONS
❿ CIVIC IDEALS AND PRACTICES

Gail Yvon's many years of "hands on" experience as a workshop leader and outreach coordinator serve the profession well in Chapter 10, "Resources for Learning and Teaching About Canada." The chapter contains a wealth of information and references which will greatly assist teachers to prepare lessons on Canada. Particularly useful is a list of resource addresses at the end of the chapter.

Chapter 11, "Technology in the Classroom," by Matthew Smith and John Preston, is another valuable chapter. In addition to useful website addresses, the chapter offers a helpful annotated list of titles of films and videos for students in grades K-12, as well as information about the availability of CD-ROMs.

The scope and tone of *Introducing Canada* make it equally useful for social studies workshops, other in-service activities, Canadian Studies courses and a variety of specific disciplines. Canada is an enigma to many Americans because of the lack of attention to the country in newspapers and magazines. The education community must be provided with more information, better materials and far more insight into the history and vitality of the Canadian presence. Only then can we expand understanding and appreciation between our two nations. This carefully and thoughtfully assembled book is a gift from Canadianists of today to students and teachers of tomorrow.

Jeanne Kissner and Marion Salinger

ICELAND

GREENLAND
(DENMARK)

Baffin Bay

Baffin
Island

Labrador Sea

Newfoundland

James
Bay

Quebec

St. John's

P.E.I.

Sydney

New
Brunswick

Charlottetown

Quebec

Fredericton

Halifax

Montreal

Nova Scotia

St. Lawrence River

Ottawa

on

Toronto

Lake Ontario

Atlantic
Ocean

Lake Erie

Canada

★ Provincial/Territorial Capital

✪ National Capital

• City

── International Boundary

── Provincial Boundary

Quebec Province Name

500 km

0   500 Miles

Chapter 1
An Introduction to the History Of Canada
Victor Howard

Educators and students viewing the history of Canada from the perspective of the United States will find similarities between the development of these neighbors, yet many striking and crucial differences as well. While the two share the experiences of accommodating great numbers of immigrants, a westward expansion, and a democratic political and social ethic, Canada and the United States have lived these experiences in different ways and with different results.

FIRST PEOPLES, FIRST SETTLEMENTS

The first human inhabitants of the area now known as Canada migrated in waves from Asia across the Bering Strait and, largely because of the geographical conditions of the areas in which they settled, evolved into numerous distinct tribes. Estimating their number in those centuries of unrecorded history is difficult, and the estimates that exist are often debated and revised as new anthropological evidence is discovered. Most sources, however, posit that there were between one and two million Natives in North America above Mexico in the late fifteenth century when Europeans began arriving, and something like 200,000 Natives and Inuit (Eskimo) in the region that was to become Canada. Tribes varied widely from the Kwakiutl (who lived along the Pacific coast, subsisting on salmon, sea and land mammals, and wild fruits, with arts including weaving, basketry, and totem poles) to the Blackfeet (nomads in the mid-continent who hunted buffalo for food, clothing, and tipis and whose culture was characterized by warrior clans, the Sun Dance, and bead and feather artwork) to the Montagnais (nomadic hunters in the semiarctic far north who followed caribou migrations and centered their religious culture on the shaman).

Although Norse sailors found their way to the eastern shores of North America between 1000 and 1400 A.D., the real exploration of that landscape which we now call Canada did not begin until 1497, when John Cabot came ashore onto Newfoundland and Cape Breton Island. In the first quarter of the sixteenth century, these regions were visited by Spanish, Italian, French, Portuguese, and English mariners who fished, stole Indian slaves, charted coastlines and went home to Europe. Jacques Cartier, a Frenchman, ventured up the great river of St. Lawrence in 1535 as far as present-day Montreal. By 1600, all competing interests from Europe had been discouraged, and France could now extend its imperial design onto the continent, calling it "New France."

The first permanent French settlement was established in 1608 at Quebec

City by Samuel de Champlain, explorer, cartographer, and agent of the French crown. Champlain brought with him three ambitions: 1) the discovery of a route to China and the East Indies; 2) the development of a fur trade with the aborigines, particularly the beaver pelt so much in demand in Europe; and 3) the conversion of the Indians to Roman Catholicism.

Champlain and his followers soon realized that, by settling along the St. Lawrence Valley, they had at their disposal a remarkable water highway into the interior of the continent. While colonists to the south had struggled across the forests and mountains until they reached the Ohio River, the French thrived along a lake and river system that led directly westward for thousands of miles. And the country to be crossed was rich in furs. The trade was risky and involved regular struggles with the Indians, but it was a profitable enterprise and played a major role in sustaining the French colony for two centuries. Moreover, the search for fur took the French into the Great Lakes Basin and south along the Mississippi River.

Jesuit missionaries arrived not only as priests but as guides, interpreters, explorers, diplomats, and recorders of an extraordinary era. As early as the 1630s, when the Puritans were founding their "City on the Hill" in New England, Father Jean de Brébeuf had already established a large mission among the Hurons far to the north and west.

However successful these initiatives were, the population of New France remained small. By 1670, little more than 8,000 French lived there. A century later, mainly through natural increase rather than immigration, that figure had risen to 70,000, most of whom were *habitants* or farm workers employed on lands owned by an aristocratic class called *seigneurs*. It is from these 70,000 that the several million French Canadians of our time are descended.

From 1690 to 1759, the French were involved in a series of wars with England and her American colonies as the two powers fought for control of North America. The French believed that the British were moving illegally into the Ohio and Mississippi valleys, where they had no right to be since those regions had first been traveled by French explorers. With Indian allies on both sides, these two European allies attacked and counterattacked along, above, and below the Great Lakes. The flaw in the French enterprise, however, was that nearly all of its supplies, reinforcements, and communications came into the continent through the fortress city of Quebec, overlooking the St. Lawrence River. The British therefore set out to capture Quebec City, which they did in 1759 when an expedition lay siege to the town and its citadel, and, in a final assault, won the day and—for a time—the continent.

In 1774, the British Parliament proclaimed the Quebec Act, which extended the boundaries of New France west and south, recognized the seigneurial system, retained French civil law and the Roman Catholic church, and appointed a legislative council comprised of French and English members directed by a governor. Thus the French presence in Canada was sanctioned by the British and allowed to continue. Nonetheless, New France

The *voyageurs* were the "water dogs" of the French fur trade during the 17th and 18th centuries, living adventurous but extremely challenging lives in the exotic North American wilderness.
National Archives of Canada (C-002774)

had become British North America.

In 1782, the British, having lost the American War of Independence, were forced to withdraw from their great empire south of the Great Lakes and the St. Lawrence just as the French had a generation before. The Canada Act of 1791, promulgated by the British government, divided the region it could now claim into two provinces: Upper Canada, now Ontario, and Lower Canada, now Quebec. British North America profited from the arrival of some 40,000 "United Empire Loyalists," refugees who fled the young United States, bearing their loyalty to English rule and law to Canada. These loyalists would thereafter be a prominent element in the population of Canada, in both reality and symbol, a vivid reminder of the historical link with Great Britain.

BRITISH NORTH AMERICA

Life in Canada in the early nineteenth-century was very much a frontier existence: great stretches of sparsely populated terrain; wretched roads; poor postal systems; few schools and churches; and marginal income from farming, lumbering, and fishing. Moreover, the lapsed fashion of beaver hats and capes in Europe ruined that trade. Nonetheless, more settlers arrived from Germany, Ireland, England, Scotland, and from the United States for that matter, to make their homes in Nova Scotia, New Brunswick, and Upper and Lower Canada.

The French and the English, while living side by side, argued constantly and furiously over language priorities, immigration policies, finances, and governmental controls. The War of 1812 briefly thrust these issues into the background as Canadians joined with British military forces in combat against the United States. President James Madison had declared war in a vague effort not only to prevent the British navy from compromising the freedom of the seas but also to extend the concept of Manifest Destiny west and north into the continent. The conflict sprawled along such scattered fronts as Michigan, Niagara, Lake Erie, Lake Ontario, New York, and Washington, D.C. It produced such legends as Laura Secord, a Canadian girl who overheard American officers planning an attack, and who then walked nearly twenty miles to deliver the information to her compatriots. After two years of weary jousting, Britain and the United States accepted the Treaty of Ghent, which effectively restored captured territories to their original owners. The American principle and dream of Manifest Destiny received a severe rebuke.

In the second quarter of the nineteenth century, roads, canals, and railways began to unite the regions; Montreal, Quebec City, and York (later Toronto) grew into active commercial towns; secondary industries such as pulp, flour, and ship construction flourished; several colleges and universities were launched. Most important, perhaps, the quest for "responsible government" gained momentum among English and French alike, particularly during and after the Rebellion of 1837 led by two patriots, William Lyon Mackenzie in Upper Canada and Louis Joseph Papineau in Lower Canada. British rule seemed so autocratic to these two men that they led several hundred other dissenters into the streets, only to be quickly overwhelmed by government troops. But the incident sufficiently alarmed Parliament that it dispatched a senior member of the aristocracy, Lord Durham, to restore order. In his report, however, Durham recommended the union of Upper and Lower Canada and the creation of "responsible government"—i.e., that the Executive Council be made responsible to the Legislative Assembly and not to the Governor. While the Act of Union of 1841 created the United Province of Canada, popular rule was not forthcoming until 1848. That same year, Nova Scotia secured self-determination, with New Brunswick following in 1854, Newfoundland in 1855, and Prince Edward Island in 1862.

Meanwhile, Canadians continued to push westward to the Pacific in search of water routes and territory. Two mighty commercial ventures, the Hudson's Bay Company and the North West Company, threw their outposts across the Prairies, into the Rockies, and beyond. Among the recruits to the North West Company was Alexander Mackenzie, the first European to cross the continent. James Frobisher and Simon Fraser gave their names to the waterways they explored. And if the population and authority of the Canadian Pacific coast could scarcely be said to equal that of the Atlantic, it could and did respond when, in the 1840s, the Oregon boundary dispute erupted. The Oregon Territory between California and Alaska had been jointly occupied by American citizens and the English, but when Yankee settlers called for including the area in the United States, James K. Polk, candidate for the American presidency, took as his slogan "54-40 or Fight!" That is, the United States wanted the northern boundary of the Oregon Territory to be set at latitude 54°40' whereas the British wanted it roughly along the 45th parallel. A compromise reached in 1846 set the 49th parallel as the permanent international line between Canada and the United States. In time, this would come to be called the world's longest undefended border.

Tensions continued to ease during the 1850s, once the two nations agreed on a reciprocal trade relationship. Although the agreement was canceled by the United States in 1866, it was evident that trade was inevitable and worthwhile.

Canada's relationship to the United States during the American Civil War was curious. By virtue of their points of contact and associations with northern states, Canadians favored the Union even though Great Britain favored the confederacy. One small band of Southern raiders moved from a Canadian hideout to attack St. Albans, Vermont, the only assault of its kind during the war. On the other hand, thousands of Canadians served with the Union army. And, as we know, the "underground railway" had already taken many escaping slaves into Canada. Their descendants form one of the enduring keystones of the black population of Canada today.

At the end of the Civil War, Canadian leaders faced both new and continuing concerns. They feared that the Americans would again cancel the trade reciprocity agreement, they were anxious about the prospect of American Manifest Destiny, they were concerned about Britain's reluctance to ensure the military defense of its colony, and they had determined the need for a greatly expanded railway system east and west. Consequently, Canadian statesmen led by Georges Etienne Cartier and John A. Macdonald, "the fathers of Confederation," began to forge the means by which nationhood could be secured. The strategy of "Federation" was seized upon as the most appropriate for numerous regions of Canada. A strong central government would still appreciate the need of Canada's regions, soon called "provinces," to have a considerable degree of autonomy.

On July 1, 1867, the British Parliament proclaimed the British North America Act, by which the Dominion of Canada, comprised of Ontario, Quebec, New Brunswick, and Nova Scotia, came into existence. Delegates would be elected to a House of Commons, but appointed to the Senate. A prime minister would lead the country in consultation with a cabinet which was responsible to the House of Commons. The provinces would tax, borrow money, maintain prisons and schools, license shops, assign property, and oversee civil rights. The federal government would look after such matters as legal tender, weights and measures, criminal law, the military, postal services, the public debt, and foreign policy.

The first prime minister, John A. MacDonald, proposed a "National Policy," a grand plan that spoke of unity, and progress, and reassurance. Tariffs on imports would be raised. A transcontinental railroad would be built. An aggressive immigration policy would be set in motion. Extensive territories were brought into Canada's orbit: the Northwest Territories in 1868, and Manitoba and British Columbia as provinces in the early 1870s. Security in these distant regions was assured by the creation in 1873 of the Northwest Mounted Police (now the Royal Canadian Mounted Police).

The peaceful momentum was soon disrupted by a rebellion of the Metis people in Manitoba. Descended from French settlers who had married Indian women, the Métis feared for their hunting grounds, their Roman Catholic faith, and their traditional freedom. Led by a flamboyant patriot named Louis Riel, the Métis launched an insurrection in 1869 that continued intermittently for the next two years. In 1875, Riel was declared an outlaw, and he moved to the United States for several years. But, in 1884, he accepted an invitation by English settlers and the Métis to assist in the redress of their grievances against the government. Out of this came the short-lived Northwest Rebellion, a series of skirmishes between Métis and federal troops. When the rebellion collapsed, Riel surrendered, was tried and convicted of murder, and died on the gallows in November 1885. Even so, he found a martyrdom unmatched to this day in Canada. Québécois, in particular, found in him a hero who resisted English control and upheld the Catholic church.

Prime Minister Macdonald's dream of a transnational railroad came true in 1885. That achievement brought hundreds of thousands of new citizens from Europe, Great Britain, Russia, and the United States. The grand design populated the western or prairie provinces where millions of acres of arable land waited for the plow. Called "homesteaders," these new Canadians contributed energy, imagination, and dedication to the settlement of that region, and, because they were encouraged to retain their original ethnic associations, they furnished an exotic cultural mosaic that persists to this day.

One important aspect of the "winning of the west" in Canadian history was that it was quite unlike the American experience. Whereas thousands upon thousands of American citizens trekked to Oregon and California between 1840 and 1860 and thousands more followed after the Civil War as the railroads came through, the overland march in Canada occurred essentially near the end of the nineteenth century by railroad. Canadians have not given this settlement the mythic dimension that the United States has

Early in the 20th century, the Canadian government used recruitment posters in many languages to attract settlers to "The Last, Best West."
National Archives of Canada (C-05218)

bestowed upon its own enterprise. No cowboys and Indians, no lean western heroes. Ironically, the Indians who overwhelmed Custer at the Battle of Little Big Horn found refuge in southern Saskatchewan. One of the few occasions when the Canadian West took on the aura of an American adventure was the gold rush at Dawson City in the 1890s which, in fact, prompted an international crisis over access from the Pacific Ocean to the interior.

Not all of the drama of the turn of the century took place in the west. Quebec faced the transition from agrarian to industrial life that had become a worldwide experience. The Québécois, by and large, lived in villages where families were large and interrelated. The local priest held considerable authority over secular as well as spiritual matters. Self-reliant economically, the villagers pursued a serene if isolated existence, their children seldom finding it necessary to attend more than a few years of school. Advanced or vocational education was almost unheard of except for the few determined to enter the priesthood or one of the professions. Within a few decades, this benevolent, somewhat authoritarian society would give way before the new demands of its citizens.

INTO THE TWENTIETH CENTURY

Canada entered the twentieth century confident and buoyant, a young nation with huge promise. The immigration program had worked. American Manifest Destiny had been permanently discouraged. Confederation had acquitted itself. By now it was apparent that the country's political destiny would be in the hands of two national parties, the Liberals and the Conservatives, although in a few years, these would be challenged by aggressive movements in the west and in Quebec.

Then came World War I. Following Great Britain's declaration of war against Germany in August 1914, Canada organized an expeditionary force which departed for Europe just two months later. Over 600,000 Canadians served in air, land, and naval units in the next four years. Sixty thousand died in action.

Military manpower was not the country's only contribution. Paradoxically, because she was so far from the battlefields and her natural resources were of such superb quality and quantity, Canada contributed greatly to the production of war materials and foodstuffs for the allies, incidentally affirming her capabilities as a modern industrial nation.

A unique crisis for Canada during the war years was the decision of the government, led by Robert Borden, to replenish the ranks of the services by conscription or the draft. Though late in coming, this policy nevertheless irritated the divisions between the French and the British Canadians, because the former did not really care to strengthen a commitment to the British Empire, which they did not wholly appreciate, or to the defense of another country, France, for whom they had no real sympathy. Many French Canadians did volunteer, but many more resented and rejected conscription.

However devastating the losses in Europe, however contentious the conscription dispute at home, Canada did earn a new stature in the British Empire and around the world. A Canadian Army Corps of several divisions led by Canadian officers won a distinct and honorable reputation. Billy Bishop, a fighter pilot, came away with the highest number of victories among the allied air forces. Prime Minister Borden was given a seat on the Imperial War Cabinet, just as each Dominion of the Empire took membership in the postwar League of Nations.

In the 1920s, the new Canadians began to make their presence felt as economic, laboring, and political forces in the western provinces. In 1919, a general strike in Winnipeg, inaccurately deemed by the federal government as "revolutionary," signaled a capacity for confrontation by workers that would never thereafter wane. Farmers pooled their resources and ambitions to purchase grain elevators and storage depots—in effect, an attempt to bypass the intransigent railroad monopolies that had previously directed the farmers' access to markets. Out of this particular reform movement emerged massive service and consumer cooperatives—the Saskatchewan Wheat Pool is an abiding example—which characterize the prairies to this day.

In foreign affairs under Prime Minister Arthur Meighen and William Lyon Mackenzie King, Canada, which as yet had no foreign office, began to assert its independence as a member of the British Commonwealth by creating a nine-member international commission which was intended to monitor Japanese ambitions in the Pacific and by withholding troops requested by Britain during a dispute between that nation and Turkey. The first treaty negotiated by Canada with another nation took place in 1923: with the United States, the subject being Pacific Coast fishing rights. By the end of the decade, the Department of External Affairs had been devised for the development and maintenance of Canadian foreign policy.

Progress but also frustration marked Quebec's gradual accommodation to the industrial age. Natural resources such as lumber and water power had to be exploited, but the need to rely on foreign investors established a pattern of "intervention" that would continue for decades. The Quebecois increasingly left their villages for life in the cities and towns, life that was often marked by sweatshops, crude domiciles, disintegration of the family, and dissipation of religious authority. Much of Quebec industry and commerce came under the management of British Canadians, who were better and more extensively educated for such careers.

The years that followed are called "The Dirty Thirties," and if they do not have quite the legendary status that they have in the United States, the economic and social catastrophes of the decade were still severe. The worst of it all fell on the Prairie Provinces, where a prolonged drought damaged an already failing wheat market, and the in Maritime Provinces, habitually impoverished in any case, where declining exports of fish and lumber proved devastating. Unemployment was the national tragedy.

Not unexpectedly, a growing chorus of demands was heard for political and economic reforms. By 1935, three new political parties had emerged with their respective programs: the Cooperative Commonwealth Federation, comprised largely of farmer-labor-socialist elements, which secured a national following and has maintained a presence in the House of Commons and in several provinces for sixty years; the Social Credit Party, located originally in Alberta where its conservative philosophy took hold for decades; and the Union Nationale, limited to Quebec and essentially conservative.

The general election of 1935 returned a liberal, William Lyon Mackenzie King, to tenure as Prime Minister. He would serve for the next thirteen years, setting in place a notable career for his party. It was King who took Canada into and through World War II. Once again, Canada mobilized, this time a million in arms. Once again, it dispatched air, land, and naval forces abroad, of whom 40,000 were killed in action including 10,000 air crew killed in the allied bomber offensive against Germany. Canada itself became a massive arsenal and granary for the allies. Among many contributions, it provided sites for the Commonwealth Air Training Command, which trained 150,000 airmen from around the Empire. The Prime Minister had his hands full with another conscription crisis although, as in World War I, only a handful of draftees were ever sent abroad. At the close of hostilities, for a brief time, Canada had become the fourth largest military power in the world. A year later, her forces had been reduced to less than 100,000.

Canadians emerged from World War II a more sophisticated people, their industrial capacities enhanced by the war effort, and their horizons extended by virtue of participation in a global conflict. The nation was now launched on a period of growth that would bring it to the point in the twenty-five years of one of the highest standards of living among modern nations. Along the way it would earn a nickname, the "Peaceable Kingdom."

AFTER WORLD WAR II

Four main themes characterized Canada in the postwar decades: 1) the relaxing of the Anglo-French monopoly in the population; 2) the emergence of Canada as an "honest broker" in world diplomacy; 3) Quebec's peaceful revolution in the 1960s; and 4) a growing nationalism among both Quebecois and English Canadians.

Whatever their feelings for one another, British and French Canadians view themselves as the "charter races" of Canada. In 1880, they were 90 percent of the population; in 1960, 74 percent. In the decade following the war, another million immigrants came to Canada, a quarter of them refugees from the catastrophe in Europe. Most immigrants chose to reside in urban centers. For example, by 1960, 88 percent of all Italians, 63 percent of all Poles, and 52 percent of all Russians lived in cities and towns, as did 66 percent of the British Canadians and 60 percent of the French Canadians. By then, less than half of the residents of Toronto were English in origin.

This considerable shift in ethnic composition raised questions about national unity and political power. The expression "mosaic" gained new meaning, as did "cultural pluralism." The country appeared increasingly willing to urge ethnic groups to perpetuate themselves while taking their part in Canadian life. John Diefenbaker, elected prime minister in the 1950s, was the first major government leader who was neither French nor English.

Though relatively inexperienced in the articulation of its own foreign policy, Canada moved firmly in those years to embrace the United Nations, to assist in the creation of the North Atlantic Treaty Organization, and to join with the Southeast Asia Treaty Organization. Its diplomats won laurels for being exceptionally temperate and inventive in the increasingly tense Cold War era. They earned for their country the accolade "honest broker," for by instinct, discipline, and intelligence, Canada was able to arbitrate international crises and to represent a neutral stance in the most difficult of circumstances. Following its participation in the Korean War in 1950-53, Canada did not engage in war until the Gulf conflict in 1991. Her soldiers and diplomats have observed wars and have patrolled the cease-fire zones of numerous battlegrounds. After the 1954 partition of North and South Vietnam, Canada provided delegates to an international team that monitored violations of the Geneva Accord which had sanctioned the division in the first place. Canadians have served as Peacekeepers in Cyprus, Lebanon, the Congo, Palestine, Egypt, and Yemen. In 1956, for his efforts to bring about a solution to the Suez Crisis created by a joint British-French invasion of that region, Lester Pearson, a senior diplomat and eventual prime minister, was awarded the Nobel Peace Prize.

At home, however, restlessness was growing in Quebec, where a wide-ranging social, economic and cultural movement, called then and now the "Quiet Revolution," began in 1960 following the death of Premier Maurice Duplessis whose long tenure as a political "boss" had greatly restricted the emotional and economic growth of that province. Though Quebec was considerably industrialized and urbanized, its managerial class continued to be British Canadian, its resources still controlled by foreign interests. The Liberal Party replaced Duplessis' National Union, formed in the 1930s, and launched a program of economic, political, and cultural enlightenment that found energy in the population's passion for being Quebecois.

The broad advance of this "revolution" was essentially peaceful, but there were those in the province who agitated for an immediate resolution to Quebec's status and for independence. The Front de Libération du Quebec, the FLQ, by 1963 had begun a campaign of terrorism that would kill several Quebecois and destroy millions of dollars in property. Though many Quebecois favored an independent status, the FLQ never won more than a few dozen actual members. Its reign of terror came to a close in 1970-71 with the arrest of two teams of FLQ who had kidnapped the British trade commissioner in Quebec and the provincial minister of labor, killing the latter. The federal government responded with the War Measures Act, which broke the FLQ and its supporters but angered many other Canadians because of its harsh implications for civil rights. All in all, it was a shattering experience for a nation which happily accepted its long heritage as the peaceable kingdom.

Despite this challenge, in 1967 Canadians threw themselves a charming birthday party to celebrate One Hundred Years of confederation. Communities and individuals devised projects and programs as gifts to the nation. Two of the best known were the Science Center in Toronto and Montreal's great Expo '67, which drew dozens of foreign entries with lavish pavilions that attracted over fifty million visitors who brought half a billion dollars in tourist revenue during the six months of the fair.

The Centennial Year commemorated Canada, but it did not exactly lay to rest a long-standing question raised by many citizens: What is a Canadian? The consequence was a social and political movement of sorts that came to be called the New Nationalism—a strong vocal popular effort to comprehend the history and character of the nation and to assert a pride in past achievements and the potential yet to be realized.

One might ask why Canadians, in the decade of the centennial anniversary, would conceive of a nationalistic spirit. Could the country not trace its history back over four hundred years? Had it not made enormous gains since confederation in its genteel pursuit of autonomy within the Commonwealth? Was it not a nation whose standard of living was one of the highest in the world?

The reasons for the New Nationalism and search for identity included the following. First, a long-standing confusion existed between the two Charter groups about their respective debts to the mother countries, England and France. French Canadians felt little real connection with France because France had done little until this time for its "family" across the ocean. The British Canadians were still cognizant of the allegiance to the Crown and the Commonwealth, but the real contact with these institutions on a day-to-day basis was relatively slight, given that many Canadians were Anglo by heritage. The growing presence of citizens of neither French nor English extraction did little to ease the confusion.

Second, the influence in Canada of the many interests of the United States had become overwhelming and overbearing, though how or whether to break away were challenges for which there seemed to be too few solutions. The import-export traffic across the border was enormous; each nation was the other's favorite customer. A growing chorus objected to the Americanization of Canadian culture by television, books, films, and magazines, all of which were either exported to Canada or beamed across the border. Paradoxically, there was some real question about Canada's capacity to meet the interests and needs of its citizens in entertainment and culture: the population was too small to pay for these services, while the United States was conveniently nearby and happy to market its products. Curiously, two of the best-known television patriarchs of the second generation after World War II, *Bonanza's* Ben Cartwright and *Star Trek's* Captain Jim Kirk, were

Canadians. Yet, so much of Canada's economy had come under the direct or indirect control of American industries and investors that a common complaint began to circulate: until confederation, Canada had been a colony of Great Britain; now it was a colony of the United States. And a branch plant.

Third, this resentment of the United States did not begin in the 1960s by any means, but it may have reached its apotheosis during that era in large part because of the tragic involvement of the United States in the Vietnam War. The civil rights disturbances as well, particularly the Detroit race riot of 1967 within sight of Windsor, Ontario, appeared to discredit the American Dream.

The benefits of this New Nationalism in Canada quickly became apparent: a new pride felt by Canadians in their country; a new excitement about the heritage and achievement of the nation; a cultural explosion that saw the creation of new publishing companies, new theaters and new endeavors in the arts; and new legislation that sought to curtail foreign investment. Plus, a new vanity: it was O.K. to be Canadian. Many Canadians who visited Europe and Britain then and even today wore a small maple leaf in their lapels so that they would not be mistaken for American tourists.

THE TRUDEAU YEARS AND THE QUÉBÉCOIS

The 1960s closed with the centennial celebration and with the emergence of Pierre Eliot Trudeau as Prime Minister, continuing the Liberal Party domination of federal politics. Since 1935, only once had a conservative government been elected, and then only for a six-year period in the late 1950s under John Diefenbaker. The Liberals had then returned with Lester Pearson, a distinguished foreign affairs specialist. With one brief interruption of several months in 1979, the party held office until 1984, with Trudeau as leader. For over forty of the fifty years following King's election in 1935, the Liberal Party had managed the nation.

A teacher and author prior to coming into government circles in 1967, enormously telegenic (some thought in the Kennedy mode), Prime Minister Trudeau proved to be a controversial multitalented leader seemingly well suited to the newly found ambitions of Canada in the 1970s. PET, as the media often spoke of him, was a bilingual, well-educated, and widely travelled federalist French Canadian, one of the most sophisticated and cultivated world leaders of his time. Trudeau's belief in confederation necessarily addressed the one certain phenomenon of late twentieth century in Canada: the tensions between provinces and dominion, between the West and Ottawa, between Ottawa and Quebec. These had to do with provincial autonomy, regional identity, and, most of all, the status of Quebec.

In the early 1970s, the Parti Québécois, led by a former journalist named René Lévesque, advocated the separation of Quebec from the rest of Canada—"separatists," they were called. And gradually the arguments began to convince a wider audience in the province. The arguments sounded these alarms: 1) the long history of subordination of French Canadians in their own province by British Canadian "managers" and by foreign investment; and 2) the danger of the loss of a pertinent, substantial French Canadian language and culture. Quebec was not France; Quebec was Quebec. Quebec was not Canadian; Quebec was Québécois.

Quebec thrived on a national movement of its own, in search of its appropriate identity. Although the Parti Québécois was a provincial and not a federal party, Prime Minister Trudeau could only look on with dismay, particularly after a bill passed in the provincial government that made French the official language there.

When the Parti Québécois became the government of Quebec in 1976, new Premier Lévesque immediately began to talk of a referendum in which he would ask the electorate to decide whether the Quebec government should negotiate some sort of separate status with the federal government. An enormous public relations campaign was set in motion, in part to persuade Québécois that separation was feasible, in part to assuage the anxieties of foreign investors. Questions abounded: If Quebec did withdraw from confederation, would the whole nation itself dissolve into a handful of angry regions? Would Quebec itself survive economically if it withdrew? Would travelers to and from the Maritime Provinces have to go through a border checkpoint, carry a passport? Who would pick up the garbage, pay out the pensions?

By the time Premier Lévesque had prepared the referendum in 1980, the concept of "separation" had been adjusted to "sovereignty association." Its features were:

1 The only taxes and laws applying to Quebec would be those adopted by the National Assembly of Quebec;
2 Every resident or native would have an automatic right to citizenship;
3 Quebec would join the International Joint Commission, a Canadian-American arbitration organization, and NATO and would respect the agreement between Canada and the United States regarding the St. Lawrence Seaway;
4 The Canadian dollar would remain the common currency in Quebec, but Quebec would establish its own investment codes and financial regulations; and
5 Free movement across common borders would be ensured.

The Quebec Referendum took place in May 1980, with Québécois going to the polls to answer one question: "Do you agree to give the Government of Quebec the mandate to negotiate the proposed agreement between Quebec and Canada? Oui? Non?" After years of debate, after years of waiting, the Parti Québécois lost the referendum. One reason was that while the younger French Canadians approved of the proposition, the older citizens felt threatened by the implied changes and so threw their numbers against the proposition. The presence of a sizable Anglophone population in the province mattered as well. Although the Parti Québécois retained its power after a general election the next year, the movement for a new status in Canada for Quebec lost momentum for the time being.

Quebec was not the only part of the country exerting and feeling pressure during these years. Both the western provinces and the Maritimes regularly expressed their resentment at the so-called "Golden Triangle" of Toronto, Ottawa, and Montreal, where it was felt the real power in and priorities for Canada rested. Both the western and Maritime regions felt that they were often ignored by the financial and political leaders of the nation who live and rule in those three cities.

The West was particularly disillusioned: the Liberal government under Trudeau, it was said, unaccountably ignored those provinces, scarcely bothering to court their support. The result was a powerful sense of indignation that began to challenge the constitutional balance. And then there was the matter of natural resources: oil, natural gas, uranium, and water power, which were abundant in these regions, and the sources of political power as well as economic bonanza.

The energy crisis of the 1970s and early 1980s affected Canada as it did so many nations. The emergency was countered to some extent by the presence in Alberta of vast oil and natural gas reserves, by the exploitation of uranium deposits in Saskatchewan, and by the water power from Northern Manitoba. In the forefront for a while was Alberta, dubbed "Texas North" because of the presence of so many petroleum technicians who came there from the American southwest. Alberta was the place to be. And the new wealth meant greater influence in dominion-provincial relations.

British Columbia, long associated with such resources as fishing, lumber, and minerals, suffered greatly from depleted markets and high costs to the extent that great numbers of public employees had to be laid off. This disaster seemed to portend similar struggles between other provincial workers and their respective governments.

Manitoba has long been frustrated by its inability to capitalize on its geographical and historic presence as the gateway to the West. The building of the Panama Canal offered an alternative route to the Pacific through which traffic could be sent with greater dispatch. The Canadian Shield, a massive rock bed that sprawls under most of the province and beyond, has made an agricultural economy something less than it might have been. Manitoba has a distinctive ethnic population, descended from the emigrations of the late 19th and early 20th centuries.

Dominion-provincial relations were further strained as the nation began to examine the prospect and significance of "repatriation" of the Constitution. The British North America Act of 1867 had been conferred by the British Parliament, which thereafter retained authority over the Act—that is, amendments had to be approved by that body, some thousands of miles away. Repatriation would return full authority over the Constitution to Canada itself. Given the nation's accumulation of powers, rights, and traditions that decreed its substantial independence, most Canadians felt that repatriation was in order—its time had come.

But a succession of meetings among federal and provincial leaders in the late 1970s revealed that such an achievement would not come easily. Although there was agreement regarding a Charter of Rights (akin to the American Bill of Rights) identifying fundamental freedoms and rights of the people, not everyone had the same opinion about the formula for amendments. What combination of provinces could assure passage of any amendment? Given the history of regional autonomy, this question became crucial. It was resolved that passage required the support of seven provinces representing 50 percent of the population of all the provinces. After considerable discussion, bargaining, and compromise, the provinces (with the exception of Quebec) completed the details and reached accord. On April 17, 1982, Elizabeth II, who remains Queen of Canada, gave royal assent.

The new Constitution, particularly the Charter of Rights, will undergo regular appraisal and interpretation by the citizenry and the courts, but there is no doubt that it is perceived as a document that assures greater unity for Canada and that it was brought about through the efforts of Prime Minister Trudeau.

Two years after the event, Trudeau stepped down as prime minister and leader of the Liberal Party, and a remarkable career drew to a close. Governing from 1968 until 1984, with but one slight interruption of a few months in 1979, Trudeau had been the longest-serving leader of a nation in the West. Though not always popular, he was one of the eminent statesmen produced by Canada this century.

TOWARD THE TWENTY-FIRST CENTURY

The "Chinese Curse," one learns, is "to live in interesting times." For Canadians, the final years of the twentieth century are just about as interesting as they could be. Tulmultuous, frustrating, fascinating. Never dull. Québécois still agitate for some sort of separate status. Federal-Provincial relations seem never to be serene. The economy is a real issue. Canadian-American accords become rather notorious. The Blue Jays win.

American students of Canada's history and culture might now ask: If the United States of America is so noisy and rowdy a nation and Canada seems so quiet and discreet, how is it that Federal-State relations are by and large placid while Federal-Provincial relations are so bumptious? One answer has to be that the founders of the two nations laid out these relationships; they bear constitutional sanction. So it is that the Canadian provinces have been given and have taken a great many more prerogatives than the American states would ever have sought: education, health, welfare for example. The provinces are considerably more autonomous than are the states; they like it that way, and they want to keep it that way. At least once a year the premiers of the provinces meet with the Prime Minister to sort out problems. On the other hand, Quebec has sought to withdraw from Confederation. By referendum at that and not by civil strife.

Between 1986 and 1992, the Mulroney government sought to build a consensus that would recognize Quebec as a "distinct society" and underwrite more liberal terms for all of the provinces. These included greater opportunities for the nomination of federal jurists, more active participation in immigration policy, and a veto on constitutional amendments. The Meech Lake Accord, which embodied this consensus, had to be approved by all of the provincial legislatures. When the deadline came around in June 1990, the legislatures of Manitoba and Newfoundland, having changed their party loyalties in the interim, voted against the accord. In 1992, a national referendum on constitutional change, the Charlottetown Accord, also failed. It would seem that the citizenry were just not that interested in sweeping constitutional revision.

Prime Minister Mulroney did score a pair of victories when Canada signed a free trade agreement with the United States in 1988 and again with the United States and Mexico in 1994 for the creation of the North American Free Trade Agreement (NAFTA). However, many Canadians objected to these agreements, arguing that Canada's self-reliance would be weakened because of the opportunities for American and Mexican firms to establish themselves there. For that matter, many Americans have frowned at the prospect of the transfer of American branch plants to Mexico.

Signal changes in the political character of Canada have also made life interesting. New parties emerged to challenge the dominance of the Liberal, Conservative, and Socialist organizations that have prevailed for well over half a century. The Bloc Québécois came forward as a national party from the chagrin of Quebec voters over the failure of the Meech Lake Accord. The Reform Party, with roots in the west, is a conservative response to the failure of the Conservatives to govern the nation.

In the general election of 1993, the Conservatives did fall from power and from the House of Commons in the most devastating loss of their history. The Liberals, led by a federalist (in the mold of Trudeau) named Jean Chrétien, won the government. The Bloc Québécois, successor to the Quebec nationalist parties of the previous generation, with fifty-three seats, unexpectedly became "the loyal opposition." And in 1997, in a general election called by the Liberals, who won again, the Reform Party replaced the Bloc Québécois as the opposition by virtue of the number of seats it had won.

Chapter 2
The Geography of Canada
Michael J. Broadway

Canada is the United States' closest neighbor and largest trading partner, yet how many American students and teachers can answer the following questions correctly?

- Canada is the world's second largest country; true or false?
- The January temperature in parts of Canada averages about 41°F.; true or false?
- Around 89 percent of Canada lacks permanent human settlement; true or false?
- Canada has the highest rate of immigration among western industrialized countries; true or false?

All of these statements are true. At 3.8 million square miles, Canada is the world's second largest country and has the world's longest coastline. Canada has a well-deserved reputation as a cold country, but while the average January temperature in central Alberta is about 5°F., at the southern tip of Vancouver Island the average is 41°F. It is also true that 89 percent of Canada lacks permanent human settlement—the 1997 population of about thirty million is concentrated along the southern border—and, averaging over 200,000 legal immigrants a year, Canada's rate of immigration is the highest among western industrialized countries.

With a country of this size, it should be no surprise that Canada's main characteristic may be said to be its diversity, for within this enormous country are enormous differences in economic conditions, culture, vegetation, climate, and landforms. British Columbia's fjord coastline, the towering Rocky Mountains, and wide open prairies attest to the variety of Canada's landforms. There is a contrast in annual precipitation levels similar to the wide range in temperature: along the northern Pacific coast, for instance, annual rainfall can exceed ninety inches, but in southeastern Alberta it seldom exceeds fifteen. Differences in climate are reflected in vegetation: the northern portions of the Yukon, Northwest Territories, and Quebec consist primarily of a treeless tundra, while coastal British Columbia has a temperate rain forest and its inland valleys have vegetation associated with a semiarid climate.

The geographic center of the country is Arviat located in the Northwest Territories, but most of its population is distributed in a series of "islands" of human settlement stretching along the border with the United States. Population growth is sustained in large measure by immigration, and Europe has been replaced by the developing world as Canada's leading source of immigrants, leading to an increasingly ethnically diverse population.

Table 2-1. Canada: Basic Population and Economic Data

Province	1996 Population	August 1997 % Unemployment	1992 Income in Canadian Dollars
Newfoundland	570,700	18.5	40,411
Prince Edward Island	137,300	14.4	37,476
Nova Scotia	942,800	11.6	39,957
New Brunswick	762,500	12.5	39,160
Quebec	7,389,100	11.5	41,784
Ontario	11,252,400	8.2	50,986
Manitoba	1,143,500	6.2	41,298
Saskatchewan	1,022,500	5.7	38,866
Alberta	2,789,500	5.9	48,596
British Columbia	3,855,100	8.5	46,603
Yukon Territory	31,500	n.d.	n.d.
Northwest Territory	66,600	n.d.	n.d.
CANADA	29,963,600	9.0	46,603

Sources: Statistics Canada, Canism Matrices 6367-6369, and Labour Force Survey.

Wide disparities in economic conditions exist among the population islands (see Table 2-1). One way to explain economic differences among regions is with the heartland-hinterland concept: southern Ontario and southern Quebec represent the heartland, and the rest of the country is classified as hinterland. The heartland possesses a favorable physical environment, access to markets, a diversified economic base, and a highly urbanized and concentrated population which has enabled it to exert political and economic control over the remainder of the country. The hinterland, by contrast, is characterized by an emphasis on primary resource production (agriculture, forestry, mining, and fishing), a scattered population, and economic dependency upon the heartland. Primary resources are typically shipped from the hinterland to the heartland, where they are processed and sold, with the value added accruing to the heartland. In recent years this pattern has gradually been eroded, with the hinterland provinces bypassing the heartland in shipping natural resources abroad, a change that has helped to narrow income differences among provinces.

The country's vast size has also decreased opportunities for interaction among the population islands and has thus helped sustain regional identities. The viewpoint of residents of these islands is often circumscribed and is sustained by an intense attachment to a local region. In Nova Scotia, for instance, Cape Bretoners (or Capers) over the past twenty years have experienced the collapse of their steel, coal, and fishing industries and endured unemployment rates between 20 and 30 percent but, instead of moving to places with jobs, many have remained, intensifying regional economic and social stress.

Regionalism takes many forms beyond the collective identification with a particular territorial unit. In the 1990s, it is evident in the desire among Quebec nationalists for a separate state; in the complaints of east and west coast fishery workers over the federal government's failure to manage the fishery; and in the resentment of Western Canadians of bilingualism and what they view as the federal government's favoritism towards Quebec. This regionalism gives Canada its unique identity, so it is appropriate to include in an introduction to Canada an introduction to its regions: Atlantic Canada, the Great Lakes-St. Lawrence lowlands, the Western Interior, British Columbia, and the North.

ATLANTIC CANADA

Atlantic Canada, the country's poorest region, consists of Nova Scotia, New Brunswick, Prince Edward Island, and Newfoundland. A hundred years ago the region had a relatively prosperous economy, but now it is characterized by high unemployment, low incomes, and slow population growth.

In 1901, Nova Scotia, New Brunswick, and Prince Edward Island accounted for approximately 17 percent of Canada's population. By 1991, the corresponding figure for those three was only 6 percent (Newfoundland became a province in 1949). During this ninety-year period, population grew by just 27 percent in Prince Edward Island, 95 percent in Nova Scotia, and 118 percent in New Brunswick; by contrast, Ontario's growth rate was over 500 percent, and Alberta's and British Columbia's populations expanded by more than 2,000 percent. Atlantic Canada's slow population growth reflects the westward shift in the country's economy away from the region's traditional resources of forestry, fishing, and mining to portions of the country with more valuable, plentiful, and marketable resources. Indeed, for most of the twentieth century, more people have left Atlantic Canada to find work than have moved into it.

Economic development efforts are hampered by the region's relative isolation from major markets in North America, its small scattered population, and the absence of a major urban center. The current regional population of

2.2 million is unevenly distributed around or near the coastline and along the Saint John River in New Brunswick, with the hilly interiors of Newfoundland, Nova Scotia, and New Brunswick being largely devoid of human settlement. All four provinces have relatively low levels of urbanization: at least 46 percent of the population resides in rural areas, compared with the nationwide average of 23 percent. The region's largest metropolitan area is Halifax-Dartmouth, Nova Scotia (1994 pop. 339,000), followed by St. John's, New-foundland (1994 pop. 177,700). Most workers are employed in the service sector. Government, finance, education, and health care are major sources of employment in the region's metropolitan areas.

Changes in Traditional Industries

The small internal market has made it difficult to attract new industries to the area because any finished product produced there has to be shipped out for sale. As a result, the region is still dependent upon its traditional industries—fishing, mining, lumber and paper, agriculture, and some manufacturing.

Fishing has been an integral part of Atlantic Canada since the early 1500s: the abundant northern cod stocks provided the basis for the existence of Newfoundland as well as many Nova Scotia coastal communities. But, beginning in the late 1980s, with fears of overfishing, the Department of Fisheries and Oceans began to reduce the amount of cod that could be caught and, in mid-1992, imposed a total ban in an attempt to protect the remaining northern cod and allow for their regeneration. Four years later the ban remains in effect and has been extended to include other species. The moratorium has resulted in over 20,000 inshore fishermen and plant workers being laid off in Newfoundland and thousands more in Nova Scotia. Although there is little agreement as to the reasons for the fishery's collapse—plant workers blame overfishing by foreign vessels, inshore fishermen blame the Department of Fisheries and Oceans for mismanagement—the reality remains: with few fish to be caught, a way of life has ended for thousands of the region's residents.

Mining, another mainstay of the economy, has also experienced substantial job losses. Cape Breton's coal mines were to be closed in the late 1960s, and a federal agency, the Cape Breton Development Corporation, was established to manage the closure. The oil crisis of the early 1970s, however, resulted in this decision being reversed, and new mines were developed for coal being used for electricity generation. Despite these investments, employment in the coal mines declined with the introduction of machinery, while cheap foreign coal imports in the mid-1990s led to a further round of job losses.

Nearly 90 percent of Atlantic Canada is forested, providing the basis for an important lumber, pulp, and paper sector. Related industries are most important in New Brunswick, which has the largest and most accessible hardwood and softwood reserves. Many of the region's pulp and paper mills are located near river mouths because water was initially used for log transport and as a raw material in the pulping process. With a small internal market, most of the pulp and paper is sold abroad, making the industry highly vulnerable to fluctuations in world demand and subject to intense competitive pressures. To remain competitive, plants invest in labor-saving technology, further reducing jobs in an area where unemployment is already well above the national average.

Agriculture is of minimal importance to the region as a whole, reflecting the area's poor soils, hilly terrain, distance from major markets, and relatively short growing season. Indeed, since the 1960s there has been widespread farm abandonment among marginal farms located in upland areas. Most of the region's farmland is used for pasture and feed grains for livestock. An exception to this pattern is the Annapolis Valley of Western Nova Scotia, which has good soil and flat land and has become an important fruit- and vegetable-growing area. Prince Edward Island is the most heavily cultivated of the Atlantic provinces, with over 50 percent of its land already cleared of forest. The island's chief cash crop is potatoes—also the principal cash crop in north-western New Brunswick, home of the McCain food-processing company. The company is a source of pride because it is one of few that is a successful world player and remains headquartered in the region.

Manufacturing in Atlantic Canada is based primarily upon the processing of raw materials. Deindustrialization is evident in traditional heavy industries, especially steel, located in the Sydney and New Glasgow areas of Nova Scotia. Shipbuilding in the port city of Saint John, New Brunswick, enjoyed a brief renaissance with the construction of twelve frigates for the Canadian navy during the 1980s and early 1990s, but the completion of the project and no new orders means that nearly 3,000 jobs have been lost.

New Developments

Against the backdrop of declining resource-based industries, the federal government provides economic development assistance through the Atlantic Canada Opportunities Agency and the Enterprise Cape Breton Corporation. These agencies seek to create new jobs by providing technical assistance and interest-free loans to local businesses.

Increasingly, governments at all levels in the region are looking to tourism as a means of job creation. Ecotourism shows particular promise; the area already contains attractions such as L'Anse aux Meadows (the site of a Viking settlement) in Newfoundland and Fortress Louisbourg on Cape Breton Island, two important heritage sites; spectacular mountain and coastal scenery in Fundy, Gros Morne, and Cape Breton Highlands National Parks; out-of-the-way places such as Sable and Grand Manan Islands; and the more traditional attractions of Prince Edward Island's sandy beaches, which are advertised as having the warmest waters north of the Carolinas. Tourism's potential as a job creator is constrained, however, by the region's remoteness from its major market—the New England states—and the relatively short summer season.

Tourism in Prince Edward Island will receive a boost from the completion in 1997 of a controversial eight-mile-long bridge connecting the island with the mainland.

GREAT LAKES–ST. LAWRENCE LOWLANDS

The region extending southwestward from Quebec City, Quebec, to Windsor, Ontario, is Canada's economic heartland, for it contains the majority of the country's population and manufacturing base. In 1996, the provinces of Ontario and Quebec accounted for 62 percent of Canada's population and 75 percent of its manufacturing employment. But the region is culturally divided between the two linguistic groups that helped found the nation, primarily English speakers in Ontario and primarily French speakers in Quebec. The 1991 census notes that 75 percent of all Ontarians had English as their mother tongue, while in Quebec the comparable figure for French speakers was 81 percent. Despite this cultural fault line, the region has dominated economic and political activity throughout the country for much of Canada's history.

The Rise of Manufacturing

In 1760, after defeating the French, Britain acquired the area north of the Great Lakes and the foundations of modern Canada were laid. Britain also inherited a well-established French colony in the St. Lawrence Valley comprised of more than 60,000 French-speaking Catholics who had cleared land for agriculture within a few miles of the St. Lawrence River, using the long lot or seigneurial system of settlement, and had developed three major settlements, Montreal, Quebec City, and Trois Rivieres. In addition to acquir-ing land and people, the British also assumed complete control of the continent's fur trade which had been the principal means of generating wealth in the colony. The region's rise to dominance began at this point, and a staples economy was developed with the addition of timber and wheat as important exports. In the mid-nineteenth century, most of the wheat came from southwestern

The extremely fertile farm lots in New France were drawn long and narrow so that all farmers would have frontage along the St. Lawrence River, their only real transportation route.
Ministère du Tourisme du Québec

Ontario, which has a warmer and longer growing season and more productive soils than southern Quebec.

Much of the economy was then controlled by Montreal merchants who exchanged staples for foreign manufactured goods. These traders and their counterparts in Toronto pressured the British administration to improve the region's infrastructure, beginning with water transportation and then railroads and telegraphic communications. The capital accumulated from the staples trade, combined with British expenditures for defense and administration, supported the establishment of a small manufacturing sector producing consumer goods. By the time of confederation in 1867, the foundations of the new country's industrial heartland had been established.

The post-confederation national policy of high tariffs or importation taxes greatly benefited the manufacturing sector by protecting it from foreign competition and enabling it to become the supplier of manufactured goods to the hinterland regions. High tariffs on farm machinery, for example, meant that western farmers would purchase their machinery from southern Ontario. The Bank Act of 1871 fostered the establishment of national banks headquartered in Montreal and Toronto, adding to the region's financial dominance, because these banks were able to set interest rates and control investment policies.

In the late nineteenth century, rapid population growth and a shortage of agricultural land forced many people into the growing industrial centers of Quebec and Ontario. These migrants provided a cheap source of labor for manufacturing tobacco, shoes, clothing, and textiles. Ontario's initial industrial strength was based upon food processing and metal working, followed by iron, steel and, beginning in the 1920s, automobiles.

Industrial expansion continued until the 1960s. The hydropower of Niagara Falls, harnessed in the early 1900s, provided industry with a cheap source of energy throughout southern Ontario. The high tariffs on imported manufactured goods meant that foreign companies wanting access to the Canadian market had to construct plants in Canada; this led to the establishment of a branch-plant economy led primarily by U.S. manufacturers. U.S. companies preferred to invest in Ontario because of its large market and the proximity of southern Ontario to U.S. offices in the Manufacturing Belt. The big three U.S. auto makers all have major plants in southern Ontario: General Motors in Oshawa, Ford in Oakville, and Chrysler in Windsor. Japanese auto makers have also constructed plants in the Toronto area. Outside of Southern Ontario, the Ottawa-Hull region is gradually developing into Canada's Silicon Valley with its concentration of computer and software companies. Although the region is the country's manufacturing center, the service sector provides most employment. Finance, insurance, real estate, business services, and wholesale trade are major employers in the Toronto and Montreal areas. Government, for obvious reasons, is a major employer in Ottawa-Hull and Quebec City.

Exploding Metro Areas

Accompanying the growth of a strong manufacturing economy has been rapid urbanization. In 1991, seven of the twenty largest metropolitan areas in Canada were in southern Ontario; four of them—Oshawa, Toronto, Hamilton, and St. Catharines-Niagara—form the so-called Golden Horseshoe around the western end of Lake Ontario. Between 1976 and 1991, the population of metropolitan Toronto increased by just over one million persons, while Oshawa gained 140,000, St. Catharines-Niagara 62,000, and Hamilton 60,000.

These population gains have resulted in the expansion of urban areas and an associated loss of agricultural land. During the 1980s it was estimated that, for every 1,000 persons added to an urban area's population, an additional one hundred acres of land was needed. The significance of these statistics is emphasized by the fact that more than half of Canada's prime agricultural land is found in the heartland. In the Golden Horseshoe, urban expansion has resulted in the loss of valuable land in the Niagara Fruit Belt between Hamilton and St. Catharines. The amount of Canadian land with soil and climate conditions suitable for the production of tender fruit crops like peaches, cherries, pears, and grapes is limited to British Columbia's lower Fraser Valley, the southern Okanagan Valley, and the Niagara Peninsula. The loss of agricultural land in this area is particularly significant in view of its accessibility to the country's largest market.

Montreal—the country's cultural and economic center during the nineteenth and first half of the twentieth centuries—has dropped to Canada's second largest economic center (after Toronto). Its more than three million inhabitants amount to nearly 46 percent of Quebec's population. Montreal's relative decline is attributable to the westward shift in the country's overall population; the loss of preferential trade with Britain once it became a member of the European Union; the construction of the St. Lawrence Seaway in 1959, which enabled oceangoing vessels to bypass the port; and, more recently, the financial and political uncertainty brought about by the election of separatist Parti Québécois governments in 1976, 1981, and 1994. Fears of Quebec separating from Canada in the late 1970s led to an exodus of corporate headquarters office functions from Montreal to Toronto and, to a lesser extent, Calgary and Vancouver. Concurrent with these changes, the city's overconcentration in traditional labor-intensive industries resulted in substantial job losses as a result of foreign competition. Between 1971 and 1986, deindustrialization resulted in the loss of over 70,000 manufacturing jobs and produced unemployment rates in traditional manufacturing areas of the city of over 20 percent. In an effort to deal with the city's long-term decline, a 1986 federal government commission proposed that Montreal build upon its existing foundation as an international city, high-tech manufacturer, and center of trade, transportation, design, culture, and tourism. It is too early to determine the success of this plan, but it is clear that the continued uncertainty over the status of Quebec has hampered investment in Montreal and unemployment remains a serious problem.

Deindustrialization is also evident in metropolitan Toronto, but the area has gained thousands of service sector jobs from its status as Canada's financial capital and headquarters for hundreds of corporations. The head offices of leading Canadian industries, banks, and investment, accounting, and law firms are located in downtown Toronto, while companies who employ large numbers of lower-paid clerical staff are moving out to the suburbs. The increasing concentration of high order decision making in the downtown area and the desire among some of these employees to reside close to their workplace are associated with inner-city population gains. High-rise apartments and condominiums have been constructed along portions of the city's Lake Ontario waterfront and in the midtown area to house the growth of well-educated, upper-income households. Indeed, this same pattern is evident among many other Canadian inner-cities, which have experienced growth in service sector employment in their downtowns.

Despite the worst recession (in the early 1990s) in Ontario since the Great Depression, metropolitan Toronto's share of Canada's total population continued to increase from 12 percent in 1971 to 14 percent in 1994, reflecting the overall strength of the region's economy. Much of the area's population gain is attributable to immigration: 38 percent (1.5 million) of the metropolitan area's residents are foreign born, and in the early 1990s over half of all Canada's immigrants chose to live initially in Ontario.

The region has maintained its status as the economic heartland of the country because of its proximity to markets and capital in the United States, its large domestic market, the presence of a large, well-educated urban labor force, its productive agriculture, and its highly integrated urban system. Indeed, Toronto's function as the national economic capital of the country may be further enhanced by uncertainty over the future of Quebec and Montreal's decline as a national business center.

THE WESTERN INTERIOR

The Western Interior provinces of Manitoba, Saskatchewan, and Alberta share characteristics similar to Atlantic Canada: they are sparsely populated and isolated, have minimal manufacturing, and are dependent upon a primary resource-based economy. But there are also significant differences between the regions in terms of physical geography, history, economic development, and population structure.

There are few landforms in the region to restrict settlement; the plains gradually rise from eastern Manitoba to western Alberta where they abut the Rocky Mountains. Glacial deposition created flat land with extremely fertile soil in southern Manitoba and central Saskatchewan. However, the climate poses major challenges for the farmer. The region has a continental climate characterized by extreme temperature variations between summer and winter, a short growing season of 90-120 days, and a rainfall that occurs during the summer but varies widely from year to year and place to place. The driest area is on the southern Alberta-Saskatchewan border, where irrigation is used to cultivate feed grains.

Settlement Patterns

The Plains are an area of relatively recent settlement. The Hudson's Bay Company was awarded a royal charter in 1670 to trade in Rupert's Land, a vast area that roughly corresponded to the area drained by Hudson Bay. For the next two hundred years, the company enjoyed a monopoly on the fur trade and prevented settlement of the region by private concerns with the exception of the Selkirk settlement north of present-day Winnipeg. In 1870, Canada acquired Rupert's Land and some of the company's trading posts that would later provide the foundations for urban growth such as Fort Edmonton.

But it was the completion of the transcontinental Canadian Pacific Railroad in 1885 that had the greatest influence on the region's settlement. Constructing the railroad served a number of important functions: it linked the western province of British Columbia with central Canada; it stimulated manufacturing in Ontario and Quebec; it provided a means of settling the Prairies; and it checked the territorial ambitions of the United States. To finance the construction, the Canadian government gave the railroad $25 million and 25 million acres of land adjoining the railway line for future sale to settlers. The company's selection of a southerly route and railway station sites greatly influenced the region's urban growth. Brandon in Manitoba and Moose Jaw and Regina in Saskatchewan were all creations of the railroad. In Calgary, the town's initial center was moved from a river junction to a site one mile further west so that the company could maximize its profits from the sale of its land.

At first, the railroad's completion failed to attract many settlers due to the harsh physical environment and the high costs associated with settling the area compared with the United States. This situation changed at the end of the century with the appointment of Clifford Sifton as Canada's Minister of the Interior. Sifton vigorously recruited agricultural workers from eastern and central Europe, with the largest single group coming from Ukraine. Between 1900 and 1914, immigration to Canada boomed, reaching a peak in 1913 when over 400,000 immigrants entered the country. Many of them chose to settle in western rural areas, and it was during this period that the region's essential character as a producer of primary products, with urban growth based upon service to the primary sector, was forged. Even though World War I effectively halted the flow of people, immigration increased again at war's end and more marginal land was brought under cultivation.

Economic Development

The collapse of wheat prices in 1929 followed by a worldwide depression and drought conditions in the 1930s brought dramatic changes to the farm economy. Saskatchewan was hardest hit as people left rural areas and migrated to the region's largest cities.

Rural to urban migration was not the only source of the region's urban population growth. During Alberta's oil boom in the 1970s, migrants from central Canada moved to the province, and metropolitan Calgary gained 189,000 persons from 1971 to 1981; the corresponding figure for Edmonton, capital of Alberta, was 161,000. By contrast, metropolitan population gains were much smaller in the more agrarian-based economies of Manitoba and Saskatchewan. Indeed, these two provinces' share of Canada's population declined from 11.4 percent in 1951 to 7.6 percent in 1991, while Alberta's share increased from 6.7 to 9.3 percent.

Agriculture's role in the regional economy has diminished over time due to the growth of other sectors of the regional economy and structural changes. Increases in the use of machinery and chemicals have improved productivity, helped transform agriculture from a labor-intensive to a capital-intensive industry, and thus led to a decline in the number of farms. Fewer farms and farm laborers have meant a decline in the demand for goods and services in small towns and have resulted in further population losses as local businesses have folded. At the same time, the closure of branch railroad lines and the consolidation of grain elevators due to improved roads and the use of trucks for grain transportation have led to even more population losses from small towns and villages.

This process is most pronounced in Saskatchewan. In 1991 the three Prairie Provinces accounted for 51 percent of Canada's farms. Saskatchewan led the nation in the amount of land in crops, with 33 million acres or 40 percent of Canada's total, followed by Alberta and Manitoba with 23 million and 11.7 million acres respectively. Spring wheat, despite recent declines in the amount of acreage devoted to it, remains the number one field crop in the region, followed by tame hay, barley, and canola. Increases in tame hay and barley cultivation reflect the expansion of Alberta's cattle industry. Cattle used to be shipped from Alberta to Ontario to be processed, but in the wake of U.S. competition, many of the old packing plants in Toronto have closed. Instead, newer plants have been constructed or expanded in Alberta: cattle and water are readily available, and the final product is then shipped directly to market.

Alberta is Canada's leading producer of oil and gas, much of which is exported to the United States. Declines in conventional petroleum reserves have led oil companies to invest in new technologies to extract oil from the province's Tar Sands located in the north in the vicinity of Fort McMurray. Recent breakthroughs have lowered the costs of extracting oil from this thick, gooey mass so that it is now economically feasible to exploit the resource. And oil companies have announced ambitious expansion plans.

Coal, found in Alberta and Saskatchewan, is exported to Japan and other parts of Asia. Saskatchewan also has some of the world's largest reserves of potash, which is used in the manufacture of fertilizer, and it too is exported out of the region.

The region has attempted to diversify its economy. Tourism has been heavily promoted in Alberta, focused especially upon the Calgary Stampede and Banff and Jasper National Parks. Calgary hosted the 1988 Winter Olympics in an effort to increase its worldwide destination awareness. Manitoba and Saskatchewan, which offer fewer such tourist attractions, struggle to attract new investment and jobs.

As an exporting region, the Western Interior's economic fortunes fluctuate with the continental and world demand for its primary resources, even as diversification efforts are hampered by the region's small population and isolation. The recent free trade agreements with the United States may have lessened the region's dependence upon the heartland and replaced it with a dependence upon a foreign country.

BRITISH COLUMBIA

British Columbia is also a resource-based hinterland, but unlike the Western Interior provinces it has developed in relative isolation from the rest of Canada. The Rocky Mountains, which run along the border with Alberta, rise to over 12,000 feet and serve as an effective barrier between the province and other parts of the country. To the west of the Rockies is the Rocky Mountain Trench, a valley that extends north from Montana's Flathead Lake to the Laird Plain in the Yukon. Between this valley and the Pacific coastline are more mountains, the interior plateau, and coast range mountains; offshore, mountains extend northwards along the spine of Vancouver Island and into the Queen Charlotte Islands. The contrast in relief between the coast range mountains and the interior plateau has produced two distinctive climates. Along the coast, mild winter and warm summer temperatures predominate, with year-round rainfall amounts increasing northwards from Vancouver's forty-seven inches. Inland, the interior plateau possesses a continental climate with little rainfall due to the rain shadow effect of the coast range mountains.

The province is heavily urbanized with nearly 75 percent of the population residing in the vicinity of the Georgia Straits that separate the southwestern portion of the mainland from Vancouver Island; within this region are Vancouver, Canada's third largest metropolitan area with a 1996 estimated population of nearly 1.9 million persons, and Victoria (1996 estimated population 320,000), the provincial capital, on Vancouver Island. Away from this region, settlement is confined to the narrow valleys that dissect the mountains and is related to the exploitation of primary resources. In recent years, internal migrants and immigrants have been drawn to the province by its relatively strong economy. Between 1981 and 1994, the province gained over 900,000 persons and increased its share of Canada's population from 11.3 percent to 12.5 percent.

A Resource-Based Economy

The economy of the province has always been oriented towards the production of staples beginning with furs, followed by gold, coal, lumber, base metals, pulp and paper, hydropower, and natural gas. Most of the province's raw materials are shipped to the United States or foreign markets in the Asia Pacific Rim region, and much of the capital associated with the development of these resources came from outside the region. Early in the twentieth century, the United States was a leading investor in the province's forest and mining industries, followed by British and eastern Canadian interests. After World War II, successive provincial governments have sought to attract foreign investment in its resource-based economy by providing infrastructure in the form of building new highways and railroads. A major component of this strategy during the 1950s was the construction of the British Columbia Railway north of Prince George into the Peace River country, giving access to that region's rich forestry and mineral resources.

More recently the government has sought Japanese capital. In the 1960s a consortium of Japanese companies made its first overseas investment in a source of coking coal for its steel industry in the Kootenay mountains in the southeast portion of the province. Coal is shipped out of the region by unit trains to the man-made port of Point Roberts, south of Vancouver. During the early 1980s the provincial government agreed to construct a new railroad line, port facilities, a highway, and a power line in return for Japanese investment in an open pit coal mine in Tumbler Ridge.

Government promotion of the forestry industry is based upon a sustained yield program. The province owns about 95 percent of the forests and allocates land to companies on long-term arrangements. Companies are permitted to cut only certain areas and are restricted in the amount of timber they remove so as to keep the forest in perpetual growth. Since 1987, companies have been required to reforest any public lands they log.

The forest industry is concentrated in the southern Georgia Straits area, reflecting the early exploitation of forests near Vancouver, Nanaimo, and Victoria and the export facilities available in the area. Over time, as local forest supplies were exhausted, logs were

The Canadian Rockies contain some of the highest and most rugged peaks in North America. Many are so high that their snowy peaks remain frozen all year long.
Tourism British Columbia

41

shipped from further away down the Inside Passage to the mills. With technological advances, plants have become larger, and it is possible to integrate pulp and paper, sawmills, plywood operations, and the manufacture of other wood products into one large mill or adjoining mills. The industry expanded into the interior with the construction of road and rail facilities in the post-World War II period, but the mills are widely dispersed, reflecting the location of companies' cutting rights. Nearly a century of forest cutting in the Georgia Straits area has left few areas of old growth forest remaining and has produced conflicts between the forestry industry and environmental groups that wish to preserve such areas. One such conflict in the 1990s on Vancouver Island in the Clayoquot Sound area resulted in the province agreeing to preserve a portion of the disputed area, while allowing some logging and expanding the amount of parkland from 6 percent of the province's land area to 12 percent by the year 2000.

The extremely mountainous nature of the province means that agriculture is confined to a few valleys, most notably the Lower Fraser Valley, east of Vancouver, and the Okanagan Valley in the interior. Irrigation has allowed farmers in the Okanagan to transform its arid conditions to support a fruit-growing area providing apples, grapes, peaches, and other fruits to markets in western Canada. In the Lower Fraser Valley, agriculture is oriented towards supplying Vancouver with dairy and vegetable products.

Other Growth Areas

The province's manufacturing sector is concentrated in the southern Georgia Straits area and consists primarily of processing raw materials for export. Of much greater importance in terms of employment is the region's service sector. Vancouver, as Canada's gateway to the Pacific, has become a major center of trade, transportation, banking, and corporate administration. The area's ties with Asia extend back to the city's founding in 1886 as the terminus of the railroad when Chinese laborers were used in its construction. Today, Chinese immigrants from Hong Kong have made substantial real estate investments in the city. Vancouver also now handles more foreign trade than any other Canadian port, exporting raw materials and importing finished goods.

Tourism in the early 1990s was the province's fourth largest export earner (after lumber, pulp, and coal), and much of its growth is also concentrated in the Vancouver area. The city boosted its international image in 1986 when it hosted the World's Fair, Expo '86, and drew over twenty million visitors. Against this backdrop of a rapidly expanding service economy, the area suffers from many of the problems associated with rapid growth, such as a shortage of affordable housing, traffic congestion, air quality problems, and losses of valuable agricultural land on the suburban fringe. Victoria is experiencing similar problems, albeit on a smaller scale, from its status as a tourist attraction, retiree center, and provincial capital. Retirees are drawn to the area by its mild climate, while its tourist appeal is based upon "a taste of England" with beautiful formal gardens, double-decker buses, and afternoon tea at the Empress Hotel overlooking the harbor.

THE NORTH

Canada's largest region, comprising about 80 percent of the country, the North includes all of the Yukon Territory and Northwest Territories and the northern portions of all of the provinces except New Brunswick, Prince Edward Island, and Nova Scotia. The region consists of two major cold climates (the Arctic and Subarctic), is sparsely populated, has virtually no agriculture due to its cold climate and poor soils, and serves as a resource hinterland for core regions and a homeland for most of Canada's Native population.

In terms of landforms, British Columbia's Cordillera and the Interior Plains extend northward in the western portion of the region, while the Canadian Shield covers the remainder of the mainland. The Shield, Canada's largest land form, is shaped like a saucer, with Hudson Bay as its center and the higher elevations located at the edges. It is comprised of extremely old rocks (mostly Precambrian) and contains a storehouse of mineral wealth. The landscape carries the scars of recent glaciation in the form of bare rock, thin soils, and gently rolling uplands dotted with thousands of lakes.

The Arctic section is characterized by extremely low temperatures. On Baffin Island, the town of Iqaluit has an average January temperature of minus 13°F. July, its warmest month, has an average temperature of 45°F. Besides being cold, the area receives little precipitation, making it one of the least productive biological areas in the world. Only grasses, mosses, and lichens are found. This severe environment, however, is home to a Native population of approximately 30,000.

The Subarctic section is covered by boreal forest in a continuous belt from Newfoundland to the Rocky Mountains. Its summers are short but warm; Chibougamau, 405 miles north of Montreal, has an average July temperature of 60°F., while the corresponding figure for January is minus 1°F. Precipitation is greater than in the Arctic but varies across the vast region, with most areas receiving over twelve inches of precipitation and the largest amounts (forty-eight inches) occurring along the Atlantic coast and Western Cordillera. The region contains about 1.5 million inhabitants, most of them non-Natives, who live in single industry towns or government centers.

Underlying nearly all of the region is permafrost—perennially frozen ground. The depth of permafrost varies from over 3,000 feet in areas of Baffin Island to less than thirty feet in southern areas. During the brief summer, melting of the so-called "active layer" occurs; the depth of this layer again varies from a few inches in the Arctic to over thirty feet in the Subarctic. This thawing poses problems for any structures built upon it, so most buildings are constructed on piles that are sunk into the permafrost and frozen in place.

Dual Economies, Competing Goals

The Native and non-Native populations support two distinct economic systems: industrial capitalism and a Native economy. The Native economy consists of subsistence and commodity sectors; the subsistence sector produces goods for direct domestic consumption, such as food, and the exchange sector produces goods for export. Industrial capitalism, the dominant non-Native economic system, is characterized by large, externally controlled, multinational corporations which extract and process primary resources for export. Governments subsidize production in the form of improvements to the region's road and rail infrastructure.

These contrasting economic systems correspond to contrasting visions for the region. To non-northerners, the region is a hinterland needing development, which means exploiting its resources. Residents of the Yukon, for instance, view gaining provincial status as a means of securing control and ownership of their natural resources from the federal government. But to Canadians living in the North and particularly Natives, the region is their home and they wish to limit and exert more control over its development.

The Native population, therefore, has pursued the goal of self-government. In 1993 an agreement was signed between the federal government and Native leaders for the creation of a new territory and government to be known as Nunavut (meaning "Our Land" in Inuktitut, the native language of the Inuit); it will come into being on April 1, 1999. The goal of the Nunavut territory—which will be located in the eastern Arctic, north of the provinces of Saskatchewan, Manitoba, Ontario and Quebec—is to assist in the preservation of Inuit culture by providing Natives with a measure of control over development.

The Challenges of Resource Development

The past one hundred years have brought profound changes to the North due to its incorporation into the world economy as a resource hinterland. The Subarctic northern coniferous forest, for example, contains about 80 percent of Canada's forest land, and most commercial logging takes place in the southern portions where climate conditions are most favorable for tree growth. Development of the forest began in the nineteenth century in Quebec and Ontario, when logs were shipped down southward-flowing rivers to saw mills for processing; the lumber was then exported to Europe. After World War I, a market for newsprint in the United States increased, and pulp and paper mills were constructed along the southern edges of the Canadian Shield in Ontario and Quebec to meet the demand. This location was easily accessible by road and rail transport from the Lowlands, as well; by damming the many rivers in the region as they dropped over the outer edge of the Shield, companies could produce the large amounts of harnessable electric power needed in the mills. The region still accounts for the majority of Canada's production of newsprint, but newer and larger pulp and paper mills have recently opened in Alberta to take advantage of more accessible forests.

Mining, developed in response to the demands of non-Canadian markets, is based upon mineral fuels and metallic ore production. Gold, which was first discovered in the Yukon in 1898, created Canada's greatest ever Gold Rush. Gold is still produced today from mines at Lupin and Yellowknife in the Northwest Territories; nickel at Thompson, Manitoba; and uranium at Cliff Lake, Saskatchewan. The vulnerability of this sector of the economy to changes in demand is illustrated by the development of iron ore deposits by U.S. iron and steel companies in the late 1940s in Northern Quebec and Labrador. Several mines were constructed along with the communities of Schefferville, Labrador City, and Wabush, and a 350-mile-long railroad connecting the region with the port of Sept Iles on the St. Lawrence River. However, a sharp decline in the demand for iron ore at the beginning of the 1970s led to mine closures and the virtual abandonment of Schefferville. Uranium City in northern Saskatchewan suffered a similar fate in 1982, when its mines closed and the town's population declined from 2,500 to 171 in five years.

The petroleum industry has discovered extensive oil and gas reserves in the Mackenzie Delta and Beaufort Sea areas, but these fields are not yet viable due to high costs of production and transportation to distant markets. Currently, the largest oil-producing field is Norman Wells in the southern Yukon. Oil was discovered there in the 1920s, but it only supplied local markets until the mid-1980s when a pipeline was constructed connecting it with Alberta's pipeline system.

Hydroelectric power has also been developed in response to external markets. This energy source remained largely untapped until increased demand for energy and technological advances in electrical transmission made northern hydro projects viable. The largest hydro project by far is the James Bay project on the southeastern section of the Bay in northern Quebec, which produces power for Quebec and the northeastern United States. It has proved to be extremely controversial because of its environmental impact. Mercury levels, for example, have risen in fish due to the processes associated with the decay of drowned vegetation, while the creation of reservoirs has destroyed valuable wildlife habitat, and native hunting grounds. Plans to expand the project were put on hold in 1992, when New York State canceled a contract to purchase electricity from the Great Whale project, to have been located north of the present hydro complexes.

The North's extensive lakes, mountains, trees, and rivers are also popular with tourists. The earliest tourist developments occurred closest to the cities of central Canada along the southern edge of the Canadian Shield in areas such as the Muskoka area northwest of Toronto and the Laurentians north of Montreal. These areas are today dotted with summer cottages, parks, and campsites. Over time, development has spread further northward with the construction of paved highways, while some tourists fly in to remote areas in order to fish and hunt, providing a significant source of employment for Native peoples as guides.

The key issue for the North's future involves balancing its economic development with the need to preserve its native environment and peoples. Natives have moved from a nomadic way of life to permanent settlement as the fur trade has declined. Their future is focused upon settling land claims and revitalizing their traditional way of life. To this end, the establishment of Nunavut is a positive step. For the remainder of the North, protecting the region's fragile ecosystem and diversifying the economic base away from its dependence upon exports are top priorities.

CONCLUSIONS

When one considers the differences among Canada's principal regions, it might appear that there is little to hold such a large and culturally diverse country together. Canada's founders recognized the problems posed by the country's vast geography and sought to unify the country by building the transcontinental railroad in the 1880s. In the first half of the twentieth century, the Canadian Broadcasting Corporation (CBC) and Air Canada were added to the list of national institutions.

But by the end of the twentieth century, Air Canada had been privatized, and successive federal governments had cut back funding for the CBC and passenger railroad service. At the same time, north-south rather than east-west linkages have been encouraged with the signing of free trade agreements with the United States and Mexico. Will these actions serve to weaken the country? Or will Canada continue to defy geography and remain united? Only time will tell.

Sources

Bone, Robert M. *The Geography of the Canadian North.* Toronto: University Press, 1992.

McCann, Larry D., ed. *Heartland and Hinterland: A Geography of Canada.* Scarborough, Ontario: Prentice Hall Canada, 1987.

Robinson, Guy M. *A Social Geography of Canada.* Toronto: Dundurn Press, 1991.

Robinson, J. Lewis. *Concepts and Themes in the Regional Geography of Canada.* Vancouver: Talonbooks, 1989.

The Canadian Geographic magazine, published six times a year by the Royal Canadian Geographical Society, Ottawa, provides a variety of interesting articles dealing with different aspects of the country's physical and human geography.

For up-to-date statistics on Canada, use the Statistics Canada search engine on the World Wide Web at www.statcan.ca/english/reference/search/search.html

Chapter 3
Canadian Government and Politics
George Sherman

Any description of contemporary Canadian government and politics must begin with an important caveat: the Canadian confederation today—including the political institutions that support it—is very much a work in progress. The structure of Parliament, federal/provincial power-sharing, and the number and influence of viable political parties may well be dramatically different by the end of this decade. Indeed, even the shape of Canada itself may radically change before the millennium as the Quebec separatist drama and other regional disputes play themselves out.

Though the United States' political infrastructure is also in a state of some flux, its devolution of power from the federal government to the states, political party realignments, and third-party movements are mere ripples when compared to the waves of change currently washing Canada's political landscape. The most obvious, and most problematic, is the radical change in the country's political party structure. For nearly fifty years, federal politics in post-World War II Canada were dominated by the same three national political parties; two of them were large, the third one was small, but it usually had a feisty, popular leader and a representation in the House of Commons too large to ignore.

That all changed, perhaps permanently, as a result of the watershed 1993 federal elections. Canada's venerable and tweedy Progressive Conservative Party, the country's oldest, not only lost its comfortable majority in the House of Commons, but managed to retain only two of the possible 295 seats.[1] The newly formed Bloc Québécois, based exclusively in Quebec and essentially dedicated to the breakup of Canada, won a majority of the province's seats in the House of Commons, finishing second to the Liberal Party in representation and becoming the official opposition party. Meanwhile, another upstart regionally based party, this one in western Canada and called the Reform Party, won nearly as many seats as the Bloc. The same election reduced the country's traditional third party—the New Democratic Party—almost to insignificance.[2] Only two years later, voters in Quebec came to within 0.6 percent of approving a referendum that would have authorized their government to begin negotiations with Ottawa to define the terms of Quebec sovereignty. Emboldened by the closeness of that vote, the Quebec government has promised another referendum in the near future.

THE EVOLUTION OF CANADA'S POLITICAL SYSTEM
After refusing to join the American Revolution in 1776, Canadians retained their colonial status until 1867 and, in some ways, remained formally

associated with Great Britain well into the twentieth century. Their association with the mother country, though friendly enough, necessarily placed limits on Canada's national sovereignty. This residual connection to Great Britain was also a major irritant among the country's sizable French-speaking community. Until 1982, a British statute allowing Canada's federal and provincial governments certain powers served as Canada's constitution. However, it contained no written guarantees regarding the rights of individual Canadians, and it could not be amended without the approval of the British Parliament.

Confederation Is Born

For ninety years following the American Declaration of Independence, what is today Canada remained a collection of British colonies: Newfoundland, Nova Scotia, New Brunswick, Prince Edward Island, distant British Columbia, and the Canada colony (formed in 1841 with the unification of Upper and Lower Canada; today, Ontario and Quebec). Each had a legislature that operated under the watchful eye of the British government.

By the end of the American Civil War, these colonies were weak, isolated, and essentially broke. The lack of any political union among them made needed economic cooperation extremely difficult. And it left them especially vulnerable to a possible invasion by the United States. Canadians had always been wary of their expansion-minded neighbor, but during the Civil War years many of their leaders, and the British as well, grew increasingly concerned that a reunited United States would use its powerful army to carry its Manifest Destiny northward to British North America. It was in this volatile and uncertain economic and political environment that the idea of a union of British North American colonies began to take shape.

During the summer of 1864, leaders of the Atlantic colonies—together with John A. Macdonald, Georges-Etienne Cartier, and other representatives of the English- and French-speaking communities of the Canada colony— gathered at Charlottetown, Prince Edward Island, to discuss a possible union. A list of resolutions drafted at this meeting by these "fathers of Confederation" was refined at a two-week conference in Quebec City in October of the same year. The resolutions, which outlined the powers of future provinces and the proposed central government, were passed into law by the British Parliament in 1867 as the British North America Act (BNA Act). The act formed the basis for an initial confederation of Nova Scotia, New Brunswick, Ontario, and Quebec. The new entity was called the Dominion of Canada. British Columbia, Manitoba, and Prince Edward Island joined before the end of the century.[3]

Geography and the French historical presence and influence dictated that Canada should be a federation. Even in 1867, its population centers were too scattered and the cultures of its founding peoples too different to be governed effectively from one central place. The challenge facing the authors of the BNA Act had been to create a central government with sufficient authority to unite the new provinces while providing them enough autonomy to deal with their individual concerns. Final interpretation of the language of the act and the settlement of federal-provincial disputes were left to the Judicial Committee of the Privy Council (cabinet) of Great Britain. Canada's central government soon found its power eroding. In 1892, the committee ruled that the provinces were "supreme" within their areas of constitutional jurisdiction. It further stated that "the purpose of the British North America Act was neither to weld the provinces into one, nor to subordinate provincial governments to a central authority."

But circumstances changed rapidly during the twentieth century. As technology placed new demands on government for regulation, as Canada's regional diversity manifested itself in the form of economic disparity, and as problems of energy development and pollution cut across provincial borders, the question of who should have responsibility for what became increasingly difficult to answer. The issues themselves were challenging enough, but Canada's problems were always compounded because the BNA Act made no provision for allowing Canadians to adjust their constitution to deal with changing realities. Some thirty amendments were added over time, but each one took effect only after having been debated and approved by the British Parliament. Until patriation of the constitution was completed in 1982, the formal amendment power remained with the British government.

The Rocky Road to Patriation

Patriation, Canadians' term for "bringing the constitution home," required both the federal and provincial governments to agree on a formula for adding amendments to the BNA Act that would transform it into a workable plan of government for a sovereign Canada. Provincial premiers at a 1927 conference failed to reach agreement on an amending formula; another conference in 1935 failed as well. World War II crowded domestic concerns from the public agenda during most of the 1940s, but in 1949, Prime Minister Louis St. Laurent brokered a consensus that gained for Canada the right at least to interpret its constitution. Canada's Supreme Court, not the British Privy Council, would henceforth be the final arbiter in cases involving interpretation of the BNA Act. Still, there was no agreement on an amending formula, so the constitution itself remained in London.

Federal-provincial constitutional conferences were held off and on for the next thirty years but, fearful of approving a formula that might lead to changes limiting their authority and autonomy, the provincial premiers balked. Western provinces, greatly outnumbered in population by the rest of Canada, feared losing control over their valuable natural resources. Quebec had other concerns. Some measure of provincial autonomy was seen as its only protection against the erosion of its French culture, and a succession of Quebec premiers refused to accept any formula unless greater constitutional powers for their province came with it. By 1980, Quebec's first separatist government tried a new strategy: it offered its citizens a referendum authorizing it to begin sovereignty negotiations with Ottawa. The referendum was soundly defeated, 60-40 percent. Still, when federal-provincial agreement on a constitution-amending formula was finally hammered out in November 1981, Quebec was the lone dissenter. That winter, over Quebec's objections, the British Parliament gave its approval to the Constitution Act, 1982. On April 17, the Queen, during a rainy outdoor ceremony in Ottawa, officially proclaimed the patriation of Canada's constitution. Signing for Canada was the prime minister whose considerable political skills were largely responsible for the historic event—Pierre Trudeau.

The Constitution Act provided for significant changes in Canada's political system. The constitution could now be interpreted and amended by Canadians without reference to the parliament of Great Britain, and federal and provincial authorities were more clearly defined. But perhaps the most significant change, and the one of most direct importance to individual Canadians, was the addition of the Charter of Rights and Freedoms. This charter also served to raise the profile of Canada's Supreme Court, whose new, greatly enhanced role as guardian of the constitutional rights of individual Canadians has made it an even more important player in the country's legal system.

A Drowning at Meech Lake; Charlottetown Discord

In 1987, with a different (Progressive Conservative) federal government in place in Ottawa and a newly elected Liberal government in place in Quebec, Prime Minister Brian Mulroney helped engineer an agreement between provincial premiers that included a series of amendments crafted to satisfy Quebec's five minimum conditions for signing on to the new constitution. But the Meech Lake Accord (forged at the federal government's resort at Meech Lake) failed to win the required unanimous approval of the ten provincial legislatures by the June 23, 1990 deadline. On the final day, the "no" vote cast in the Manitoba legislature by Native member Elijah Harper prevented the unanimous consent required by its rules. Meech Lake was dead. Hours later, Newfoundland's legislature called off what would have been the final (and probably "no") vote.

After three years of anticipation that the June 23 date would represent Canada's finest hour, defeat of the Meech Lake Accord sent much of the country, bewildered and disappointed, into a profound depression. Almost immediately Prime Minister Mulroney launched a fresh series of initiatives to discern just what the "rest of Canada" wanted in the way of constitutional change before making still another offer to Quebec. This second try, however, would prove more difficult, divisive, and ultimately disappointing than the first. Debate over the Meech Lake Accord had heightened the awareness of other constituencies in Canada who also felt poorly served by the constitution, including women, western Canadians, and Elijah Harper's fellow Native peoples.

With the pulse-taking in high gear, Mulroney appointed a special constitutional committee of English-Canadian premiers, led by former Prime Minister Joe Clark, and charged it with the formidable task of crafting a constitutional reform package that would better accommodate the varied and often conflicting interests of Canada's ever-growing number of ethnic and regional groups. After nearly two years of reports, white papers, public discussions, and private brokering, Canadian leaders—by then including Quebec Premier Robert Bourassa—struck a constitutional deal like no other in Canadian history. The so-called Charlottetown Agreement represented the first consensus on constitutional reform between the federal and provincial governments since 1867. But, weary of the bickering, anxious to vent their frustrations with the ruling elite, and suspicious of the agreement's arcane language and complexity, the people of Canada rejected the plan in an unprecedented national referendum held October 26, 1992. Many Quebecers, however, including their angry premier, interpreted the referendum defeat as representing their second rebuff from the rest of Canada in as many years. The opposition Parti Québécois, which had itself urged Quebec voters to reject the agreement, immediately began to exploit the referendum result to breathe new life into the separatist cause.

In the 1994 provincial elections, the Parti Québécois won control of Quebec's Assemblée Nationale (the provincial legislature), and its leader, Jacques Parizeau, became premier. Just one year later, a provincial referendum on sovereignty failed by less than 1 percent of the popular vote in an election rife with charges of false counting and ballot fraud. The day after the vote, Parizeau resigned. His successor, the charismatic (now former) leader of the Bloc Québécois, Lucien Bouchard, immediately promised another referendum "sometime in the near future." For his part, Prime Minister Jean Chrétien immediately promised a renewed effort to find the elusive magic formula for a confederation that everyone can live with. Those efforts continue to this day.

THE CHALLENGE OF GOVERNING CANADA

Canada's considerable geographic and cultural diversity presents a special challenge for lawmakers. Trying to satisfy the desires of so many different regions and groups within a single country is no easy task. Laws acceptable to one region or one group of people often will create problems for another. The issue of language is but one example. Canada's official policy of bilingualism, a guarantee that French Canadians may receive government services in French wherever they live or travel in their country, is a major annoyance in western Canada where, for most people, French is still a "foreign" language. Another complaint: the necessity of printing government booklets, forms, and signs in two languages requires twice the time, paper, space, and money.

A Federal System

Its huge size and considerable regional and cultural diversity explain why Canada, like the United States, adopted a federal system of government.

Government powers and responsibilities are shared between the national government and the governments of the individual provinces and territories, but with a balance of power different from that of the United States. In the United States, the 10th Amendment to the Constitution grants to the states all powers not specifically given to the federal government. In Canada, however, only powers not delegated to the provinces are left to the federal government—and the powers granted to the provinces are considerable. They maintain almost exclusive jurisdiction over education, property laws, health services, and natural resources. Provincial governments may even regulate trade with other provinces to protect threatened industries. (Canada's participation in the North American Free Trade Agreement, of course, prevents provinces from regulating trade with the United States or Mexico.)

The national government, on the other hand, is responsible for military matters and defense, international affairs, trade with other nations, currency and banking, criminal law, the mail, and most taxation. The national capital is Ottawa, Ontario, although Canada's recently created "National Capital Region" extends across the Ottawa River to embrace Hull, Quebec. The bridges that connect the two cities form a symbolic linking of the British and the French, Canada's two official founding peoples.

Political Parties

One of the most portentous recent trends in Canadian politics has been the development of a divisive multiparty system. Five national parties now enjoy enough support to place delegations in the House of Commons of sufficient size to prevent the formation of a majority government. Some fear that, were this wide dispersal of power to become a common occurrence, it could lead to the kind of paralysis that has long plagued many of Europe's multiparty parliaments. Of equal concern to some observers is the fact that Canada's fractious politics divide along lines of regional self-interest. This situation makes secession a tempting option (or at least a powerful tool of influence) for disgruntled losers in national politics.

From east to west, Canadian politics reflect the regional diversity of the country's geography and culture. In Atlantic Canada, the Liberal Party historically has been the most popular, largely because that party has most consistently supported an active role for the federal government in reducing economic disparities among regions. Atlantic Canada, the poorest region, would be the biggest loser in any decentralization of power in Canada or in any move towards a more laissez-faire economy.

In the Western Provinces, frustration with what is perceived as Ottawa's preoccupation with central Canada, especially Quebec, has found its voice in the new Reform Party, the most conservative of Canada's five national parties. Its members oppose official bilingualism and have urged cutbacks in social welfare spending and increases in provincial autonomy. They have also been at the forefront of the movement to relax Canada's gun control laws.[4]

The West is also, ironically, the last bastion of support, ebbing though it may be, for social democrats. The New Democratic Party (NDP) has its roots here, the seeds having been planted during the Great Depression. After winning brief control of the government of Saskatchewan some fifty years ago, social democrats created the country's first provincial universal health care plan—a model for the current national system, one of Canada's proudest achievements. The NDP still has strength in the West, mainly at the provincial level and especially in Saskatchewan and British Columbia. But with the welfare state in retreat around the globe, the future of the party that for years fancied itself as "the conscience of Canada" is very much in doubt.

In Quebec, the Bloc Québécois, formed in 1992, won enough seats in the House of Commons to make it the official opposition party in the Canadian Parliament. Ontario, which elected the NDP to form its provincial government in 1990, has since returned to its more traditional Progressive Conservative roots. But, before doing so, in the 1993 federal election, Ontario voters returned not one member of that party to Parliament.

Parliament

Like most democracies in the world, Canada has a parliamentary form of government. The Canadian Parliament consists of an appointed Senate of 104 members and an elected House of Commons whose 301 members represent legislative districts called "ridings." When Canada holds a national election, voters in each riding go to the polls to select their one representative to the House of Commons. The number of candidates can vary greatly from riding to riding, depending on the number of active political parties in a given region and on how many independent candidates qualify for a place on the ballot.

Federal elections in Canada must be held at least every five years, but traditionally, prime ministers have called them during the fourth year of their mandate. When a new House of Commons meets after an election, the political party that has won the most seats has won the right to "form the government," as they say, and take charge of the civil service and the bureaucracy. The party's leader becomes Canada's prime minister. (Party leaders are chosen by delegates to leadership conventions that are similar in appearance to the national nominating conventions held every four years in the United States. Unlike their American counterparts, however, leadership conventions in Canada usually are called only after the death or resignation—voluntary or not—of a current leader.)

The prime minister administers the government with the assistance of a cabinet whose members are usually, but not always, selected from the governing party in the House of Commons (or, occasionally, the Senate). Each cabinet minister has one or more assignments within the bureaucracy, referred to as "portfolios," such as Defense, Foreign Affairs, and Fisheries. Unlike the president's cabinet in the United States, whose structure is a creature of legislation passed by the Congress and whose members must be

The Canadian Parliament

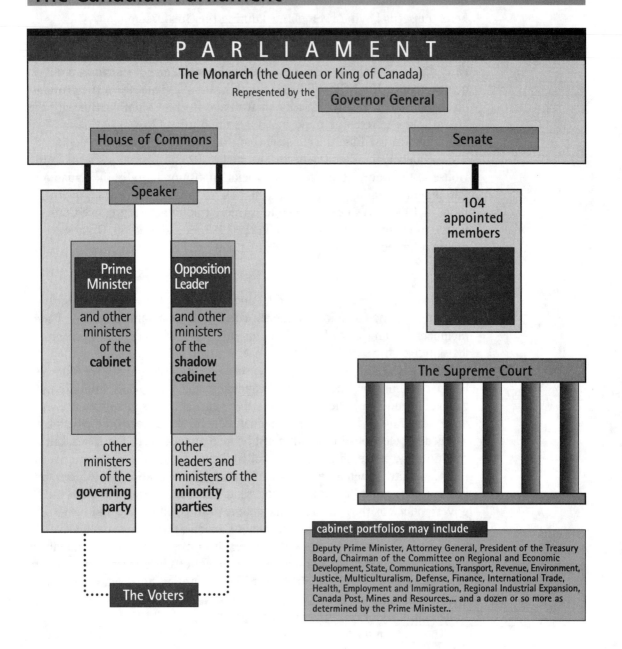

PARLIAMENT

The Monarch (the Queen or King of Canada)

Represented by the **Governor General**

House of Commons

Senate

Speaker

104 appointed members

Prime Minister

and other ministers of the **cabinet**

other ministers of the **governing party**

Opposition Leader

and other ministers of the **shadow cabinet**

other leaders and ministers of the **minority parties**

The Voters

The Supreme Court

cabinet portfolios may include

Deputy Prime Minister, Attorney General, President of the Treasury Board, Chairman of the Committee on Regional and Economic Development, State, Communications, Transport, Revenue, Environment, Justice, Multiculturalism, Defense, Finance, International Trade, Health, Employment and Immigration, Regional Industrial Expansion, Canada Post, Mines and Resources... and a dozen or so more as determined by the Prime Minister..

The gothic beauty of the Canadian parliament buildings in Ottawa.
Ottawa Tourism and Convention Authority

approved by the Senate, the cabinet in Canada is the sole preserve of the prime minister. The number of cabinet ministers, therefore, often changes from government to government, or even from year to year within the mandate of a single government. The size of the cabinet, which usually ranges from twenty to thirty members, depends on many factors, including the ambitiousness of the government's legislative agenda, various political considerations, and sometimes, public opinion.

Regardless of their number, members of the cabinet, including the prime minister, play a dual role in the government. They remain legislators and representatives of their constituents back home but, as cabinet members, they are also managers of the government bureaucracy. This fusion of legislative and executive authority is the most significant difference between the governments of Canada and the United States. Each would-be prime minister is elected by the people of one riding to be their representative in the House of Commons and becomes the country's chief executive only if his or her party wins the most seats. The president of the United States is elected, even if indirectly through the electoral college, by voters across the country to lead an executive branch that is separate from the lawmaking Congress.

The leader of the political party with the second greatest number of seats in the House of Commons becomes leader of Her Majesty's Loyal Opposition. Its members sit directly across the center aisle from the governing party in the rectangular House chamber (see diagram). Some members of the opposition parties are assigned by their leaders the special task of monitoring the policies and actions of a specific cabinet minister across the aisle. These members, known as "critics," form the so-called "shadow cabinets" of the opposition parties. They are the most vocal critics of the sitting government and prepare themselves to assume cabinet positions of their own should their party win the next election. They are given the opportunity to challenge the government almost on a daily basis while Parliament is in session. With few exceptions, every meeting of the House of Commons (called a "sitting") features a Question Period of forty-five minutes. With opposition members face-to-face with government leaders, the House of Commons chamber provides a perfect arena for confrontational debate and criticism. Question Period ensures a continuous accountability from government leaders by requiring them to defend their day-to-day actions in public view. It is televised, and usually quite lively.

Almost all proposed laws are introduced by a cabinet minister after consultation with other members of the cabinet, especially the prime minister. The fact that cabinet members are part of the governing party all but guarantees passage of their agenda.[5] The legislative tug-of-war that so often occurs in the United States when Congress and the White House are controlled by different parties, whatever its advantages or disadvantages, is alien to the Canadian system. Party solidarity is rigid. The odd member who may disagree with a party position is more likely to change affiliation or resign than to cast an independent vote.

Bills passed by the House of Commons must also be passed in the Senate, although today's Senate has considerably less legislative authority. In an earlier time, the Senate gave closer scrutiny to the work of the House, but as the parliamentary system has evolved in Canada, the appointed Senate has grown increasingly reluctant to challenge the will of the democratically elected House. In fact, the Senate has not rejected a House bill since 1940. Still, the Senate has played a useful role in adding amendments to improve bills and has conducted important in-depth investigations into a number of significant, often controversial issues. The fact that members of the Senate are appointed and can retain their seats until age seventy-five serves to insulate them from political pressures and may allow them to be more objective and forthcoming in their deliberations and investigations.

That, of course, is the charitable view. It must also be said that, for years, the Senate has been the object of considerable criticism from many quarters. The generous salaries and perks enjoyed by its members, who spend much less time on the job than members of the House of Commons, have soured public opinion across the country. Critics have charged that the Senate today is little more than a plush reserve for the political supporters of the prime ministers who appointed them. It is little wonder that Senate reform has been on the agenda of every serious set of constitutional talks since Meech Lake.

The Monarch

Though completely independent of Great Britain since 1982, Canada continues to invite the British monarch to serve as the Queen (or King) of Canada, too. Because the monarch cannot be in two countries at the same time, she or he, with the advice of the Canadian prime minister, appoints a prominent Canadian to the post of governor general to serve as a royal stand-in. (From 1763 to 1867, the governor general, then always a British appointee, ran the British North American empire—some with greater benevolence than others.) The governor general, in the monarch's absence, welcomes international leaders on their visits to Canada and presides over such special events as the

Canada Day celebration held each July 1st on Parliament Hill.[6]

The "GG," as he or she is known, also still formally opens each new session of Parliament during a day filled with many traditional ceremonies. The capstone of these ceremonies is the Speech from the Throne, written by the prime minister, but read by the governor general or, on rare occasions, by the monarch. The speech reveals the government's legislative goals for the new session to a rare joint sitting of the House and Senate and members of the Supreme Court.

A LOOK AHEAD

It is a historical cliche and a matter of pride among many Canadians that their country gained its independence and built its constitution through a process of evolution rather than revolution. But it could be argued that all three elements of their widely admired political system—peace, order, and good government—have been in increasingly short supply in recent years.

Many years ago, one of its prime ministers observed that Canada was "geographically ridiculous and politically impossible." Before too long, Canadians will have to decide once and for all whether they will continue to savor the irony of that observation—or live out its prophecy.

Notes

1. This was the party of Brian Mulroney and also of Canada's first woman prime minister, Kim Campbell, who inherited the position after being chosen party leader after Mulroney's resignation in June 1993. The Mulroney government, first elected in 1984, successfully negotiated two major treaties with the United States: the first on acid rain; the second, the Canada-United States Free Trade Agreement (now with the inclusion of Mexico, NAFTA). It also crafted the Goods and Services Tax (GST), an extremely unpopular national sales tax. When the global recession of the late 1980s sent unemployment in Canada soaring into double-digits, both free trade and the GST made convenient scapegoats. But the Mulroney government also had more than its share of political scandal—and the extravagant lifestyles of the prime minister and his wife did not go down well with Canadians, especially during difficult times. By the time he left office, Mulroney's approval rating hovered at around 15 percent, the lowest rating of any prime minister since polls began measuring such things in the 1940s.
2. All five parties retained their viability in the June 1997 federal election, which featured Canada's first five-way leaders' debate. In that election, the Liberals lost seats but managed to retain a majority in the House of Commons. Reform picked up seats to replace the third-place Bloc as the official opposition party. Both the NDP and the Progressive Conservatives made small gains that will guarantee their active participation in the House of Commons.

3. Newfoundland did not join. It remained a British colony until 1949.

4. But only for guns associated with hunting. No national party in Canada has even broached the subject of easing the country's ban on handguns and assault rifles.

5. The existence of a third party in any parliamentary system raises the possibility that no party will win more than 50 percent of the seats in an election. That possibility is even greater with four or five parties in the mix. In such an event, whichever party wins the most seats still takes charge of the prime minister's office and forms the cabinet, but this so-called "minority government" must build bridges and make certain concessions to another party, or even two, in order to secure the majority votes necessary to pass legislation. (If not, the government is considered defeated and another election must be called.) Such bridges and concessions might include appointing some third-party members to the cabinet, modifying legislation, or adjusting budget allocations. A number of Canada's most progressive social initiatives were the result of concessions to the NDP by past Liberal governments courting their support.

6. *The National Lampoon* once cracked that "Canadians celebrate the Fourth of July three days early in order to get ready for American tourists." In fact, Canada's independence day is April 17 (the date of the signing of the Constitution Act, 1982), but the anniversary passes each year virtually unnoticed. Canadians have been celebrating their July 1st birthday since the signing of the British North America Act on that date in 1867. Until the constitution was patriated in 1982, the holiday was known as Dominion Day. Then it was renamed Canada Day to reflect the country's, and the holiday's, new status. Further comparison of patriotic holidays in both countries reveals an interesting difference. Americans celebrate the birthdays of two presidents and a civil rights leader, whereas the only birthdays celebrated in Canada are those of Queens Victoria (who gave royal assent to the BNA Act) and Elizabeth II, the current monarch. No Canadian—not even the country's first prime minister—has been honored with a national holiday.

SOURCES
Books

Forsey, Eugene. *How Canadians Govern Themselves*. Ottawa: Government of Canada, 1988. A readable and succinct overview by a former member of the Senate of Canada who is also one of the country's foremost constitutional scholars.

McTeer, Maureen. *Parliament: Canada's Democracy and How It Works*. Toronto: Random House, 1987. A student text (middle-junior high), well illustrated and easy to understand. The author is the wife of former Prime Minister Joe Clark.

Merritt, Allen S., and George W. Brown. *Canadians and Their Government.* Toronto: Fitzhenry and Whiteside Limited, 1986. A well organized and readable mini-text written for Canadian high school students, which would also be useful as a teacher reference. The book concludes with an interesting comparison of the political systems of Great Britain, Canada, and the United States.

Sherman, George. *Teaching about the Canadian Parliamentary System.* Plattsburgh, New York: Center for the Study of Canada, SUNY Plattsburgh/North Country Teacher Resource Center, 1989. Includes teacher backgrounders, student readings, learning strategies, transparency masters, bibliography, glossary, and more.

Thompson, Wayne C. *Canada, 1996.* Washington: Skye Corporation/Stryker-Post Publications, 1996. A multidisciplinary overview of Canada that includes a substantial section dealing with Canadian government and politics, including leader and party profiles, provincial politics, and Canadian international policy. This book is updated on a biennial basis.

Videos

Canada's Governmental System. Government of Ontario, 1987. (30 min.) Instructional video on Canada's federal system, its geographic and historical setting, the division of federal and provincial powers, the workings of Parliament, and the provincial legislatures.

The Canadian Parliamentary Video. Canadian Broadcasting Corporation/New York State Education Department/Center for the Study of Canada, SUNY Plattsburgh/North Country Teacher Resource Center, 1989. (30 min.) A fast-paced overview that includes elections; Parliament's geographic, historical and cultural setting; and opening ceremonies.

Chapter 4
Canada and the World
Donald K. Alper and Matthew Sparke

Canada's relationship to the world beyond its borders is defined in the popular Canadian imagination by the country's continuing commitment to multilateral cooperation and to global peacekeeping in particular. However, this cooperative and multilateralist world view also has to be understood in terms of the overshadowing effect of Canada's proximity to the United States. Thus, as well as documenting Canada's commitments to global security and human rights protection, we also focus here on the changing nature and ramifications of Canada's relationship with its southern neighbor.

This relationship has intensified during the twentieth century as free trade agreements have coincided with what might be termed a new "economism"—a narrowed focus on the so-called "bottom line" in Canadian foreign affairs. This same economic interest has also oriented much of Canada's international outreach to the Pacific Rim, as well as innovative, high-tech regional developments.

CANADA AND MULTILATERALISM

Canadian Foreign Minister Lloyd Axworthy, on his first official visit to Washington in 1996, called on the United States to work with Canada "in pursuit of internationalism and engagement to achieve common foreign policy goals." With these words, the foreign minister emphasized a corner-stone of Canada's approach to international affairs: the pursuit of foreign policy objectives through a range of cooperative, multilateral actions, as opposed to operating unilaterally. In its relations with the United States, Canada has tried to equalize the power imbalance between the two countries by working in the context of multinational organizations like NATO, the G-7, and in recent years the Organization of American States (OAS). Canada, however, cannot avoid the necessity of giving priority to its crucial bilateral relationship with the United States, which provides the market for 80 percent of Canadian exports and is the source of 65 percent of foreign direct investment. This partnership has become even more important to Canada in recent years as prosperity and jobs are increasingly seen to be tied to a stable and well-managed relationship. With nearly half of Canada's manufacturing output heading south of the border, the U.S. market is now more important for Canadian manufacturers than the Canadian market.

The single area where multilateralism is best reflected is in Canada's commitment to the United Nations. Since the creation of the UN in 1945, Canada has been one of its strongest supporters. Today, Canada is proportionally one of the UN's larger financial contributors and is a leading advocate for further strengthening its role in international conflict resolution. In a major foreign policy review in 1995, Canada stressed its belief that the UN was as important as ever in promoting global peace. One recommendation strongly supported by Canada was to make the UN more proactive in troubled areas by providing quick reaction to world crises before they become severe and potentially unresolvable.

The UN is an area where Canada and the United States have different viewpoints. At a time when the United States is reconsidering its UN involvement and perhaps drifting towards greater isolationism in terms of international cooperation, Canada is working to revitalize the UN's capacity to respond to military as well as social and humanitarian crises. Canada has recently expressed its displeasure with the U.S. Congress for withholding payment of dues and calling for cuts in spending to the UN.

Promoting international security through multilateral forums like the UN has been and continues to be a central element of Canadian foreign policy. As a medium-sized power traditionally in the shadow first of Britain and then of the United States, Canada has emphasized participation in multilateral organizations. This internationalist outlook reflects Canada's dependence on international trade, but it also stems from the belief that Canadian interests are best pursued in forums where the voices of many countries can be heard and the potential domination of the most powerful can be offset. Moreover, multilateral cooperation fits the view that in the post-Cold War world, the major threats to security—regional conflicts, weapons proliferation, drug trafficking, human rights violations, and environmental degradation—require broad-based international cooperation.

Canada participates in many multilateral organizations that link security, political, and economic concerns. Canada is a member of the sixteen-member North Atlantic Treaty Organization (NATO), which was formed in 1949 as a western European defense alliance. Today, NATO functions to maintain stability and security in Europe, not only through an integrated military structure, but also by working to extend western democratic practices. Although NATO remains a Cold War-era collective security alliance—in which an attack on one NATO country is regarded as an attack on all—Canada increasingly supports NATO as a peacemaking and peacekeeping body, including participating in the mission to Bosnia. Canada also sees NATO as a promising framework for fostering democratic and liberal values in the formerly Eastern Bloc countries. Some Canadian officials believe their country can play a unique role in eastern Europe because the large number of immigrants from those countries now living in Canada forms the basis for a natural affinity. Although Canada's contributions of military personnel and cash to NATO have been reduced in recent years, NATO remains important because it provides an avenue for Canada to play a role in Atlantic-European affairs.

The Canadian government also actively participates in the newly formed

World Trade Organization (WTO), which has a membership of 121 nations. The purpose of the WTO is to put into place a multilateral worldwide trading system based on freer trade and institutionalized procedures for resolving trading disputes. In recent years, the WTO has discussed how to promote environmental concerns and international agreements on trade and labor standards.

In the Asia Pacific region, Canada has become an active player because of expanding trading ties and the enormous influx of immigrants from many Asian countries. Although Canada lacks the security commitments and traditional ties in the Asia Pacific region that it has in the Atlantic region, it has a strong interest in contributing to Asian Pacific stability, security, and prosperity, and in taking advantage of the enormous trade potential of this rapidly expanding area.

A major aspect of Canada's approach has been to work closely with such multilateral frameworks as the Asia Pacific Economic Cooperation Forum (APEC) and the Association of Southeast Asian Nations (ASEAN). APEC links seventeen economies in the region and provides a forum for government officials to meet, discuss common problems, and promote better understanding. APEC embodies an ambitious vision of free trade among countries in Asia and across the Pacific Basin to North and South America. ASEAN is made up of six Asian states (Brunei, Indonesia, Malaysia, the Philippines, Singapore, and Thailand) and a broader group of "dialogue partners," which includes Canada, the United States, and the European Community. Through the ASEAN Regional Forum, created in 1994, the governments engage in discussion on topics ranging from regional peacekeeping to nuclear nonproliferation, from maritime security cooperation to human rights.

These multilateral forums are designed to foster the habit of constructive dialogue aimed at building cooperation within and across the region and eventually supplanting the traditional structure of military alliances. Canada's commitment to this approach reflects the belief that its long-term security and economic interests are best enhanced through broad-based consultation processes among the diverse interests in the Asia Pacific region. Active participation in these evolving multilateral forums facilitates the expansion of trade with the rapidly growing Asian economies. With the ASEAN member nations alone offering a market of 300 million people, APEC country economies as a whole are undergoing unprecedented growth, on which Canada is trying to capitalize. In addition, companies from Canada and other industrialized countries are increasingly moving their production activities and capital into these ASEAN countries.

Another multilateral forum of which Canada is a member is the Commonwealth, made up of Great Britain and most of its former colonies—representing about one-quarter of the world's population. As a multiethnic, multiracial organization, the Commonwealth serves as a forum where member nations can make their views known and gain access to a network of economic, social, and educational programs. The Commonwealth makes possible regular and often close contact among nations rich and poor, north and south.

A similar multicultural organization to which Canada belongs is La Francophonie, an association of French-speaking countries, most of which share the experience of being former French colonies. Like the Commonwealth, it provides mutual assistance to its members in all fields and builds bridges between cultures and peoples.

CANADA AND PEACEKEEPING

When people think of Canada's activities abroad, peacekeeping is one of the first to come to mind, and indeed Canada is often one of the first countries to offer peacekeepers to the United Nations. Since the end of World War II, Canadians have participated in all major peacekeeping operations mandated by the UN. In 1997, Canadian personnel were involved in ten UN missions, making Canada the sixth largest contributor. Canadian forces form the third largest contingent of peacekeepers in the Balkans, and recent missions have been as varied as assisting Cambodians in de-mining their countryside and sending Royal Canadian Mounted Police training personnel to Haiti (along with military personnel) to help professionalize the Haitian army and police force.

Since the end of the Cold War, an important civilian component has been added to the traditional military aspects of peacekeeping. In 1995, Canada established the Lester B. Pearson Canadian International Peacekeeping Training Center to offer research and instruction on all aspects of peacekeeping. Pearson was a Canadian diplomat, and later prime minister, who won the Nobel Peace Prize for his contributions to restoring peace during the 1956 Suez Crisis. The Pearson Center's program involves traditional peace enforce-

Canadian soldiers in UN tanks in Croatia. Canada is one of the most respected peace-keepers in the United Nations. Canadian Department of Defence

ment training focusing on military missions and cease-fire monitoring, as well as developing expertise to meet the new challenges of the post-Cold War environment—ethnic and regional conflicts, humanitarian disasters, human rights violations, and struggles to reform corrupt and undemocratic governments. The new generation of peacekeepers is trained to work with civil police, human rights organizations, the media, and elections officials in

preventing conflict, promoting democratic development, and helping countries help themselves. In addition to training peacekeepers, the Pearson Center conducts seminars and conferences on challenges of mass refugee migration and human disaster relief.

CANADA AND THE PACIFIC

By the year 2000, more than 70 percent of all world trade will be among or with the economies of the Asia Pacific region, and today this region is Canada's second largest market after the United States. Japan is Canada's second largest individual trading partner, and trade with the Asia Pacific region surpasses that with the European G-7 nations combined. Moreover, the vast majority of those who apply to come to Canada as refugees are from Asia. In 1996, *Macleans*, Canada's national weekly news magazine, introduced a Chinese edition.

Until relatively recently, the Pacific was not an important part of Canada's international consciousness, and Canada's treatment of Asian immigrants was deplorable. The opening of the Canadian west in the late nineteenth century, the establishment of gold fields, and the completion of the Canadian Pacific Railway to the Pacific coast resulted in a large influx of immigrants from Asia, mainly from China and Japan. Until the second half of the twentieth century, Asian immigrants were the victims of severe discrimination and exploitation. For example, exclusion policies for a time prevented Chinese from immigrating to Canada; Japanese Canadians were forcibly sent to "relocation" camps during World War II; restrictive covenants in Vancouver prohibited Chinese Canadians from buying property outside the "Chinatown" area until the 1930s; and Chinese Canadians were not permitted to vote until 1947. Yet, despite this history, Asians came to Canada in great numbers because of the country's reputation as a land of opportunity and because, in later years, of a more relaxed, even proactive, immigration policy and increasingly enlightened attitudes toward multiculturalism. Now the Asia Pacific region is the source of nearly one-half of all immigrants to Canada.

After World War II, Canada defined its interests in the Pacific in the context of the Cold War and the western alliance. Canada sent troops to join UN forces in Korea, and throughout the 1950s and 1960s generally supported the anticommunism policies of the United States. Although commercial ties were growing, Canada's primary orientation remained with Europe and North America.

The late 1960s, however, brought a discernible change. Buoyed by the enormous commercial potential of Asian markets, especially Japan and China, Canada embarked on a policy of increasing commercial trade relations with the Asia Pacific region. In 1970, partly to show independence from the United States, Canada officially recognized the People's Republic of China—then successfully negotiated an enormous wheat deal with China.

Promotion of transportation and tourism and the penetration of the "closed" Japanese market were also part of Canada's efforts. By the mid-1970s, Japan had become Canada's second largest trading partner, and China became the other major commercial opportunity in Asia. New and expanded commercial ties were also established in Southeast Asia following the end of the Vietnam War and the increased stabilization of the region's governments.

By the 1980s, government officials, businesspeople, and academics were referring to the dawn of the Pacific era and taking measures to respond to it. Rapid economic growth in Japan and China continued to attract the interest of the Canadian business community, and newly industrializing countries (NICs), such as South Korea, Taiwan, and Singapore, were recording growth rates unequaled anywhere in the world. Trade with South Korea grew rapidly, and it soon became Canada's second largest Asian trading partner.

Western Canada, in particular, had begun to see its future as closely integrated with the Pacific basin countries. Vancouver experienced a significant shift from its traditional role as service center for British Columbia to a major service center for Asia Pacific economies. The Asia-Pacific Foundation (APF), created by an Act of Parliament in 1984, has as its primary objective the furthering of the Canadian role in Asia Pacific. Headquartered in Vancouver and with liaison offices in Tokyo, Taipei, and Singapore, the APF has received substantial federal funding to develop Asian language and awareness programs across the country. The province of British Columbia has also taken action to strengthen Vancouver's position as Canada's Pacific center for trade, commerce, and air travel. In 1987, the province instituted the Pacific Rim Educational Initiatives program designed to prepare its students for the twenty-first century marketplace by focusing their studies on the culture and history of the Asian Pacific. Partnerships have also been created among the federal government, the province of British Columbia, and the city of Vancouver to promote trade and investment across the Pacific.

By the 1990s, Canada had clearly given priority to North America and the Asia Pacific in foreign political and economic activity. The government's foreign policy "White Paper" issued in 1995 announced as its first priority the promotion of prosperity and employment through trade. Using the "Team Canada" approach, high level Canadian officials, led by the prime minister, journeyed in search of new markets and investment opportunities in China and other growing Asian countries. While multilateral frameworks like APEC and ASEAN are viewed as critical in building good will and facilitating business opportunities, the Canadian strategy has increasingly focused on selective targeting of specific nations.

On political/security issues, Canada has favored new multilateral frameworks as opposed to reliance on traditional big power military alliances. Multilateral forums are seen as best suited for dealing with the new security issues such as nuclear testing and proliferation, ethnic strife, and migration. Canada has taken the lead in the North Pacific Cooperative Security Dialogue, an organization attempting to foster working relationships among countries in the region without formal ties. Further, many Canadian-led nongovernmental organizations (NGOs) involving academics, nonproliferation advocacy groups, and military experts have opened up dialogues in areas where government officials are constrained by official relations.

One of these areas of concern to both Asian countries and Canada is the environment. Large forested areas of southeast Asia are being depleted to provide tropical timber for Japan and other developed countries, and by 2020 there are expected to be at least fifteen cities with populations of more than fifteen million in the Asian region. Rapid growth and urbanization have already resulted in severely overloaded infrastructure, heavy pollution, traffic congestion, housing shortages, and environmental degradation. These problems have increased the demand for specialized services such as environmental consultants, pollution-control equipment, and engineers for which Canada, and particularly Vancouver, has a comparative advantage. Today and into the future, the markets that provide the greatest export opportunity for environmental industries are in the Asia Pacific region.

A more difficult and internally controversial aspect of Canada's relations with Pacific countries arose over the trade-human rights conflict—an issue in Canada's dealings with many Asian countries but most prominently with China. Since the massacre of protesting students in Tiananmen Square in 1989, many Canadians have opposed enhanced relations with China. The Canadian government, however, has not been willing to accept exclusion from the Chinese market. Since 1989, Canada and China have signed several joint partnership agreements, Canada has provided China with substantial loans and export credits, and Canadian businesses have signed deals worth more than $1 billion. When critics condemned Ottawa for its bottom-line approach, Jean Chrétien's Liberal government retorted that the relationship with China is not a matter of team Canada versus human rights. Instead, they claim, the goal is to link, not separate, the political, trade, and aid aspects of foreign policy. The Chrétien government's argument is that trade fosters engagement, which makes possible the advancement of other issues and values from the inside. Although this approach seeks to link hard-nosed business with value agendas that reflect the Canadian democratic tradition, many Canadians have spoken out against engagement until such time as significant progress is made on human rights.

BRITISH COLUMBIA AND "CASCADIA"

Although all of Canada has been affected in some way by the country's connections with Asia, the impact on the province of British Columbia (B.C.) has been extremely significant and is manifest in a multitude of ways. The largest number of Asian-Canadians are in British Columbia, and the proportion of Vancouver's population with roots in Asia has surpassed 30 percent (up from approximately 10 percent in 1980). The steady stream of immigration has given parts of Vancouver the flavor of Hong Kong and has fostered a booming trade with Asia that now accounts for one-third of the province's exports. Asian languages are prevalent in the city's public schools; neighborhoods and popular culture reflect Asian themes; and businesses increasingly are geared to Asian markets and Asian Canadian tastes. Two Chinese Canadians were elected to the B.C. legislative assembly for the first time in 1996.

British Columbia's connections to the peoples and countries of Asia Pacific have given this province a view of itself and its future that is quite different from the rest of Canada. One *Vancouver Sun* writer termed the province's new orientation as "transPacific." Others refer to British Columbia as a "distinct society," given its Pacific-oriented economy and cultural kinship with Asia. In fact, some—in a parody of the politics of Quebec's claim to constitute a distinct society—have argued that B.C. should be understood as an abbreviation for "Bye, Canada." Insofar as these sentiments have become associated with a new notion of a transnational region linking B.C. with the United States, they may represent an equally significant threat to the coherence of Canadian confederation.

B.C.'s position is paralleled in the U.S. states of Washington and Oregon, where the similar proximity of Asian economic opportunities align with comparable, if less pronounced, immigration-based linkages. Laying claim to an older environmental vision of a cross-border "ecotopia," economic boosters in the region have argued that the future success of Washington, Oregon, and British Columbia lies in their partnership as a transnational region called "Cascadia." This Cascadian vision offers its B.C. boosters and American counterparts an attractive and appropriately internationalist image with which to accomplish two goals at once. On the one hand, Cascadia can be advertised as a way of attracting investment dollars. The concept envisions a transnational region perfectly positioned on the Pacific Rim, but also somehow alienated from the distant federal control centers of Ottawa and Washington, D.C., and therefore inherently well suited to an age and area of free trade unfettered by governmental regulation. On the other hand, Cascadia has also simultaneously been proposed as a regional vision that will enable B.C. and its southern neighbors to better position themselves in the global competition for consumption dollars. On this basis, Cascadia's boosters have initiated a promotional campaign in, among other places, Japan and Australia, advertising the region as a site for a so-called "Two Nation Vacation." Along with this transnational tourism campaign, other attempts to attract tourism dollars into the region have included plans to host a transnational Olympic games where sporting activities would be scheduled simultaneously in Victoria, Vancouver, Seattle, and Portland.

Along with the dual projects of attracting investment and tourism to Cascadia have come a series of infrastructural initiatives geared towards reducing the friction of distance and borders on movement into and through the region. A high-speed rail link between Vancouver and Seattle is continually being proposed, and improvements in passenger as well as freight transportation by rail are already under way. At the same time, boosters of the region are working on border initiatives to speed up customs and immigration processing between Canada and the United States. The most notable of these developments to date is the so-called "PACE lane" through which drivers purchasing the Peace Arch Crossing Experiment decal from either Canadian or American authorities are assured of speedy, "pre-clearance" passage across the border. These border-eroding initiatives also indicate in quite substantive ways how Cascadia constitutes something more than just an environmentally attractive "region-state" in an age of niche markets and global imagineering. As a transnational region made more possible by the erosion of the international border, Cascadia also illustrates the productive synthesis of transnationalism and regionalism in the economic context of what has come to be known as globalization.

CANADA AND GLOBALIZATION

As a buzzword, "globalization" has suffered the fate of overuse. However, as a way of describing the changes in the world economy following the collapse of Bretton Woods, the oil-shocks, and the more general crisis of capitalism in the early 1970s, the word remains useful. Indeed, the term is appropriate not only to understand regional developments such as Cascadia, but to more generally comprehend Canada's changing relationship with the world at large.

As economic historians remind us, the world economy has always been global to some extent, and the global trading links connecting the big vertically integrated and nationally based companies of the middle part of the twentieth century were, in this sense, no exception. However, after the crises of the early 1970s (and, in fact, as one of the underlying reasons for those crises), the organization of production, trade, and consumption increasingly became reconfigured globally. Global trade has become less about the exchange of finished products between autonomous companies located in autonomous nation-states. Instead, we have witnessed the growth of large transnational companies that organize the production process on a global scale, subcontracting subprocesses to the most globally competitive bidders.

As a result, intra-firm trade (trade between components of the same transnational conglomerate) now accounts for approximately 40 percent of all global trade, and the significance of national trade policies, indeed the significance of nation-states as regulatory entities more generally, has been considerably reduced. Now, nation-states are increasingly forced to compete in the global divisions of labor, investment, and consumption. To be sure, the nation-state has not, contrary to some of the globalist gurus of this new world order, simply "ended." Evolving would-be region-states such as Cascadia are still very much emergent. But given that nation-states now compete globally in much the same way as regions like Cascadia, the ability of national governments like Canada's to set policy and regulate business has been considerably weakened.

In many ways the form of border-corroding dynamics evident in Cascadia is emblematic of the more general weakening of national governance in developed countries like Canada. In fact, Cascadia is by no means the only example of a transnational region mediating and thereby redefining Canada's new relationship with the world economy. In the Prairies, there is talk of the Red River Corridor linking Winnipeg in Manitoba with Minneapolis–St. Paul in Minnesota. A private consortium plans to turn Winnipeg airport into a continental cargo-hub which—employing a new duty-exempt regional designation for the airport—would seek to serve the whole metropolitan Northeast from Toronto to Chicago with European and Japanese freight. Of course, transnational linkages between southern Ontario and U.S. cities like Detroit and Buffalo go back long before the recent round of free trade-led restructuring, but they may, for the same reason, be seen as avatars of the new world order. Further east, the provinces of New Brunswick and, to a lesser extent, Nova Scotia are also increasingly pinning hopes of development on transnational partnerships with New England states. These developments can easily be overstated, but they enable and exemplify a certain integration of Canada with the United States and thus introduce the larger issues surrounding the changing Canada–U.S. relationship.

CANADA'S CHANGING POSITION VIS-À-VIS THE UNITED STATES

During its early colonial history and even up until the end of World War II, Canada's major continental axis of economic development followed the trajectory of its relationship with the world across the Atlantic, from east to west. The great St. Lawrence River was to become the major conduit of this activity, as the economic exploitation of Canada's natural resources turned from cod, the fish staple of the Maritimes, to fur and timber from what became known as the "empire of the St. Lawrence." From the river port cities of Montreal and Quebec, these staples were transported on ships bound for England and France. Finished goods from Europe entered Canada by the same route, turning Montreal in particular into

Canadian fishing boats blockade an Alaskan passenger ferry, their owners furious over "unfair tactics" by American fishers. Defining the rights of Canadian and American fishers as Pacific salmon travel through Canadian, international and American waters without passports is a major source of conflict in the Canada-U.S. relationship.
Ian Smith/*Vancouver Sun*

Canada's linchpin of east-west trade.

From confederation in 1867 until World War II, the east-west pattern remained dominant, even as the frontier of colonial development moved west with Toronto slowly coming to eclipse Montreal as the major staging post of east-west relations. During this time, U.S. economic and political might was often at the forefront of Canadian consciousness—the desire to reach the west coast by railroad before the United States being symbolic of a wider effort to articulate a coherent nation-state as a bulwark against apparent U.S. eagerness to command the whole continent. However, economic activity in Canada (most notably the railroad and a high tariff) was organized around east-west links, and connections to the south were often economically infeasible.

One example of this lack of integration was the failure in 1911 of the first bid to implement a free trade agreement, then called a "reciprocity agreement," with the United States. This failure brought down the Laurier government, but it was because of more than party politics. It also symbolized how most businesses in Canada were then uninterested in free trade with the United States. The east-west system was serving them well enough, they had fixed capital invested in the system infrastructure, and they did not want to see it threatened.

After World War II and the growth of the United States as the preeminent global economic powerhouse, all this was to change—but it was a slow evolution. While Canada's links with the old colonial powers declined and connections with the U.S. industrial northeast intensified, Canadian social and political life remained organized by a form of regional balancing act in which the provinces rather than social classes were the fissiparous elements brought together through national policy-making. Canada, with its widely varied geography and regionally distinct cultures, seemed to demand even more of a national redistribution system—a system that could not only provide a social-welfare safety net, but could also hold all the inequalities of the diverse regions together in the grander equality of nationhood. America, as the seemingly political opposite to the massive projects of public investment in Canadian infrastructure (e.g., a national rail service, airline, and health care system), came in these postwar years to be construed as the embodiment of all that Canada was not. Given the parallel Great Society programs in the United States, this was a mistaken simplification. But it nevertheless became a form of national self-identification around which Canadians could rally—all the while their economy became ever more interwoven with American industrial development.

An indication of how today's dominance of north-south links has come to threaten the whole postwar system of Canadian confederation is clearly illustrated by the case of Quebec. Given that Quebec's early economic development was predicated on east-west trade with Europe, it was no surprise that the province was badly affected by even the early postwar changes. With north-south development coming to define Canada's most significant relationship with the world economy, Quebec became geographically marginalized. This marginalization has increased as American development has moved west, first away from New England to the Chicago-Detroit region, and, subsequently, to the west coast. In the resulting climate of unemployment and economic insecurity, the call to separatism found an increasingly eager audience. With the federal government's resources already stretched, the system of regional redistribution has not been able to address all of the economic problems caused by marginalization, and so Ottawa's critics in Quebec have found it easy to find fault and inadequacy.

Of course, Canada's constitutional quandaries have had a relatively independent political logic to them as well, and as other chapters in this book explain, Trudeau's patriation of the constitution in 1982 and the constitutional conferences at Meech Lake and Charlottetown had their own destabilizing effects on confederation. However, it must be remembered that these governments of the 1980s were also those most involved in framing the conditions and organizing the entry of Canada into free trade agreements with the United States. Indeed, for many critics, the legalistic constitutional developments and the advent of free trade are linked as two sides of the same free market currency—a currency that is seen to indicate an inexorable and undesirable Americanization of Canadian politics.

FREE MARKET DEREGULATION

After winning the general election in 1984 and announcing in New York that Canada was once again "open for business," Prime Minister Brian Mulroney was only too eager in 1985 to celebrate the results of a Royal Commission on Economic Union, the so-called Macdonald Commission. The commission had concluded that Canada's economic future lay in embracing the free market reforms already being implemented in countries like the United Kingdom and in formalizing those reforms internationally in a free trade agreement with the United States. The Reagan administration was happy to oblige in this regard, and eventually, after a contentious general election in which the anti-free trade vote was split between the New Democratic Party and the Liberals, Mulroney's Conservatives were reelected and enabled to ratify the Canadian-U.S. Free Trade Agreement.

Implemented in January 1989, this agreement has been blamed for the terrible recession in Canada from 1989 to 1991. Certainly, some of the job losses were due to U.S. branch plants moving from Canada back to America, now known as the "New South" of lower wages and inferior health and safety regulations. Likewise, the recession had much to do with the high interest rates and overvalued Canadian dollar imposed by the Bank of Canada in the name of monetarist money supply policies. However, the more significant implications of free trade and the new dominance of north-south linkages in Canadian affairs go deeper than all the effects of the early 1990s recession. Rather, they consist of the entrenchment of a fundamentally free-market, deregulatory approach to governance in everything from regional redistribution to the welfare system that has left many Canadians complaining vociferously about Americanization.

The Americanization argument in many ways misreads the symptoms as the illness. Certainly, because free trade has seemed to lock the Mulroney reforms in place, Canadians are increasingly unable to contrast themselves with the United States in terms of possessing a more communitarian system of welfare provision. Indeed, Jean Chrétien's Liberal Party, which in 1988 was a zealously patriotic critic of free trade, quickly became a free trade fan and signed on to the North American Free Trade Agreement (NAFTA) as soon as it was elected in 1993. The party was reelected in 1997. This about-face indicates the profundity of the entrenchment of free trade thinking and commitments.

But Americanization is not the best way to describe this phenomenon. First, it ignores the degree to which Canadian capital has become a powerful continental player in its own right, often buying out smaller American competitors. The four big Canadian banks are among the ten largest on the continent, and Canada's other corporate giants include the world's largest shoe manufacturer, North America's second largest producer of telecommunications equipment, the world's largest and third largest distillers, and its largest and second largest nickel producers.

Second, the Americanization argument also ignores the degree to which Canada's embrace of the whole free market vision of governmental cutbacks and monetarist fiscal policy was orchestrated by Canadian, as opposed to American, elites. The same business organizations that rejected reciprocity in 1911 saw in the 1980s that the east-west system was no longer tenable and that free trade north-south was far more likely to secure a profitable return on their increasingly north-south investments in fixed capital.

Finally, and most significantly, the Americanization argument is inadequate insofar as it offers ever more outdated nationalist arguments as answers to a serious threat to the socioeconomic system of Canadian confederation. American politics is not the cause of the sweeping decentralization and tremendous strains on Canadian unity. Simply bashing Yankees will not enable Canadians to regain control over their economic interactions with the world outside. Likewise, heaping scorn on American individualism will not prevent the way even left-leaning provincial governments have had to conform to the new economic dictates of competition and make cutbacks in the welfare state. As the new economic logic forces the provinces to compete with one another in a grisly race to the bottom, it is not at America so much as at the way free market deregulation policies have been internationalized to which criticism should be directed.

Perhaps, though, it is in Canadians' fabled national skills as communication specialists that an alternative future lies. After all, it was the Canadian Marshall McLuhan who first anticipated the impact of globalization when he spoke about the "global village." Links across the continent between Canadian environmental groups, Canadian feminists, and Canadian unions hold open another way of integrating Canada with the world in north-south directions. These groups are increasingly working together with their Mexican and American counterparts to build new transnational coalitions.

For the moment, however, it is the skills of Canada's free marketers that have proven themselves most successful, and the neoliberal Canadian engagement with the world, east-west across the Pacific, as well as north-south, proceeds apace.

Sources

Cameron, Maxwell, and Richard Grinspun, eds. *The Political Economy of North American Free Trade.* New York: St. Martins, 1991.

Canada, Department of Foreign Affairs and International Trade. "Backgrounder: Canada and Peacekeeping." World Wide Web site: www.dfait-maeci.gc.ca/english/foreignp/disarm/peacek.htm.

Gertler, Meric, and Daniel Drache, eds. *The New Era of Global Competition: State Policy and Market Power.* Montreal: McGill-Queen's University Press, 1991.

Jenson, Jane, Rianne Mahon, and Manfred Bienefeld. *Production, Space, Identity: Political Economy Faces the 21st Century.* Toronto: Canadian Scholars' Press, 1993.

McMillan, Charles. "Canada, Asia, and the Pacific Century." *The Annals of the American Academy* 538 (March 1995): 96-114.

Chapter 5
The Canadian Economy
Anthony Cicerone and Mark J. Kasoff

Why should American students study the Canadian economy? First, most Americans do not realize that Canada, not Japan, is by far the most important international economic partner for the United States. In fact, the province of Ontario alone does more trade with the United States than Japan. In 1995, total trade (goods, services, and investment income) between the United States and Canada amounted to $334 billion (U.S.),[1] the largest two-way trade in the world. Second, many of the products that Americans use each day are Canadian-made. Americans live in homes built with Canadian lumber, read newspapers printed on Canadian newsprint, eat pasta made with Canadian durum wheat, and enjoy listening to such popular Canadian singers as Céline Dion, k. d. lang, and Alanis Morrisette. Commuters traveling to work in Boston ride on light rail trains built by Bombardier, a Canadian company. WordPerfect is now owned by Ottawa-based Corel. Third, by studying the Canadian economy, American students will learn economic concepts, including those of international trade, and will gain a better understanding and appreciation of their own economy.

SIMILARITIES BETWEEN THE CANADIAN AND U.S. ECONOMIES
In many respects, the Canadian economy is very much like the American economy. The two countries face similar economic problems, have similar goals and business structures, and are among the wealthiest nations in the world. Canada's economy, like that of the United States, is a mixed capitalist system in which individuals own property and most economic decisions are made in the private market, but the government is an active participant.

A comparison of the two demonstrates that, although the U.S. economy is much larger, their per capita income and the standard of living are similar. The most widely used measure of a nation's income is Gross Domestic Product (GDP), defined as the total current value of all the goods and services produced within a nation for a particular year. In 1995, per capita GDP was $19,169 (U.S.) in Canada and $27,571 (U.S.) in the United States. Although it is true that the Canadian GDP per capita was less than that of the United States, this does not necessarily mean that living standards were lower. Other measures of living standards indicate that, while Americans have more passenger cars and televisions per capita, Canadians have more telephones and a lower infant mortality rate. Based on its high standard of living, quality of life, abundant natural resources, and strong democracy, the United Nations named Canada the best country in the world in which to live in 1996.

As in the United States, Canadians have established a set of economic goals and expect their government to pursue them actively. The Economic Council of Canada, a federal government agency established in 1963 to advise the government and inform the public, originally agreed upon five basic goals for Canada's economy: 1) full employment, 2) a high rate of economic growth, 3) reasonable price stability, 4) a viable balance of international payments, and 5) an equitable distribution of rising incomes.

Historically, government has played an important role in the Canadian economy through mega-infrastructure projects, publicly owned crown corporations (e.g., Canadian National Railways), equalization payments to poorer provinces, and agricultural policy (e.g., the Canadian Wheat Board). Even so, private businesses continue to use most of the country's resources and to produce most of its goods and services. In recent years, financial pressures have reduced the share of governmental economic activity. Many crown corporations have been sold to private investors, and federal transfer payments to the provinces have been reduced. Canadian businesses are organized as proprietorships, partnerships, corporations, and cooperatives and vary widely in size and scope of operation, but corporations are the predominant form. According to the *Financial Post* 500, in 1995 the ten largest Canadian businesses ranked by total sales were: General Motors of Canada Ltd., BCE Inc., Ford Motor Company of Canada Ltd., Royal Bank of Canada, Northern Telecom Ltd., Chrysler Canada Ltd., Seagram Co. Ltd., Canadian Imperial Bank of Commerce, George Weston Ltd., and Alcan Aluminum Ltd. Of these, three—General Motors of Canada Ltd., Ford Motor Company of Canada Ltd., and Chrysler Canada Ltd.—are completely owned by their United States parents.

Canada's economy is still very resource-dependent. Fish, wood and mineral products—including off-shore oil—provide millions of dollars worth of exports every year.
Bow Valley Energy, Inc.

Most of the wide range of Canadian goods and services are produced for consumers. In 1995, Canadians spent 60 percent of GDP on consumer goods and services, while Americans spent 68 percent. Many Canadian consumer products have brand names familiar to Americans. Canadians may eat Kellogg's Corn Flakes for breakfast, drive to work in a Chevrolet, stop at McDonald's for lunch, and brush their teeth with Crest toothpaste before bed. Even the sacred Canadian doughnut, best known by the name of Tim Horton, has recently merged with Wendy's American fast food chain.

DIFFERENCES BETWEEN THE CANADIAN AND U.S. ECONOMIES

Although the Canadian economy appears at first glance to be simply a smaller version of the American, this is not the case. The American economy *is* more than ten times larger than Canada's: in 1995, Canadian GDP was $565.8 billion (U.S.), and the U.S. GDP was $7,253.8 billion (U.S.). But while the Canadian mixed market economy is structured much like that of the United States, there are differences between the two. In the Canadian economy, natural resources have had greater historical importance, greater reliance has been placed on international trade, and there is more extensive government involvement, a more centralized banking and financial system, and large regional economic disparities.

Staples Thesis

A nation's economic system develops over time, but its basic structure depends in part on its natural resource endowment. The "staples thesis," developed by Professors Harold Innis and W. A. Mackintosh to explain the Canadian economy, proposes that a country's economic growth and development are based on the export of staples (raw materials or primary resources) for which it has a comparative advantage.

The extent to which the staples trade affects the economy depends on three linkages. First, backward linkages involve investment in those industries that produce inputs for the staples sector. In the wheat industry, for example, farmers require fertilizer, irrigation equipment, tractors, and harvesting machinery. Second, forward linkages involve investment in those industries that process the staples. In the forest industry, processed goods include pulp, paper, lumber, ships, housing, and furniture. Third, final demand linkages involve investment in the sectors in which the income earned in the staples industry is spent. The owners and workers who earn their incomes in the staples industry spend their income on consumer products, from food, clothing, and shelter to automobiles, health services, and entertainment.

Staples products with strong linkages help the economy grow and develop into a vibrant, diverse, independent economic system. Staples products that do not establish strong linkages, on the other hand, are apt to create an economic system that is almost totally dependent on income earned from the staples product and never becomes self-sustaining.

For Canada, the economy has historically been based upon four staples: fish, fur, forests, and farming. Portuguese, French, and British seafarers fished off the coasts of Newfoundland and Nova Scotia in the seventeenth and eighteenth centuries, but because of its structure, the fishing industry did not initially lead to large-scale settlement in Canada. Some small outposts were established, but the fishermen came ashore only to dry or salt their catch, then headed back home to Europe.

Trapping of fur-bearing animals, especially the beaver (Canada's national symbol), also became important during the seventeenth and eighteenth centuries. Beaver pelts were exported to Europe, where they were processed and made into the broad-brimmed hats that were stylish at the time. The famous Hudson's Bay Company, the oldest joint-stock company in the English-speaking world, was chartered on May 2, 1670, and became the predominant purchaser and exporter of pelts to Europe. Because beavers were relatively easy to trap, the rapidly diminished supply pushed trappers further and further into the north and west. The fur industry, however, did not have the necessary structure to establish strong backward and forward linkages.

By the early nineteenth century, the lumber industry was operating at its peak. Timber, which is a large, bulky cargo, was shipped to England for use in shipbuilding, while return crossings brought immigrants and manufactured goods to Canada. Unlike the fur trade, the timber industry was complementary to agriculture and established more linkages to other industries such as shipbuilding, saw mills, and furniture manufacturing.

Agriculture became increasingly more important in the nineteenth century, and with the introduction of new strains, wheat became an engine of growth for the Canadian economy until the Great Depression. Moreover, growing wheat established numerous forward, backward, and final demand linkages. These included demands for farm equipment, grain elevators, food

Table 5–1. Changing structure of the Canadian economy
Output by Sector as Percent of Total Production

Industry	1870	1926	1970	1994
Agriculture	34.3	18.1	3.3	2.5
Forestry	9.9	1.3	0.8	0.6
Fishing/Trapping	1.1	0.8	0.2	0.1
Minerals and Petroleum	0.9	3.2	4.0	5.1
Manufacturing		21.7	23.3	21.6
Construction		4.1	6.3	6.1
Transportation and Communications	22.6	9.6	8.9	5.2
Electric Power, gas and water		2.8	2.9	2.8
Wholesale and retail trade		11.6	12.4	15.1
Finance, real estate, insurance	31.2	10.0	11.6	19.2
Public administration		3.4	6.9	7.5
Service		12.9	13.5	14.1

Source: About Canada, *Center for Canadian Studies, Mount Allison University, from M.C. Urquart, R.H.A. Buckley, Historical Statistics Canada, 1995.*

Table 5–2. Canadian foreign trade, 1994

Top 20 Canadian Exports to U.S.	Top 20 U.S. Exports to Canada
1 Motor cars and other motor vehicles	1 Motor vehicle parts and accessories
2 Paper and paperboard	2 Motor cars and other motor vehicles
3 Special purpose motor vehicles	3 Thermionic, cold cathode valves, etc.
4 Motor vehicle parts and accessories	4 Internal combust piston engines and parts, n.e.s.
5 Crude oil from pet. or bit. minerals	5 Automatic data process machines and units thereof
6 Special transactions and commodities	6 Special purpose motor vehicles
7 Wood	7 Electrical machinery and apparatus, n.e.s.
8 Aluminum	8 Measuring/checking/analyzing and contr instruments
9 Natural gas	9 Telecommunications equipment, n.e.s.
10 Pulp and waste paper	10 Electrical apparatus for switching or protecting electronic circuits
11 Parts for office machines and auto data processing machines	11 Parts for office machines and auto data processing machines
12 Furniture and parts; bedding, mattresses, etc.	12 Miscellaneous low-value shipments
13 Road motor vehicles, n.e.s.	13 Printed matter
14 Telecommunications equipment, n.e.s.	14 Special transactions and commodities
15 Thermionic, cold cathode valves, etc.	15 Manufactures of base metal, n.e.s.
16 Oil (not crude) from pet, and bit. minerals, etc.	16 Furniture and parts; bedding, mattresses, etc.
17 Internal combustion piston engines, and parts, n.e.s.	17 Heating and cooling equipment and parts
18 Aircraft and associated equipment	18 Aluminum
19 Low valued import transactions	19 Pumps, air or other gas compressors and fans
20 Gold, nonmonetary (excluding ores)	20 Aircraft and associated equipment

Source: International Trade Administration, U.S. Department of Commerce, October, 1996.
Note: n.e.s. = not elsewhere specified

processing plants, consumer products for farmers, and transportation to export the wheat. Between 1886 and 1914, prairie wheat emerged as a major Canadian export, the GDP increased 150 percent, and the population grew from 5.1 to 7.9 million. Ten thousand miles of railroad track extended from the prairies to Thunder Bay on Lake Ontario. Much of this growth was tied to wheat.

The twentieth century has seen large quantities of Canadian exports in wheat, pulp and paper, minerals, oil, and natural gas. Although the production of these staples has served as an economic stimulus, today Canada has a mature, sophisticated economy that produces a variety of goods and services besides primary resource commodities. As Table 5-1 indicates, the Canadian economy looks much different now than it did in the eighteenth and nineteenth centuries.

In 1994, agriculture, forestry, fishing, minerals, and petroleum accounted for 8.3 percent of Canada's GDP; manufacturing, construction, transport and communications, and utilities accounted for 35.7 percent; and service-producing industries accounted for 55.9 percent. This compares to 1870 when the figures were 46.2 percent for agriculture, forestry, fishing, minerals, and petroleum; 22.6 percent for manufacturing, construction, transport and communications, and other utilities; and 31.2 percent for service-producing industries. Canada, like most mature economies today, is evolving into one in which the goods-producing industries' share of GDP is decreasing and the service-producing industries' share is increasing. While the staples theory accurately explains the historical evolution of the Canadian economy, it has become less important given the growth of manufacturing and services.

International Trade

In the relatively small Canadian domestic market, foreign trade is more important than in a large economy like that of the United States. In 1995, Canadian exports of goods and services were about 32 percent of GDP, while imports were 33 percent. In the United States, with its much larger market, exports were 11 percent of GDP and imports were 12 percent. This means that about 66 percent of Canadian GDP occurs in the foreign trade sector compared to 23 percent for the United States—and foreign trade is three times more important to Canada than to the United States.

Trade can be based on comparative advantage—the principle that the relative costs of producing different goods or services vary across nations. With its vast forests, prairies, and natural resources, Canada's comparative advantage in the production of commodities such as wheat, timber, minerals, metals, and other primary products is reflected in its exports. International trade can also be based on economies of scale. Economies of scale operate when a firm produces a sufficiently large quantity of one product to capture the cost advantages of using specialized, large-scale equipment and of dividing different tasks among workers. Intra-industry trade exemplifies how the principle of economies of scale leads to trade. Approximately 26 percent of Canada's total commodity exports and 23 percent of its total imports consisted of motor vehicles and parts in 1994.[2] (See Table 5-2 for a comparison of Canadian and U.S. exports to each other in 1994.)

Canadian trade is not only specialized in the products it trades, but also in the nations with which it trades. Historically, Canada's greatest trading partners have been the United Kingdom and the United States. As a British colony, most of Canada's trade was with the United Kingdom. Canada exported a long list of natural resources to England and imported manufactured goods in return. In the nineteenth century, the United Kingdom and the United States were roughly equally important trading partners with Canada. In 1874, 51

Quebec's Bombardier (bom-bar-dee-ay), inventor of the snow mobile, is also a world leader in the production of transportation equipment, including the newly popular short-haul commercial jet aircraft.
Bombardier of Canada, Inc.

percent of Canada's imports and 49 percent of its exports went to the United Kingdom, while 42 percent of its imports and 40 percent of its exports went to the United States. Then, beginning in the 1880s, the United States replaced the United Kingdom as Canada's major trading partner, and in 1995, about 80 percent of Canada's foreign trade was with the United States.

In 1854, the United States and British North America signed a reciprocity treaty that lasted until 1866, when it was abrogated by the United States. The treaty allowed many commodities, including all primary products, to cross the border free of tariffs. Until the 1870 recession, Canada maintained a policy of low tariffs and appealed to the United States to renew the reciprocity agreement.

The period 1878 through 1935 was one of high tariffs and the National Policy. Prime Minister John A. Macdonald introduced the National Policy in 1878 in order to foster long-term economic growth through railroad subsidies, farm supports, a few primary product exports, and high protectionist tariffs. Most economists agree that the National Policy helped Ontario and Quebec, which produced manufactured goods with high tariffs keeping out foreign competitors, but that it hurt the other provinces. The 1920s and 1930s saw a tremendous increase in Canadian tariffs and those throughout the rest of the world, an ill-advised effort by nations to offset the disastrous unemployment and other dire effects of the Great Depression. When the United Kingdom joined the European Economic Community in the 1960s, special trading preferences with Canada were no longer permitted, causing a greater reliance on the U.S. market.

After seeing the damage that high protective barriers could do, Canada, along with most other nations, adopted a policy of reducing trade barriers. In January 1988, after nearly two years of tough negotiations, the Canada-United States Free Trade Agreement (FTA) was signed. The agreement, which took effect on January 1, 1989, was to remove all tariffs between the two countries over ten years, extend the principles of right of business establishment and national treatment of investment on a nondiscriminatory basis, and provide a trade dispute settlement mechanism. Subsequently, Canada, the United States, and Mexico enacted the North American Free Trade Agreement (NAFTA), which took effect on January 1, 1994. The NAFTA Agreement was patterned on the FTA, but remains weak in the areas of agriculture, transportation, and financial services.

Government Role

The importance of government involvement in the economy is enormous, though often difficult to measure. Government plays a number of important roles, including producing and owning goods and services, regulating and subsidizing businesses, redistributing income, and protecting the consumer.

The amount of general government disbursements (expenditures on goods and services plus current transfers and payments of property income) and current receipts relative to GDP are widely used indicators of the degree of government involvement in the economy. Canadian government outlay as a percentage of GDP has increased from around 13 percent in 1926 to around 49 percent in 1993. In 1995, Canadian general government disbursements were 46 percent of GDP, while current receipts were 39 percent. In the United States the figures were lower, at 32 and 31 percent respectively.

The Canadian government's social expenditures have increased from 18 percent of GDP in 1980 to 23 percent in 1995, exceeding the average expenditure for the G-7 countries[3] and exceeding government social spending in the United States, which amounted to less than 14 percent of GDP in 1995.

The health care system provides a good example of one area in which Canada and the United States are at opposite positions with respect to government intervention. The Canadian government plays a major role in funding and regulating the health industry, and all Canadian citizens and legal immigrants, including the unemployed and homeless, have equal access to quality health care. In this single-payer system, the government finances health care through payroll and general taxes and pays private health care providers.

The Canadian Health Act governs the twelve separate health care systems, one for each province and territory. Funding is done through a federal-provincial mix. The federal government awards grants to the provinces, provided they adhere to the five basic principles: 1) comprehensive benefits, 2) universality of coverage on equal terms and conditions, 3) accessibility, 4) portability between provinces, and 5) public administration of the system.

Canadian health care expenditure as a share of GDP has been growing rapidly and today is second highest to the United States among member nations of the Organization for Economic Cooperation and Development (OECD). As the population ages, this poses a serious financing problem for the system, especially in light of the federal and provincial budget problems.

The Banking System

Settlement of the Canadian west was much more orderly than in the United States, and the centralized banking system that evolved reflects this. In

Table 5–3. Provincial economic data 1994–96 (millions of dollars)

Province	GDP/Capita	Personal Income/ Capita	Unemployment Rate	Net Debt March 1994	Deficit 1994/ 1995	Deficit** 1995/ 1996
Newfoundland	16,716	17,464	20.4	4,565	41	(33)*
Prince Edward Island	18,112	17,746	17.1	524	13	(7)*
Nova Scotia	19,662	18,917	13.3	7,535	255	176
New Brunswick	19,771	17,939	12.4	4,127	(17)*	(75)*
Quebec	22,946	21,020	12.2	57,763	7,245	4,680
Ontario	27,639	23,666	09.6	69,253	8,378	—
Manitoba	22,187	20,156	09.2	6,962	344	191
Saskatchewan	22,820	18,621	07.0	7,098	(575)*	(257)*
Alberta	30,272	22,603	08.6	2,936	108	477
British Columbia	27,236	23,432	09.4	5,630	(27)*	(362)*
Yukon/ Northwest Territory	30,553	24,745	—	(271)*	36	(1)
CANADA	25,595	22,143	10.4			

Source: Economic Reference Tables, August 1995, Department of Finance, Canada, Ottawa; Statistics Canada-
Cat. NO 68-212-XPB. * Surplus, ** Estimate

Canada, a limited number of large banks with numerous branches across the country were established, while in the United States many banks with few branches were the rule. Today the Canadian banking system is referred to as multiple branch banking, while the American system is a mix of branch and unit banking. At present there are just sixty-eight Canadian chartered banks (incorporated by the government). Seven are classified as Schedule I banks (domestically owned), and sixty-one are classified as Schedule II banks (primarily foreign owned). The seven Schedule I banks, with their numerous branches, dominate the Canadian banking industry.

In part because bank regulators have discouraged mergers, the relative size of Canadian banks on the international market has decreased to the point where at present no Canadian bank is listed among the sixty largest in the world. Presently, the clear-cut differences that once existed between the Canadian and American banking systems are starting to blur as financial institutions of all sorts perform many of the same functions and as more American bank mergers occur.

Foreign Investment

Investment in new capital equipment, infrastructure, health, and education all help to foster economic growth. Investment funds come from savings, both domestic and foreign. Canada's openness to foreign investment dates back to when it was a British colony and the United Kingdom was its principal foreign investor, providing funds to build railways and canals. After World War I, the primary form of investment in Canada shifted from portfolio (investment in government bonds and the stocks and bonds of companies) to direct investment (which involves control as well as owner-ship of securities), and the United States became its principal foreign inves-tor. By 1992, the United States owned approximately 64 percent of all foreign direct investment.

In the early 1950s, Canadians became concerned about the large amount of foreign direct investment in their country. Foreign companies, particularly American, were building new plants, expanding already-owned plants, and buying stocks in foreign-controlled companies. Much of this expansion occurred in resource sectors, such as petroleum, gas, and mining. A major concern was that Canada would become a "branch-plant-economy," in which foreign owners would extend local laws to their Canadian operations, provide for very little research and development in Canada, and permit few upper management positions to exist. In response, the Trudeau government established in 1974 Canada's first investment screening body, the Foreign Investment Review Agency (FIRA), to screen all but the smallest foreign takeovers and newly established businesses in order to ensure a "significant benefit" to Canada.

With the election of the Progressive Conservative party in 1984, restric-tions on foreign investment were reduced (FIRA was replaced by Investment Canada), and the government declared that "Canada is open for business."[4] By

1994, foreign investment in Canada had reached $637.6 billion, while Canadian investment abroad had grown to $295.9 billion. The percentage of direct foreign investment in Canada, however, had decreased substantially, from about 60 percent in 1974 to about 25 percent in 1994. The U.S. share of foreign investment in Canada declined to 65 percent from 75 percent over the 1984–94 period. Large increases were recorded for the European Union (especially the United Kingdom), Japan, and Hong Kong.

The United States remains the most important recipient of Canadian investment, accounting for 54 percent of the $125 billion in 1994, but the share has dropped from its peak of 69 percent in the mid-1980s. Canadian investment has risen more rapidly in the European Union, Hong Kong, and the Asian countries.

Thus, Canada is moderating its foreign investment dependence on the United States. This is due to higher rates of economic growth of Canadian investment in Asia, increased levels of Asian investment in Canada, and increased levels of European investment in Canada. However, the U.S.-Canadian direct investment relationship will remain the largest for the foreseeable future.

Regional Disparities

Large and persistent differences in income and standard of living exist among the different Canadian regions and provinces (see Table 5-3). In 1995, GDP per capita ranged from $17,306 in Newfoundland, the poorest province, to $31,092 in Alberta, the wealthiest province. The most populous province, Ontario, had the second highest GDP per capita of $28,384, while the average for all of Canada was $26,347. The degree and pattern of regional differences in income have persisted for decades. In 1961, for example, the Atlantic provinces region was the poorest in Canada, with GDP per capita averaging between only 49 and 65 percent of the Canadian average.

A wide variation in unemployment rates throughout Canada is another indication of the magnitude of regional economic differences. In December 1996, for example, the unemployment rate varied from a low of 5.9 percent in Saskatchewan to a high of 20.4 percent in Newfoundland. In the Atlantic region, unemployment rates were 20.4 percent in Newfoundland, 15.9 percent in Prince Edward Island, 13.3 percent in New Brunswick, and 12.9 percent in Nova Scotia. Quebec and Ontario had unemployment rates of 12.1 and 9.1 percent respectively. In the Prairie region, Manitoba's unemployment rate was 7.5 percent, Saskatchewan's was 5.9 percent, and Alberta's was 6.3 percent. The province of British Columbia had an unemployment rate of 8.7 percent, while the rate for all of Canada was 9.7 percent. Historically, unemployment rates have been consistently higher in the Atlantic region than in the rest of Canada.

Canadian policy makers have called for a federal system of assistance for the poorer provinces in an effort to equalize living standards throughout the country. An "equalization payments program" exists to compensate the

poorer provinces in their efforts to raise revenues and allow for an equivalent level of public services across Canada. Twenty-three percent of total
federal transfers to the provinces in 1994–95 was for equalization payments.
For years, unemployment benefits and other social assistance payments have
been higher and made on better terms in the poorer provinces, although
fiscal constraints have forced the current government to make cutbacks.

While the exact reasons for the wide differences in income among the
provinces are not fully known, certain plausible explanations exist. Economic
development and growth in the different regions have been based in part on
staples products. The Atlantic region depended on fish and timber for its
growth and development and to a large extent still does so today, but the
linkages necessary to create a robust economy did not occur with these
staples. Moreover, the Canadian government has declared a virtual fishing
moratorium in the North Atlantic in order to replenish depleted stocks, throw-
ing thousands out of work in Newfoundland and the other Atlantic provinces.
The moratorium is expected to remain in effect for many years. Wheat, on the
other hand, provided Ontario and the Prairie Provinces with the means to
prosper because of the strong linkages that the wheat industry created.

Equalization payments, unemployment insurance, and other social
services may have exacerbated the problem of large regional economic
disparities by discouraging mobility. High unemployment rates are a signal
that workers should move to rapidly growing areas, thereby raising their
own incomes as well as the level of those who remain. But generous government programs tend to restrict labor mobility, allowing the unemployed to
remain in their region and perpetuate the problem.

CURRENT ECONOMIC CHALLENGES

Over the last few years, large government operating deficits have been a
serious and persistent problem confronting the Canadian economy. Total
Canadian government (federal, provincial, and local) expenditures have
exceeded revenues every year since 1974. These accumulated deficits led to a
massive debt for both federal and provincial governments. In 1994, the
Canadian ratio of net public debt to GDP was about 64 percent, 25 percent
higher than it was in the late 1980s, while the net government debt to GDP
ratio in the United States was about 40 percent. This represents more than
$14,000 debt for every Canadian citizen. Government debt as a percentage of
GDP was second only to that of Italy among the G-7 countries. Furthermore,
total net external debt—debt owed to foreigners—was about 45 percent of GDP.

Persistent Canadian federal deficits started in the 1970s with tax rate
reductions without reductions in spending, increasing interest rates, and economic recessions in the 1980s and 1990s, which reduced tax collections. Provincial and local deficits had been quite small until the 1980s when they soared
because of reduced revenues and increased spending. When recessions hit,
provincial deficits increased, and by 1994 they accounted for roughly one-third

the general government debt. The federal government and every province have been forced to reduce deficits and look towards the eventual retirement of some debt. This budget drain has contributed to the sluggish performance of the Canadian economy and caused cutbacks in social services such as health care and education. Some provinces like Alberta and Ontario have actually reduced tax rates at the same time. As Canada stays the course on reducing budgetary deficits, overall economic performance should improve.

Unemployment and Job Growth

Unemployment, a second serious and persistent problem, has been much higher in Canada than in the United States in recent years. This is due to lower rates of economic growth, the structure of the Canadian economy with a greater share of less productive industries, Canadian labor laws that favor unionization and make it more difficult for companies to dismiss employees, and more generous unemployment benefits.

The prospects are favorable for lower unemployment rates in the future. Trade liberalization through NAFTA and the World Trade Organization (WTO) has favorably altered the structure of Canadian industry and made companies more competitive, while tight government budgets have trimmed unemployment benefits. Most important, the Canadian economy is expected to grow more rapidly than most industrialized countries in the years ahead, creating new jobs at a healthy pace.

The Quebec Sovereignty Movement

What are the economic implications of the sovereignty movement in Quebec and the rest of Canada? Sovereignty supporters dismiss those who predict dire economic consequences should independence occur, citing their commitment to the Canadian dollar, free trade, and NAFTA membership. They might be right, but only if separation is friendly and occurs quickly.

Major stumbling blocks would be the following: that Quebec assume at least one-quarter of Canada's huge public debt; that aboriginal groups residing in Quebec be allowed to remain in Canada; and that NAFTA membership be extended to Quebec (adding members requires unanimous consent of existing members). Without NAFTA membership, an independent Quebec's products would be subject to Canadian, U.S., and Mexican tariffs, so Quebec would be less desirable to foreign investors because goods produced there would not qualify for duty-free export to the rest of North America. A smaller Canada would also strengthen the U.S. economic domination of North America. Uncertainty about Quebec has caused weakness in the value of the Canadian dollar and dampened the Canadian private investment climate.

For these reasons, sovereignty would result in economic damage to Quebec and the rest of Canada. The failure to resolve this issue on the political level will continue to impose economic costs.

The Global Economy

While the Canada–U.S. economic relationship is amicable, it is not without disputes and problems. Also, Canada would like to reduce its dependence on the United States.

The Helms-Burton Act is an example of a current dispute. In an effort to expand the Cuban embargo, the United States government recently passed legislation that allows U.S. citizens to sue foreign businesses that profit from using property expropriated from them and to ban high level executives and their families from entering the United States. The Canadian government has objected strenuously to what it considers an illegal attempt to extend U.S. laws beyond its borders, contrary to accepted international legal practices. In response, Canada has strengthened its 1985 Foreign Extraterritorial Measures Act (FEMA), designed to defend against attempts by foreign governments to apply unreasonable laws or rulings and forbid compliance in Canada with "extraterritorial" measures such as Helms-Burton. Canada, with support from the European Union, is pursuing the issue under NAFTA and the World Trade Organization. A recent Canadian parody of Helms-Burton mockingly suggests that the three million descendants of Tory ancestors should be compensated for land expropriated by the United States!

Canada has begun developing an initiative to build trade and investment ties throughout the Asia-Pacific region. It is hoped that Canadian business can take advantage of this growing market while becoming more independent of the United States.

Despite these developments and Canada's attempts to reduce dependence on the U.S. market, the long-standing bilateral economic relationship will continue to be the most important for both countries.

CONCLUSION

Long-term prospects for Canada's economy look good. The International Monetary Fund predicts a 2.9 percent rate of growth in 1997, compared with an average of 2.6 percent for the G-7 countries. In 1993, the federal government established a serious program to reduce the deficit to 3 percent of GDP by 1996-97, and so far the program is on target. Cuts in federal programs (notably in agriculture and other business), reductions in transfers to the provinces, lower unemployment insurance assistance, and a 15 percent reduction in the number of federal employees constitute the main goals of the program.

The goal of Canadian monetary policy is to maintain good economic performance through price stability. Over the last few years, the Bank of Canada, the Canadian central bank, has been quite successful in attaining this goal. The Bank of Canada is even more independent than the U.S. Federal Reserve system when it comes to using monetary policy to fight inflation. Inflation has not been a serious problem in Canada since 1982, when the Consumer Price Index (CPI) increased by 10.6 percent. Between 1983 and 1995, the CPI increased by more than 5 percent in only two years,

1983 and 1991; between 1992 and 1995, it has been within the target range of 1–3 percent.

The federal government has focused its economic program on increasing business productivity and innovation, expanding markets through trade, modernizing infrastructure, and promoting science and technology. Further, it is reforming the unemployment insurance system, which in its current form has tended to encourage frequent use and helped to perpetuate regional variations in unemployment while raising the overall unemployment rate.

The provinces, too, are putting their economic houses in order. *Canada Quarterly* reports that six provinces have already posted balanced budgets for 1995-96 and that Ontario and Quebec have announced balanced budget plans. Some of the budget cuts have been difficult and will require long-term adjustments, but the provincial governments are facing up to their problems and soon will reap the benefits.

Altogether, the Canadian economy, with its large resource base, well-educated labor force, and commitment to free trade, has many long-term strengths. The national and provincial governments appear to be making the necessary changes that will enable Canada to compete and succeed in the global economy, maintaining its high standard of living and reputation as one of the best countries in the world in which to live.

Notes

1. All figures expressed in dollar amounts are Canadian dollars unless otherwise noted. Making international comparisons of economic data is fraught with pitfalls: definitions of economic variables from one country to another may not be exactly the same, and the method used to convert one currency to another affects the values.
2. The 1965 Automotive Products Agreement, "Auto Pact," between Canada and the United States, which with some modifications was extended under the FTA and NAFTA, makes the auto industry a special case. The pact allows virtually unrestricted trade between manufacturers in the two countries, subject to certain stipulations ensuring a degree of balance in the quantities crossing the border.
3. The G-7 countries are Canada, France, Germany, Italy, Japan, the United Kingdom, and the United States.
4. Not all restrictions on foreign investment have been eliminated. Restrictions still exist in the cultural industries, including broadcasting and publishing.

Sources

Armstrong, Muriel. *The Canadian Economy and Its Problems.* 4th ed. Scarborough: Prentice-Hall Canada Inc., 1988.

Knight, Malcolm. *The Canadian Economy.* 2nd ed. Washington, D.C.: ACSUS Papers (The Association for Canadian Studies in the United

States and the Michigan State University Press, 1996).

Kresl, Peter. "An Economics Perspective: Canada in the International Economy." In *Understanding Canada*, edited by William Metcalfe. New York: New York University Press, 1982.

Lipsey, Richard G., Paul N. Courant, and Douglas D. Purvis. *Economics*. 8th Canadian ed., New York: Harper Collins College Publishers, 1994.

Norrie, Kenneth, and Douglas Owram. *A History of the Canadian Economy*. Toronto: Harcourt Brace and Company, Canada, 1991.

Organization for Economic Cooperation and Development. *OECD Economic Surveys Canada*. Paris: OECD, 1995.

Strick, J. C. *Canadian Public Finance*. 4th ed. Toronto: Holt, Rinehart and Winston of Canada, Limited, 1992.

Chapter 6
Canadian Culture in the Late 1990s
William Metcalfe

What is culture, anyway? The *Oxford Universal Dictionary* (1955) defines the term as "the intellectual side of civilization," whereas Bobbie Kalman, in *Canada, the Culture* (1993), calls it "the way we live." These two definitions, both simplistic and misleading, illustrate the problem of describing "Canadian culture" to anyone. Is one to concentrate upon "high culture," the sophisticated creative products in art, music, drama, and dance that may appeal chiefly to an elite few? Or upon "popular" or "mass culture," widely disseminated manifestations of creativity that, banal or sophisticated, touch the majority of citizens in their daily existence? Or should one think in a more anthropological sense of "culture" as some summation of "the way we live," of things believed in, of shared values and practices and artistic tastes? Ultimately, our goal here is to discover the societal norms and signposts that, taken all together, make Canadians "Canadian" and differentiate them from "Americans."[1]

CANADIANS VS. AMERICANS: SOME TRADITIONAL ASSUMPTIONS
The most important fact about Canada's culture is that Canadians know it to be different from American culture—different in ways that may seem so obscure and subtle as to escape our attention, but may also seem so obvious as to be taken for granted (just as bad, from a Canadian point of view). For example, colloquial Canadian speech may differ from American, sometimes including the interjection of the word "eh?" as a kind of equivalent of the common American "you know?" or "right?" While there is no single "Canadian accent," people with sensitive ears will quickly recognize a Canadian speaking on the radio by his or her speech patterns and characteristic inflections. Students who have access to Canadian radio broadcasts (even more "Canadian" than Canadian TV) should be encouraged to listen to accents and idioms and to understand how they differ from the American.

More generally, scholars have emphasized basic differences between Canadian and American attitudes and behavior patterns. The writings of Northrop Frye, William Kilbourne, and Margaret Atwood are pertinent here, but the most recent summary of defining aspects of Canada's "differentness" is Seymour Martin Lipset's *Continental Divide* (1989).[2] Incorporating a good deal of historical causation in his sociological analysis, Lipset contrasts Canadian with American attitudes, beliefs, values, and norms. He necessarily emphasizes national differences more than similarities, but then these differences are the very things of which Americans—who tend to assume that Canadians are just "colder Americans"—need to be aware.

Lipset demonstrates that Canada has historically been a "counterrevolutionary" nation devoid of a defining, liberating revolution of independence; a place of "peace, order and good government" rather than one that emphasized the sacredness of individual liberty; and a fundamentally Tory/conservative rather than a Whig/liberal land. Canadians have shown more deference to authority and hierarchical elites, have been willing to accept more governmental and bureaucratic paternalism and intervention in the economy, and have only recently (in 1982) adopted a Charter of Rights and Freedoms which, nevertheless, is considerably more equivocal on the matter of individual, as distinct from collective, rights than the American Bill of Rights. Canada's huge geography and relatively small population have also encouraged direct governmental actions, on a scale unimaginable in the United States, to provide services in the absence of sufficient capital and a viable marketplace. These actions have ranged from a national railway system to a single-payer, guaranteed national system of health care.

Canada's political style is determined by its being a British-style parliamentary democracy, not a U.S.-style democracy with a strong tradition of checks and balances among executive, legislature, and judiciary. Indeed, the principle of judicial review, theoretically introduced by the 1982 Charter of Rights, seemed to most Canadians very American indeed, truly "foreign" to British-derived Canadian tradition. Arguably, Canada's political parties are stronger than those in the United States, and the percentage of citizens who vote in national elections is higher (around 75 percent vs. perhaps 50 percent on a good day in the United States), although it can also be argued that political activity at the grassroots level in Canada is more sporadic and generally less dynamic than in the United States. Canadians these days do not much love their politicians and are beginning to question seriously the way the parliamentary system is operating; nevertheless, they look upon American politics with a mixture of amazement and repugnance.

Modern Canadians are more law-abiding and Canada's crime rates are much lower than America's; Lipset quotes popular-historian cum-TV-personality Pierre Berton's dictum that Canadians are "cautious, prudent, elitist, moralistic, tolerant (of ethnic differences), cool, unemotional and solemn," more laid-back, in effect, perhaps "solid, reliable, decent . . . [but] a little bit dull," "the quiet North Americans." Not surprisingly, therefore, Canada is said to have produced few national heroes (John A. Macdonald? Louis Riel? Terry Fox? Wayne Gretzky?), few philosopher-pundits (George Grant, nationalist philosopher, is known only to an intellectual elite in Canada, and while even Americans have heard of Marshall McLuhan, few anywhere fully understand his prose), and no national ideology or sustaining national myth. Yet Canadians do have a strong sense of separate identity, which they are at times hard-put to define except that it is not American. Proud of their "kinder, gentler society"—by which they mean their better "social safety net," especially their (increasingly troubled) system of univer-

The grandeur of the National Gallery and its location on Parliament Hill reflect the importance Canadians attach to their own culture.
National Art Gallery of Canada

sal health care—they see themselves as inhabiting "a better, less aggressive, gentler, more peaceable, but also more mediocre, country."[3]

American scholar Mary Jean Green has spoken of a pervasive feminine quality in contemporary Canadian, especially Quebecois, literature.[4] It is certainly true that Canada's celebrated women writers—Margaret Atwood, Margaret Laurence, Alice Munro, and Carol Shields are perhaps the best known—have been at the forefront of literary achievement for the past thirty years, at precisely the time when the country's writers seem to have found, after much searching, their true national voice. English Canadian literature has clearly matured and no longer seems to reflect Canada's historical sense of being merely a nation in the making, trying to break out of its colonial adolescence.

Canadians have, however, often felt themselves victims of two successive colonial empires—the British (in the classic sense of empire) and the American (in the economic/cultural sense). Because they have also inhabited a harsh, northern land, they have been obsessed with, and proud of, their very survival—in the words of their national motto, *a mari usque ad mare* ("from sea to sea")—as an independent country which the United Nations persists in calling one of the best countries on earth in which to live. (Paradoxically, they are statistically more urbanized than Americans; most Canadians prefer to "survive" no more than a short drive from the nearest Tim Horton's Donuts drive-in, and the vast majority live within one hundred miles of the American border.)

Perhaps it is the awareness of the odds against prosperous survival in a harsh, almost-empty northern land that has led Canadians to espouse the seemingly opposed phenomena of big government (almost state socialism, in the U.S.—needless to say, not the Canadian—view) and organized labor (twice as important, relative to population, as in the United States). Canadian politics has been characterized by fundamentally middle-of-the-road "progressive conservative" government (from both the old-line parties, the Liberals and the Conservatives) and fairly radical socialist third parties, of the principle of "redistributive equalitarianism" in lieu of the more American "egalitarianism" (i.e., in Canada, competition is healthy so long as the weakest are provided for and not too many live in poverty).

The Lipset litany of Canadian differentness is a long, but enormously instructive and thought-provoking one of which Americans should be aware as they try to understand what makes Canada and Canadians tick. It should also, as with all litanies and academic analyses, be taken with a grain of salt. Lipset himself reminds us that, when we talk of national characteristics, we must remember that we are doing this comparatively and that everything we highlight must be understood relative to another country's norms. Moreover, his somewhat historical bent may lead him to deemphasize the fact that Canada has been changing rapidly in the past twenty-five years. As the world's economic, business, and communications systems have marched almost unhindered across national boundaries, as Europe has lost its position as the source of imperial control and of attitudinal imperatives, as western democracies have struggled with huge economic and economically driven policy swings and with the increasing intolerance (and, some would say, incivility) of special interest groupings of their citizens, some of Canada's comfortable, historical, and self-congratulatory assumptions about the nature of its culture have been challenged, and perforce modified. Above all, vast numbers of non-European immigrants have come to Canada, bringing different cultural norms and expectations and quite literally changing the public, adult face of a country long "deadset in adolescence."[5]

WINDS OF CHANGE

We live in a postmodern age, dazzled by the magic and mountebankery of rapidly changing technologies, by the increased globalism of communications and economic interactions, by the promise and potential of NAFTA (North American Free Trade Agreement), WTO (World Trade Organization), EEC (European Economic Community), and the like. Business (and, concomitantly, political) decisions are often driven by international imperatives and perceived opportunities. Communications technology (a field in which Canada has been a leader), now totally integrated with the technology of computerization via the Internet, direct-to-home TV via satellites, or merely worldwide e-mail chatter, knows no natural boundaries and respects no national borders. Furthermore, no amount of national cultural protectionism can, realistically, keep these technologies from crossing those borders and reaching eager consumers in all parts of the global village.

The Canadian Radio, Television and Telecommunications Commission (CRTC) is charged with ensuring that Canada's airwaves (radio and TV, including cable- and satellite-originated TV) retain generous measures of "Canadian content" and thus are vehicles that support the all-important cultural industry infrastructure that nurtures Canadian performers and creative artists (choreographers, set designers, theater directors and actors, writers, composers and musicians, both classical and pop). But clearly the CRTC is now facing an ever-more-difficult, some would say hopeless, task. Indeed, cultural protectionists in all countries, united by a desperate feeling that culture the world over is being relentlessly homogenized by the twin forces of U.S. cultural-industry commercialism and the technological revolution that allows it to flood into homes in the farthest corners of the world, may be excused for fearing that a cultural Armageddon will soon be upon them! Canada, predominantly English-speaking and absolutely proximate to the United States, is especially vulnerable to invasions of America's cultural industries, be they TV, mass culture music, films, books, or magazines. And however would Canada go about ensuring that there was sufficient "Canadian content" on the Internet?

In such a climate, it is not surprising that the most persistent (although not ultimately effective) public resistance to the Canada-U.S. Free Trade Agreement of 1988 (NAFTA's immediate predecessor) was that of Canada's cultural elites, especially its writers. Ironically, although NAFTA ostensibly protects the independence of Canadian cultural industries, it has really engendered American challenges to hitherto successful cultural protectionist measures, while at the same time a governmental obsession with deficit reduction has led to the weakening of one of the strongest agents of Canadian cultural development—the Canadian Broadcasting Corporation (CBC), which in 1996 celebrated its sixtieth year as an advocate for and sponsor of much Canadian high and mass culture. Of course, globalization can cut both ways: 1996 was the year that saw the triumph of Canadian country star Shania Twain at the U.S. Grammy Awards, plus signal successes by Alanis Morissette, k. d. lang, and others (although just what is decisively and identifiably "Canadian" about their material, especially as their successes mount and their addresses take on American ZIP codes, is questionable). In light of these developments, American students should think about the real implications of the processes of cultural assimilation and cultural takeover, about "the Americanization of the world," about the value of meaningful cultural diversity on a worldwide, i.e., truly multinational, basis.[6]

In this last regard, Canada can serve as a wonderful case study for American students. They can learn, in general, the historical, defining characteristics of Canadian society and "culture." They can discover that Canadians are more obsessed with hockey than Americans, that Canadian "snowbirds" in Florida tend not to tip as readily as canoes, that Canadians have recently been willing to accept not one, but two new coins in lieu of familiar, old paper currency (the $1 "Loonie," then the $2 "Two-nie" or "Doubloon"). They should know that most Canadians now think in kilometers, kilograms, and degrees Celsius, not in miles, pounds, and degrees Fahrenheit, a change Americans have adamantly refused to make. They should also learn that Canada has since 1971 had a ministry charged with the encouragement of multiculturalism, that Canadians have been willing to see millions of tax dollars given to ethnic groups for the preservation and fostering of their cultural traditions and customs, and that the Canadian Constitution of 1982 defines the country as being multicultural as well as bicultural in essence. Indeed, ignoring its actual history, Canada has long prided itself on being a cultural mosaic rather than an American-style melting pot. Ironically, the country has recently become much more of a mosaic than its population may now be willing to tolerate: an interesting amount of both anglophone and francophone nativism (i.e., we were here first, you had better conform to our cultural norms) has surfaced in the past half-decade.

Canadian Sikhs can now, thanks to the Supreme Court of Canada, wear their turbans when in Royal Canadian Mounted Police uniforms. When some Iranian Canadians publicly refused to condemn the *fatwah* (a religious decree) issued by the Iranian hierarchy against novelist Salman Rushdie, which was, in essence, a license to kill him, the Canadian press quickly enough reminded them that such intolerance was decidedly "un-Canadian." Similarly, Iraqi Canadian supporters of Saddam Hussein were generally condemned by the Canadian media, despite the fact that some Canadians viewed the Persian Gulf War with an un-American lack of enthusiasm.

On the other hand, Canadian cultural creativity is becoming ever less Anglo- and Eurocentric. If Canadians have long been proud of the music of Healey Willan (born in England, longtime resident of Canada), they have recently learned to take pride in that of the Chinese Canadian Alexina Louie. The 1996 winner of Canada's prestigious Guiller Prize for Fiction was Indian Canadian Rohinton Mistry (for a magical novel about life in India, not Canada), and the very multicultural Michael Ondaatje has had commercial success in Canada as well as abroad equal perhaps to that of the clearly Canadian Alice Munro, Timothy Findley, and Margaret Atwood. Soon more than half the members of the Canadian House of Commons will be of neither British nor French descent.

Canada is much more conscious of the presence, rights, aspirations, and demands of its aboriginal Indian and Inuit populations, the former collectively referred to as the First Nations of Canada. These native peoples have not, historically, been treated by Canadian governments and society as humanely, or as differently from their U.S. counterparts, as Canadians have wanted to imagine. Nevertheless, they have, in the past three decades or so, increasingly been acknowledged as peoples with the inherent right to some kind of sovereignty. Native land claims are gradually being acknowledged, understood, and negotiated with a view to settlements that will be both just and practical in the light of late twentieth-century realities. The First Nations of Canada, proportionately twice as numerous in Canada than their counterparts in the United States (approximately 2 percent vs. 1 percent of the respective populations), are vocal, well led, and well represented in public and legal arenas. Their presence is infinitely more visible and psychologically important to Canadian politicians and to Canada's general public than is the case of Native Americans in the United States.

No consideration of Canadian culture can overlook one essential, fundamental, historical, cultural distinction about Canada: the presence, since 1763, of two "founding nations," England and France, who united to form a British

North America that resisted the American Revolution and went on, by an extraordinary act of pragmatism, hope, and political-societal compromise, to become the Dominion of Canada in 1867. These two founding peoples may have shared a Canadian political and geographical entity, a Canadian citizenship, and some sense of common achievement, but in fact from the beginning they constituted two distinct societies and learned two very distinct histories of their own country. The division of Canada into these two societies has had a huge impact on the culture of both, though chiefly on that of what in Quebec is now called "the Rest of Canada" or "English Canada" (which we have seen is now multicultural, not merely British in nature).

In recent decades, moreover, the arrival in all parts of Canada of vast numbers of non-British and non-French Europeans, followed by West Indian, Middle Eastern, and Asian immigrants, has ultimately had a troubling effect upon both of Canada's founding peoples, whose latent nativist assumptions that all Canadian culture should derive from Anglo-French patterns seem more and more irrelevant. Ironically, Canadians have recently been treated to the spectacle of American politicians justifying legislation to make English the official language of the United States by pointing to Canada's problems with separatism in Quebec. These problems—simplistically and inaccurately—are presumed to be the result merely of official bilingualism and toleration of a "distinct society" in that province.

There is a good deal of geographic diversity in Canada, for the country is highly regionalized in its geography, politics, economics, populations, and attitudes. Canada's constitution, especially its division/distribution of powers between the federal and the provincial governments, has meant that the ten Canadian provinces are individually much more important in the daily course of events and in the psychology of the people than the fifty American states. All ten Canadian provincial premiers meet often, in rather grand "federal-provincial conferences," with the prime minister of Canada to discuss and formulate policy. Provincial cabinet ministers also meet (as a group, as well as individually) with their counterparts, both provincial and federal, and important interaction occurs between provincial and federal civil service departments on a daily basis. These practices are radically different from the way the U.S. federal government deals with its state counterparts, and they substantially enhance the ways in which citizens of each province identify with provincial, as opposed to national, causes.

Moreover, the Province of Quebec constitutes a region in and of itself (arguably Ontario does likewise), while in other parts of the country, provinces combine to form vast regions that command intense personal loyalty from their inhabitants. Thus Atlantic Canadians (from Nova Scotia, New Brunswick, Prince Edward Island, and Newfoundland), Prairie Westerners (from Manitoba, Saskatchewan, and at least part of Alberta), those who live on the Pacific Rim (residents of British Columbia and at least part of Western Alberta), and those who live in the North (the Yukon and the Northwest

Territories, the latter soon to be divided into the territory of Nunavut and another yet-unnamed area) constitute groupings of people whose feelings about themselves and their way of life give them a clear sense of regional identity within the broader Canadian one.

WHO'S WHO IN CANADIAN CULTURE

While students should know about the salient elements of Canadian culture that make it different from general American culture, they can also be directed to think about that culture in terms of its creators, its performers, its transmitters, and its achievements. Some of these elements are readily accessible, as close to Americans as their television sets, their bookstores, and their CD outlets. Others, regrettably, are harder to come in contact with, accessible only to those who can utilize a first-class library or who live close enough to the radio and television signals of the CBC, its Quebec equivalent (Radio Canada), or the many private, commercial radio and TV stations emanating from Canada. Some Canadian material is now available on cable or satellite TV, although radio listeners can arguably learn more about Canadian culture than can television watchers, since most of the revealing "talk" about the country takes place on radio.

The CBC—in the words of its advertising messages, "radio [or TV] we can call our own"—was created during the Great Depression with the specific mandate of promoting Canadian unity in a very large country with a population spread out along over three thousand miles of railway lines. Now under attack by governments determined to cut spending and reduce deficits, the hitherto heavily subsidized CBC has been a magnificent success, giving opportunity to generations of radio and TV producers, designers, and technicians; to playwrights, composers, orchestras, and their musicians; to pop, folk, rock, and every other variety of mass-culture music groups; to dancers and choreographers; and to academic and journalistic elites, as well as to the ordinary people whose knowledge of their own country comes into their homes over the airwaves.

The most popular program on CBC radio—a national phenomenon listened to across the country by hundreds of thousands and dealing with national, regional, and even local issues with national resonance—is "This Morning." This was once called "Morningside" with the popular Peter Gzowski, three hours of high-quality conversation that might be compared to, although it far surpasses in national significance, American National Public Radio's "All Things Considered." But "This Morning" is only one of many radio and TV shows available to the entire country, which give Vancouverites more than a little in common with Haligonians (residents of Halifax, Nova Scotia) and Torontonians. One thinks of the sophomoric yet incredibly popular, topically satirical "Royal Canadian Air Farce" (and its several spin-offs); of TV's "Kids in the Hall"; of "This Hour Has 22 Minutes" (the original was called "This Hour Has Seven Days"); of Lister Sinclair's brilliant, long-running evening radio show, "Ideas"; of CBC radio's "Cross Country Check-Up" (discussion and phone-in), its zany "Basic Black," and its immensely informative, weekly "Sunday Morning"; of the weekly summary of parliamentary activity called "The House"; and of the stunningly successful nightly radio news program, "As It Happens." Programs such as these can give students a variegated, multilayered, and thought-provoking idea of the kinds of issues that Canadians think about and of how they tend to think about them in ways that are occasionally quite different from American norms.

Canada has supported the development of a good deal of classical music, film, theatre (note Canadian spelling), drama, and dance with generous governmental funding. CDs of the Montreal Symphony Orchestra (l'Orchestre Symphonique de Montreal, which has been called "the best French orchestra in the world" and is conducted by a Swiss, Charles Dutoit) are bestsellers in the Decca/London catalogue (another Canadian spelling). Somewhat less readily available in the United States are discs featuring the Toronto, Vancouver, and Calgary symphonies, occasionally playing music by Canadian composers, often featuring Canadian soloists. Canadian tenor Ben Heppner is a sensation on several continents at the moment, assuming the mantle worn in the past by the legendary Jon Vickers, while Canadian soprano Nancy Argenta is a major player in the world of "early music," starring on many current discs. Years after his death the phenomenal talent of Glenn Gould still astonishes record collectors. Pianists Louis Lortie, Marc-Andre Hamelin, and the chamber orchestra I Musici de Montreal are big CD sellers. Toronto's Tafelmusik Baroque Orchestra may be the best "baroque band" playing and recording in North America; Montreal's Cirque du Soleil is so popular internationally that it has opened permanent company shows in Las Vegas and Florida; and several Canadian ballet companies tour the United States regularly.

The problem with thinking of these successful Canadian performers of "high culture" as examples of "Canadian" culture is that in large part they perform works that are international, often not at all contemporary, in origin or essence. Students of national cultures might also ask themselves how American is the work of the New York Philharmonic, or the Metropolitan Opera Company. While the performers involved may mostly be American, the repertoire of both organizations is only marginally American. Moreover, if one offered a list of modern Canadian classical musical compositions as evidence of "Canadian" cultural development, it could be argued that listening to them would reveal much about trends, fashions, and fads in contemporary classical music, but little that would be recognized as particularly Canadian, in musical content at least.

It is possible to imagine that listening to Canadian performers in musical genres with mass appeal would give one a clearer sense of Canadian culture. Thus the discs of Shania Twain, Bryan Adams, and Terri Clark; of k. d. lang and Joni Mitchell; of Gordon Lightfoot, Ian and Sylvia Tyson, Bruce

Cockburn, and Leonard Cohen; of the astonishing Cape Breton Island fiddler Ashley MacIsaac; of Celine Dion or Anne Murray might be sought out by students.[7] Yet again students should reflect on what the works of performers, especially those performing in genres that are inherently international in style and content, can tell us about a nation's cultural fabric (except that the cultural scene is alive and well, producing successive generations of performing artists who can succeed anywhere). Exceptionally, the songs of many real "folk" artists, including the Newfoundland "Irish" groups who were so popular in New York in 1996, tell listeners much about that beleaguered island's preoccupation with the sea and the absence of the cod, while Stompin' Tom Connors and the madcap Nancy White have made many records that are full of very Canadian ideas and attitudes.

Many Canadians work in the Hollywood movie industry as highly visible performers. Others are technicians in the huge infrastructure of people who don't appear on screen but support the entire operation with their talent and skills. High-tech animation studios, for example, are at present dominated by graduates of one Canadian college program. All this is proof positive of the vibrancy of Canadian cultural industries, but at the same time a clear illustration of how the magnet of one giant American industry sucks creative and performing talent out of Canada itself. Jim Carrey, Michael J. Fox, Keanu Reeves, Tantoo Cardinal, Leslie Nielsen, Dan Ackroyd, Donald and Kiefer Sutherland, the late John Candy, and many other movie and TV luminaries are Canadian. Journalists Robert MacNeil and Peter Jennings are familiar faces in millions of American homes; so too are Pamela Anderson Lee, Shannon Tweed, William Shatner, and Matthew Perry.

Encouraged by Canadian government policies, many American TV shows and feature movies are now made in places like Toronto and Vancouver, utilizing hundreds of Canadian technicians. As a group, then, Canadians in the media are so influential that they are often referred to as "the Canadian mafia," but decades of governmental tilting with U.S. film mogul Jack Valenti have yet to get Canadian feature films decent exposure in Canada's own first-run movie houses, so powerful is the American grip on the film distribution industry. Students might, nevertheless, seek out Canadian films, either those made by the National Film Board of Canada or those made by independent producers.[8]

A mature, rich body of work of considerable depth and variety, Canadian literature in English should be explored by all American students and teachers for its intrinsic interest and merit as well as for clues to what makes Canadians tick. But the short stories, poems, and longer fiction of the best Canadian writers really do combine universal human themes with culture-, time-, and place-specific details that give readers a strong sense of a particular society. Margaret Atwood, Margaret Laurence, Alice Munro, Carol Shields, Timothy Findley, and Michael Ondaatje have already been mentioned. Students should also look for the works of Robertson Davies, Rudy

Wiebe, W. P. Kinsella, Hugh MacLennan, and Mordecai Richler and for the mystery novels of L. R. Wright, Ted Wood, and Howard Engel. Much Quebecois literature has been translated into English, although little of it is likely to be available in U.S. shops; one might begin by looking for names such as Gabrielle Roy and Roch Carrier (whose wonderful children's story, "The Sweater," speaks to kids of all ages in book or video form, and whose antiwar novel *La Guerre, Yes Sir!* is an astonishing tour de force).

Finally, Canadian art also provides clues to the Canadian character. William Kurelek's brilliant pictures of kids growing up on the Saskatchewan prairie; Ken Danby's almost-photographic cultural icons (including his terrific "Goalie"); Alex Colville's only apparently realistic, darkly ambivalent studies of people and animals; Emily Carr's dramatic, instantly recognizable West Coast canvasses; the iconoclastic works of David Milne; and the abstract modernists known as "Painters Eleven"; but above all the stunning, often apocalyptic landscapes of the legendary "Group of Seven"—all have something essentially Canadian to reveal to practiced eyes. So, too, do the brilliant images of the Inuit and Canada's First Nations people, expressed in wood, bone, and soapstone carvings, sculptures, paintings, woodcuts, totem poles, and engravings. Arguably these works are better known and their imagery more a part of the average Canadian's visual world and sensibility than their equivalents in the United States.

THE IMPORTANCE OF BEING CANADIAN

Understanding a foreign culture is complicated, time-consuming, and difficult at best. Of course, understanding one's own culture in an articulate, sophisticated way is almost as hard. Yet such understandings form a well-educated mind; and, fortunately, by trying to understand someone else's culture, one almost always has to define more clearly the essence of one's own. The study of Canada's society, people, and culture is an ideal way for American students to come to grips with differences, both obvious and subtle, that differentiate two peoples whom many assume to be essentially similar. While it is far easier to see that Chinese or Somali or Mexican culture is different from American than it is to perceive the contrast with the culture of Canada, this very challenge makes studying Canada all the more interesting—a discriminating, perceptive activity that can sensitize students to cultural diversity in ways they have not yet imagined.

The important thing to remember is that Canada is, by conscious choice, a North American alternative to the United States. For Canadians, nothing is more important than their independent identity—they're Canadian, eh? Thus Canadian culture may seem slightly anti-American—it is certainly by definition non-American—but it flourishes proudly in a northern land that is readily accessible to our students. Americans are more likely to respect this identity, and possibly to understand their own as well, if they learn something about what being Canadian really means.

Notes

1. Because this chapter attempts to deal with the culture of Canada generally, it has no space to even begin to do justice to the rich and distinct francophone society and culture of Quebec. It is obvious that Quebec's presence within Canada has had major ramifications for the development of cultural attitudes in the "Rest of Canada" (or ROC, a term of rather ominous implications, popularized first in Quebec during the early 1990s). The reverse is also true, although to a much lesser extent: in many ways, Quebec and the ROC still constitute "two solitudes" which talk at, not to, each other. Sadly, one might now say the same about the City of Montreal and the Rest of Quebec.

2. Originally published by the Canadian American Committee and the National Planning Association of Washington, D.C., *Continental Divide* was subsequently published by Routledge, New York, in 1990.

3. Lipset, *Continental Divide*, pp. 44-45. Sondra Gottlieb, wife of Canada's former Ambassador to the United States, is the original source of the description "solid, reliable . . . [but] dull."

4. Lipset, *Continental Divide*, p. 63.

5. The description is from Earle Birney's satirical poem, "Canada: Case Study."

6. In February 1997, Canada faced squarely the issue of whether its traditional government policies designed to protect and nurture cultural industries and the creation of "national" cultural products could continue in the face of increased challenges to these policies brought before the World Trade Organization by the United States. It seemed clear to the then Liberal government, as well as to experts in the field of cultural policy, that Canada's determination to foster and to market Canadian cultural creativity would of necessity have to be implemented in a combination of old, and as yet undetermined, new policy initiatives attuned to the trade politics and the technological realities of the coming half decade. Michael Dorland, ed., *The Cultural Industries in Canada: Problems, Policies, and Prospects* (Toronto: Lorimer, 1996) is an excellent summary of the state of play through the end of that year.

7. For students who may be surprised by how many Canadians are "famous" in one field or another, the Web site at www. alvin.lbl.gov/ Canadians.html will open their eyes. For example, in addition to the music industry names mentioned in the text, one might cite the following musical groups: Pearl Jam, Barenaked Ladies, Snow, Crash Test Dummies, Tragically Hip, Nine Inch Nails, Blue Rodeo, Dream Warriors, the Band, and the Jeff Healey Band.

8. Canadian feature films come and go, as varied in quality and subject matter as current Hollywood offerings. A few are distributed in commercial video form, usually at prohibitive prices in the United States.

The best reference for NFB films is *Canada in Film and Video*, updated regularly by the Canadian Film Distribution Center of SUNY Plattsburgh's Center for the Study of Canada (Feinberg Library, Rms. 124-128, Plattsburgh, NY 12901-2697, tel. 518-564-2396, fax 518-564-2112, from which one can rent Canadian video materials very inexpensively).

Sources

Berton, Pierre. *Why We Act Like Canadians: A Personal Exploration of our National Character.* Toronto: Penguin, 1987. As opinionated and provocative as one would expect from the noted TV personality and popular historian.

Dorland, Michael, ed. *The Cultural Industries in Canada: Problems, Policies, and Prospects.* Toronto: Lorimer, 1996. An excellent summary of the state of play in these industries and of the complex nature of Canada's dilemma as its government tries to continue to protect and nurture Canadian culture in the face of increasingly "globalized" trade policies, ever more aggressive American competition in the cultural marketplace, and rapid technological change.

Lipset, Seymour Martin. *Continental Divide: The Values and Institutions of the United States and Canada.* New York: Routledge, 1990. Sociologist's study of many ways in which Canadian society has differed from American. Convenient, wide-ranging summary.

Macleans. "Canada's Weekly Newsmagazine" is an invaluable aid to staying current in terms of Canadian cultural developments and issues. So too, of course, would be any of several important Canadian newspapers, Toronto's *Globe and Mail* in particular.

Web site: www.alvin.lbl.gov/terning/Canadians.html "Well-Known People Who Happen to Be Canadian," arranged by categories, updated frequently.

Chapter 7
Quebec, Past and Present
Richard Beach

Quebec, Canada's largest province, represents a massive piece of the world's real estate—close to 600,000 square miles. The province ranks eighteenth in size among the nearly 200 member countries in the United Nations. In fact, the U.S. states of Vermont, Massachusetts, New York, California, Texas, New Jersey, New Hampshire, Maine, Rhode Island, and Pennsylvania combined would all comfortably fit inside the province. It is three times larger than France and seven times that of Great Britain, Canada's two "European founding nations."

Quebec's terrain is mostly rolling and hilly; only a few mountains are more than several thousand feet high. Much of Quebec's territory has, during the past 100,000 years, undergone extensive glaciation, and the evidence is everywhere in its rocky soil, massive sand hills, gravel pits, erratic boulders, moraine-dammed bodies of water, and fertile dried-up lake bottoms. Many thousands of small- and medium-sized lakes, hundreds of rivers, including the enormous aquatic umbilical cord, the St. Lawrence, and a fjord, the Saguenay River, ebb and flow throughout the territory. Straddling the international border with New York and Vermont are magnificent Lake Memphremagog in the Eastern Townships, an archetypal glacial body of water, and its more renowned cousin, Lake Champlain, located south of Montreal.

Quebec is inhabited by the descendants of the two so-called "charter" groups that immigrated from France and the British Isles, by many immigrants from the United States, and also by thousands of First Nations peoples—the Cree, Neskapi, and Inuit in the north, and the Mohawk, Montagnais, Abenaki, and Micmac, among others, in the center and south. To this mix have been added people in ever-increasing numbers from countries all over the world. French is the official language and is the spoken mother tongue of more than 80 percent of the people. Most of the remainder are native English speakers. Many Quebecers, in fact, are bilingual, some trilingual, and Italian, Portuguese, and many other European, African, and Asian languages can also be heard in the Montreal metropolitan area.

Quebec's diverse economy, traditionally resource-based especially in forest products, minerals, water, and agriculture, today focuses on the service trade, manufacturing, transportation, and biotechnology sectors. A prosperous, aggressive, confident, and outward-looking middle class has emerged during the past thirty-five years to propel the economy. There are problems of course—stubbornly high unemployment, the dominance of Montreal over the rest of the province, and Quebec's place in Canada, to name a few. But there are more successes than weaknesses.

QUEBEC'S LAST 100 YEARS[1]

Quebec entered the twentieth century different in many ways from the other provinces and territories of Canada. The economy remained primarily agricultural and provinces and territories in Canada. The economy remained primarily agricultural and resource based. Mineral exploration, lumbering and farming retained an importance in Quebec far greater than in most other areas of Canada. While foundries, textile and paper mills, breweries, and banks—most controlled by the English minority or American investors— flourished in towns and cities, overall, Quebec lagged behind the rest of Canada, especially Ontario, in industrial development. And, of course, French-speaking and Roman Catholic Quebecers, a significant majority in the province, remembered and cherished a history quite different from their English-speaking fellow citizens.

Cleavages between the French-speaking majority and the English-speaking minority remained within the province. (Hugh MacLennan, the noted English Canadian writer, coined the term "two solitudes" during the 1940s to describe the situation.) Not surprisingly, the two linguistic groups tended to cluster, whether in cities or rural areas. Religion was a powerful force in both communities (French-Roman Catholic; English-Protestant) and remained a divisive factor as well. Immigration gradually became an important concern. Since there was minimal immigration of francophones[2] to Quebec, replenishment and growth of the original French-Canadian community[3] was dependent upon indigenous expansion or the assimilation of non-francophone immigrants. But a significant majority of people from a variety of ethnic backgrounds who moved to the province eventually assimilated into the English-speaking minority population, primarily because the "public" school system was based on religion (Catholic or Protestant) and because of the ever increasing attraction and importance of the

English language in Canada, in North America and indeed throughout the world. The schools, therefore, served as natural "sorting mechanisms" for immigrants—Catholics, the majority, attended Catholic (French) schools while Jews, Orthodox and Protestant Christians and others originating from all over the world attended Protestant (English) schools. Some francophone elites, including a few who displayed pronounced ethnocentric tendencies, were quite content with this process until the 1960s. Thus, while the majority population remained more or less homogenous, the English-speaking community gradually developed a multi-ethnic character, color and perspective.

In many social, cultural, religious and economic domains, therefore, rural Quebec, geographically if not in terms of numbers of people, remained relatively static, despite rapid change elsewhere on the continent; successive conservative and nationalistic political regimes in the province found it convenient to maintain the status quo for decades. When change inevitably arrived, it was dramatic and profound, affecting all Quebecers and, for that matter, the rest of Canada.

World War II and Its Aftermath

World War II was, for Quebec and its people, a pivotal event in several important respects. First, many of Quebec's religious, intellectual, and political leaders did not possess the fervor, loyalty, or patriotism for France that was exhibited by English Canadians for Britain prior to and during the war. Young people were strongly discouraged by the elites from joining the Canadian armed forces. Despite these objections, thousands of French Canadians did enlist and fought bravely and heroically shoulder to shoulder with their English-speaking countrymen. Some also joined the U.S. Army.

For those at home, news about the war from radio and newspaper reports and stories from returning veterans, as well as the sad reality that thousands of loved ones had died in remote European towns and villages, significantly broadened their geographic horizons and provided them with a more worldly perspective. Quebec's relative isolation and slow industrial development was soon to end—and abruptly.

Indeed, the complexity, magnitude, and pace of change that took place in Quebec during the years following World War II are difficult fully to comprehend. The economy was undergoing a rapid transformation. Pressure for change, impatience, and unrest were increasingly in evidence by labor, university students and professors, some intellectuals, and a few courageous journalists. And, of course, politics became involved.

During its heyday from the mid-1930s through the 1950s, the Union Nationale (UN), Quebec's dominant political party, had resisted change, instead voicing traditional conservative French Canadian themes such as the "nobility of the plow," religion, anticommunism, and greater provincial autonomy. Maurice Duplessis, the venerable UN leader and premier for some twenty years (1936-39, 1944-58), facilitated church control over a network of educational, health, and social welfare institutions—even the boy scouts and trade unions—as well as savings and loan associations.

Through the Duplessis era, the Quebec government invested comparatively few resources in social and economic development. The economy remained dominated by English-speaking managers who broke unions, kept wages low, and limited overall economic opportunity for the French-speaking majority. Federal institutions, though more benign, perpetuated English domination as well. Also characteristic of this period was considerable censorship of films and books, repression of women (who were not allowed to vote in Quebec provincial elections until 1944), a still very high birth rate (families of twelve to twenty children were not uncommon), and the suppression of both religious minorities and political dissent. All the while, French language education in the province continued to follow the classical Catholic humanist model, which was out of step with the economic requirements of an increasingly urban society and industrial economy. Clearly, the "Duplessis era" had to end before the "Quiet Revolution" could begin.

Many developments that contributed to the post-Duplessis upheaval had their roots in changes before his death. The rural exodus continued apace as French-speaking Quebecers flocked to the cities because of better employment prospects and improved ground transportation; investors came to Quebec from other parts of Canada and from the United States after World War II to seek their fortunes; and Quebecers traveled more frequently to the United States to visit family or to vacation.[4] As a result, French Canadians became more familiar with the materialist aspirations, lifestyles, urban values, practices, and institutions of anglophones in the rest of North America. Growing interaction with foreign science and technology, and related skills, philosophies, and concepts, eroded traditional support for an insular French Canadian community. The advent of television, seasonal work opportunities in U.S. border towns, an improved literacy rate, the growth of an influential artistic community, and a more assertive and nationalistic intelligentsia all contributed to an undercurrent of rising expectations. Such feelings had been manifested graphically by labor unrest and violent strikes in Quebec as early as the late 1940s. A number of future leaders such as journalist René Lévesque and the globe-trotting bon vivant Pierre Trudeau were already expressing their impatience with the repression of the Duplessis regime, the irrationalities of the old order, and the irrelevancy of traditional French Canadian nationalism.

Many francophone Quebecers for the first time began to question the restrictive controls the Church had over their lives. Some also realized what little influence they had within the federal government in Ottawa. Still others came to understand, to their surprise, discomfort, and sometimes outrage, the extent to which Quebec's economy was dominated by English Canadians and by American entrepreneurs. These awarenesses led a growing number of Quebecers to demand greater control over their own destiny as well as a greater appreciation of the distinctiveness of their own culture and a desire to preserve and cultivate it.

The sudden death of Duplessis in September 1958 marked, in effect, the end of an era in Quebec. Duplessis's power had been close to absolute and no successor had been groomed by him or his party. Within two years, an election was held, and the Union Nationale was out of power. Reformer Jean Lesage and the Liberal Party now guided the destinies of the province. Thus began the fateful era of the Quiet Revolution.

The Quiet Revolution

Lesage and his colleagues were convinced that Quebec needed to modernize right away through vigorous state intervention in order to catch up with the other provinces of Canada and the United States. His government aggressively sought additional powers from the federal government, insisting upon greater participation or even total provincial control, in such matters as social welfare, immigration, resource exploitation, transportation, and, in particular, cultural and linguistic affairs, some of which were already constitutionally the province's purview. A rallying cry or motto of the reformers that represented this new assertiveness was *maîtres chez-nous* (masters in our own home).

The Liberals won a second election in 1962, primarily on a platform promising to nationalize enterprises judged essential to fostering more rapid economic development. The subsequent expansion of Hydro-Quebec, for example, through the consolidation and nationalization of many anglophone-owned-and-managed private hydroelectric power companies outside of Montreal, epitomized the new aggressive economic order. Political opponents, especially within the Union Nationale, viewed the nationalization as hostile to the principles of free enterprise. A number of anglophone business elites expressed doubts about the ability of predominantly French-speaking state monopolies to manage their affairs competently. They were proven wrong. Hydro-Quebec soon became a model of efficient and dynamic state capitalism. The new utility was transformed into an economic powerhouse employing legions of young Quebec engineers and, importantly, creating a sense of pride that spilled over into many other economic and entrepreneurial pursuits.

Even though the old party defeated the Liberals in 1966—in part reflecting the fears of many conservative francophone voters in rural areas that the nature and pace of change was becoming too rapid and extreme—they themselves continued on the path of major reforms. The civil service was greatly expanded, the Quebec Civil Code, unique in Canada, was updated, and the rights of women were strengthened. Quebec joined Canada's hospital insurance and medical care programs. More state-owned or "crown" corporations were created, and state intervention in economic and social development continued. The reforms of the Quiet Revolution were irreversible; the "Old Quebec" of the Duplessis era would never return.

Reports of federal commissions in the 1960s demonstrated the need for more and real "French power" in Ottawa. The selection of Pierre Trudeau to replace the retiring Lester Pearson as leader of the Liberal Party of Canada (and, therefore, as prime minister) in 1967 was due in large part to his Quebec roots. To many French-speaking Québécois, he represented a native son who would provide tangible advantages for them. At the same time, English-speaking Canadians concerned about the growing threat to national unity from some independence-minded groups in Quebec saw in Trudeau, an avowed federalist and an outspoken critic of the excesses of Quebec nationalism, someone who could resist pressures for special consideration and privileges for Quebec.

During the 1960s, the urban and suburban middle classes became the new power brokers in French Quebec society. Its intellectuals, cultural leaders, journalists, public bureaucrats, and many teachers articulated a new version of nationalism, now called "Québécois nationalism," in that it was territorially based, assertive, and in some circles ethnocentric.

It should be stressed that independence for Quebec was not a popular concept at that time. A variety of other constitutional arrangements and modifications, short of political sovereignty, were widely debated among the Quebec intelligentsia, journalists, and bureaucrats. These included demands for "special status" for Quebec within Canada, official recognition of "two nations" within the Canadian state, and the establishment of a more loosely administered federation.

Nevertheless, other elements in French Quebec society became impatient with the politicians, their options, and both the rate and the direction of political, social, and economic change. Soon the restless energies of a few radicalized francophones, frustrated by a process of change that did not correspond to their expectations, went well beyond constitutional means to obtain redress of their grievances and turned violent. The principal manifestation was the October Crisis of 1970, during which one small cell of nationalist radicals kidnapped the British trade commissioner in Montreal. Another cell abducted and then murdered the province's Minister of Labor. The terrorists were soon captured and either

Quebec City is the oldest city in Canada—and the only "walled city" in North America.
Ministère du Tourisme du Québec

convicted and jailed or exiled. Thereafter, the political evolution of the province has followed traditional and legal means.

By the late 1960s, intellectuals and labor activists with links to the mass media and others had paved the way for the emergence of another political party to rival the Liberals (then led by a young economist, Robert Bourassa). The new Parti Québécois (PQ), under the leadership of the charismatic René Lévesque, was an amalgamation of several separatist groups, as well as former Liberals who bolted the party when it failed to adopt a more nationalistic agenda. It took advantage of widespread disaffection with the alleged lack of recognition or accommodation of Quebec's distinctiveness by English Canada. Now separatism had a legitimate, and moderate, political voice.

The Sovereignty Referendums

Two of the most momentous, divisive, exciting and, for many, traumatic events in the province's history were referendums on some form of Quebec sovereignty in 1980 and recently again in 1995. But, in spite of the pain they caused, little was resolved by either.

The Liberal government of Robert Bourassa, first elected in 1970, was tired, divided, and demoralized in 1976 when he called an election, hoping to rejuvenate the party. Pundits and Liberal politicians alike underestimated two things: the popularity of the Parti Québécois, and the decline of the Union Nationale as a viable political force in the province.

Under the leadership of the mercurial populist René Lévesque, the PQ conducted the provincial election campaign using a platform that focused on "good and honest government" and the shortcomings of the Liberals, while downplaying the party's *raison d'être*—the sovereignty of Quebec. This strategy was adopted for practical reasons, as polls indicated that the party would lose the election badly if the campaign was fought primarily on the issue of independence or even the party's soft sovereignty policy (the seemingly oxymoronic "sovereignty-association," as party strategists called it). The PQ only promised that, if

Nearly half the population of Quebec is concentrated in and around cosmopolitan Montreal.
Ministère du Tourisme du Québec

111

elected, a referendum on the issue would be held sometime during its mandate. The strategy worked, and the PQ was elected. Soon thereafter, a number of major pieces of legislation were passed that fundamentally changed Quebec society still further. The most significant was the controversial Law 101 that, in 1977, legislated the primacy—some would suggest almost the exclusivity—of the French language in many parts of the province.

The crescendo toward Referendum 1 began soon thereafter. The formulation of the question itself became divisive. The people were ultimately asked, in a forty-five-word question, merely to give the government a mandate to negotiate sovereignty-association with English Canada. Following months of emotional, torturous debate, the referendum was held in May 1980, and the "no" side won conclusively by a majority of 60-40, though the vote was roughly split among francophone voters. The Nationalists were bitterly disappointed; scars remain today. Sadly, many francophone families were permanently divided as a result. That was not the case among all other Quebecers—immigrants, anglophones, Native peoples alike—all of whom had voted overwhelmingly "no."

During a fifteen-year period following Referendum 1, a number of efforts were undertaken to reconcile the different views of the country espoused by some French and English Canadians, but without success. The apparent insolubility and interminability of the problem was particularly frustrating and stressful to the average Canadian, especially because most realized that their country was paying a high economic and social price for its inability to get its act together. Indeed, observers in other countries, including in the United States, expressed disbelief that a country so rich in human and natural resources could be wasting so much time and energy on constitutional bickering. Others suggested that the flames of discontent were intentionally being fanned by ambitious bureaucrats, politicians, frustrated nationalists, and other individuals with their own racial or linguistic axes to grind in order to keep themselves in the limelight (and in jobs), and that the citizens were being victimized as a result.

Several attempts were made to reach a consensus, but to no avail. These included the Constitution of 1982 (agreed to by nine provinces, but the Quebec government refused to sign); the Meech Lake Accord of 1987 (two English-speaking provincial legislatures refused to endorse the provisions by the time the three-year statute of limitations had expired in 1990); and the Charlottetown Accord of 1992 (which was voted down by seven of the ten provinces, including Quebec, in a national referendum).

Alas, the soup continued to simmer. After a period from 1985 to 1994, when the federalist Liberals were in power in the province, the PQ was elected in 1994, defeating a tired and missionless Liberal Party. Once again, the promise of "good government" and a referendum sometime during the mandate had won popular appeal. Another national crisis was inevitable. Many citizens predicted, or at least hoped, that a promised second referendum would settle the issue once and for all. It did not. Referendum 2, held in October of 1995, asked the people of Quebec to vote for or against sovereignty. The campaign created frantic and sometimes fanatical reactions on both sides, bringing out the best and the worst in Quebecers and other Canadians. Federalist ("no") leaders both in and outside Quebec were overconfident and realized too late how close the vote was likely to be. Though the uninspiring Premier Jacques Parizeau was legally the leader of the "yes" camp, the "yes" forces were led in reality by the popular and charismatic Lucien Bouchard, who was relatively new to the separatist scene. The margin of victory for the "no" forces was razor thin: 51-49 percent. Canada breathed an enormous sigh of relief.

Premier Parizeau resigned the day after having made what many observers interpreted as racist remarks in his emotional election night "concession" speech.[5] Bouchard succeeded him as leader of the party and became premier, with three years left in the PQ's mandate. Bouchard has promised to hold a third referendum before the turn of the century, prompting cynics to refer to Quebec's "neverendum" condition. Canada is no closer to solving its most vexing problem than it was thirty years ago.

EDUCATIONAL AND CULTURAL OUTCOMES OF THE QUIET REVOLUTION

One of the great yet less widely known transformations that occurred during the Quiet Revolution has been in the field of public education. Throughout the 1960s, Quebec's educational system was overhauled from top to bottom. A Ministry of Education was only created in 1964; before that, the Roman Catholic Church had been the de facto controlling and administering body. Remarkably, within a decade, most Catholic schools, by far the most numerous, had become secularized after more than 300 years of near total church control. Dozens of community colleges—none of which had existed previously—were created. The province's four comprehensive universities—the Université de Montréal, Université Laval, Concordia University, and McGill University, all of which had been relatively elitist and exclusive until the 1960s—were expanded enormously. And an entirely new public system, the Université du Québec, was created, with campuses located throughout the province.

The impact was enormous. Thousands of teachers, professors, and support personnel had to be trained and hired. Secular boards of education and councils were created. Job opportunities for immigrants from Belgium, France, Switzerland, and francophone Africa especially became available, the domestic pool of appropriately trained personnel being inadequate. The construction industry boomed to create the many buildings and facilities required. This entire work force was soon unionized, and their leaders became a powerful force in the Quiet Revolution.

The cultural life of the province was also vibrant during the 1960s and '70s: raconteurs and balladeers performed everywhere, new theatre was created, and a good deal of great and not-so-great literature was written, all supported enthusiastically by students, professors, and bureaucrats and much of it funded or at least touted by the government. No longer was the Church able to censor movies, prevent the construction of drive-in theatres, or ban books from libraries. Influence and prominence shifted rapidly from religious leaders to government bureaucrats, professors, and cultural figures. University rectors and union leaders were esteemed as well. The 1970s became the decade of the visionaries—those who heralded the need for greater provincial authority and power, or even independence, and those who wrote or sang about Quebec and its people.

During the 1980s, however, successful business leaders emerged as the new champions of Quebec society, eclipsing the cultural elites, government bureaucrats, and politicians. Huge Quebec corporations such as Bombardier (transportation), Québecor (printing), and Lavalin (engineering), expanding rapidly and prospering with thousands of small- and medium-sized enterprises successfully and prominently producing everything from bicycles to bromides, brought tremendous wealth to a new strata of francophone Quebec society.

An Evolving Economy

Agriculture traditionally has been relatively more important to the economy of Quebec than in most of the other industrialized regions of the continent. Until the Quiet Revolution, the industrial sector remained heavily dependent upon the labor-intensive manufacture of goods such as textiles, clothing, footwear, leather items, and furniture. The "feast or famine" nature of these businesses over the years, as well as their somewhat antiquated production methods, contributed to consistently higher unemployment and lower overall productivity than existed in Ontario and other regions. Moreover, while protective tariffs, quotas, and other trade barriers guaranteed a domestic market for many manufactured goods, Quebec products were seldom competitive in the international arena.

The Quebec economy has also been characterized by the export of unprocessed or semiprocessed products, such as iron ore, asbestos, pulp and paper, copper, zinc, and gold—primarily to the United States—and massive sales of hydroelectricity to New England and New York. A substantial aluminum industry has prospered for decades thanks to the availability of cheap hydroelectric energy. Many of these economic activities until recently have overwhelmingly involved capital investments by English Canadian and foreign firms, the latter primarily U.S.-based multinational corporations and banks.

The Quebec economy today continues to change. Private sector and government initiatives are focused on the province's becoming more export-oriented and internationally competitive in areas that utilize its comparative advantages (e.g., the abundance of relatively cheap, renewable hydroelectric energy and access to large markets in the United States). In particular, for products such as electronic goods, office and communications equipment, pharmaceuticals, transportation equipment, and processed natural resources, market expansion is and will be in the United States more than in the rest of

Canada. Moreover, for high technology industries to expand to the large scale required in today's global market, major U.S. participation will have to continue in the form of expanded private investment, joint ventures, North America-wide marketing systems, and technical expertise. This has already been accomplished by Bombardier, a rising star on the international scene. Indeed, the "draw" of this transportation equipment powerhouse has resulted in the location of half of Canada's aerospace industry in Quebec (Bombardier also owns plants in Ontario).

Quebec's desire for market expansion naturally affected its attitude toward the recent trade agreements. The FTA (Free Trade Agreement) negotiated between Canada and the United States by the Mulroney and Reagan governments took effect in 1989. While it received only lukewarm support in the rest of Canada, Robert Bourassa's provincial Liberal government and many Quebecers were solidly behind this bold initiative. Similarly, Quebec enthusiastically embraced the implementation of NAFTA in 1994. Creative and entrepreneurial small- and medium-sized businesses in Quebec have moved aggressively into the U.S. market under provisions of these trade agreements. Separatist politicians also saw the emergence of greater north-south rather than east-west economic trends as weakening Quebec's dependence on the rest of Canada, and thus wholeheartedly supported the treaties as well.

In spite of these advances, however, a feeling of political uncertainty and instability has slowly emerged during the 1980s, and these elements have unquestionably hampered economic expansion. Thirty years of explosive expansion of bureaucracies at the provincial and municipal levels and enormous growth of the educational system and social services—all of which were generous to employees and liberal with construction funds and other ex-

Table 7-1. Population of Quebec by ethnic origin, 1851-1991

Census Year	French number (percent)	British number (percent)	Other number (percent)	Total number
1851	669,887 (75.2)	215,034 (24.2)	5,340 (0.6)	890,261
1871	929,817 (78.0)	243,041 (20.4)	18,658 (1.6)	1,191,516
1901	1,322,115 (80.2)	290,169 (17.6)	36,614 (2.2)	1,648,898
1931	2,270,059 (79.0)	432,726 (15.0)	171,470 (6.0)	2,874,255
1951	3,327,128 (82.0)	491,818 (12.1)	236,735 (5.8)	4,055,681
1971	4,759,360 (79.0)	640,045 (10.6)	628,360 (10.4)	6,027,765
1981	5,105,670 (80.2)	487,385 (7.7)	776,015 (12.2)	6,369,070
1991	5,068,450 (74.4)	284,960 (4.2)	1,456,890 (21.4)	6,810,300

Source: Government of Canada, *Census of Canada,* 1851-1991.

penses—have been costly to the government and to Quebec society. This was the price the province had to pay to accomplish what it did during the Quiet Revolution. Nevertheless, in so doing, Quebec has amassed a huge provincial debt (proportionately higher than the country as a whole and than most other provinces) and tolerated ever-increasing annual deficits. As a result, the continental economic downturn of the early 1990s, with its high interest rates, dealt a huge blow to Quebec. Official unemployment has hovered around 12 percent for years, a figure well above the Canadian average and one that

Who Are Canadians of French Ancestry?

The word "Canadian" in an ethnic, geographical, linguistic, and political sense has had an interesting and somewhat varied history as it relates to Canada's two founding nations. The term gradually emerged during the early 1700s to refer to native-born people of French or French-Indian ancestry, most of whom were trappers, traders, or peasants living a subsistent existence in the wilderness or on the seigneuries owned by the aristocrats. Therefore, until the conquest, there were two peoples in *Nouvelle France*: *les français* and *les Canadiens*.

After 1763, no common terminology evolved to describe both founding peoples of Canada. *Canadien* was associated primarily with French-speaking people, who constituted a majority of the population of British North America from 1763 to about 1850. According to les Canadiens, all other inhabitants of the new British colonies—United Empire Loyalists, British settlers, and indigenous English alike—were *les Anglais* (the English). The English-speaking population commonly referred to themselves during the early years as "English," "British North Americans," or more often, "British" and seldom "Canadian," although most were residing in a Canadian colony. According to them, the French-speaking population residing in the St. Lawrence Lowland and in Atlantic Canada were "the French." Thus, the descriptive terms used by both groups to describe each other were ethnically, rather than politically, linguistically, or geographically based.

This tendency was reinforced during the British period of 1763-1867 because the names of the colonial entities located in the northeastern half of the continent were constantly changing. The territory along the St. Lawrence was, for example, referred to sequentially as the Quebec Colony (1767-91), Lower Canada (1791-1841), Canada East (1841-67), and the Province of Quebec (1867 to the present).

Confederation, the establishment of distinct provincial subunits, and the emergence after 1850 of English as the language of the majority in Canada as a whole resulted in and indeed necessitated the development of new terms to describe the two founding nations. To distinguish themselves from *les autres*, Canadians of French origin became known as *les Canadiens français* (French Canadians), though little attempt was yet made to identify with any specific region of French Canada. The remainder of the population—the economic and demographic majority of British extraction—referred to themselves as "Canadians" or, less frequently, "English Canadians." Thus, for the first time, there were linguistic undertones to the ethnic terms. The singular term "Canadian," used in a political and territorial sense, was still less important.

The twentieth century has witnessed several changes in what Canadians call themselves and are referred to by others, particularly within the French Canadian communities. A trend emerged that identified the two founding groups more by language, territoriality, and ethnicity. During would not be tolerated in the United States. By the mid-1990s, it became obvious that only through major cutbacks and a restructuring of government could the province begin to get its fiscal house in order.

Many investors outside Quebec's francophone mainstream have argued that, among other irritants, the province's powerful unions and the government's persistent efforts to promote French in the workplace and educational system have created an unattractive economic environment for investment—there being many other locations on the continent and beyond

the past two decades, the terms "francophone" and "anglophone" have been used and accepted more and more, not only because political and cultural leaders wanted to separate language from nationality, but also to accommodate the many "new Canadians" who have arrived in Quebec during this century.

Traditionally, a *Québécois* was a person from the City of Quebec (in the same way a *Montréalais* is a Montrealer and a *Beauceron* is someone from the Beauce, a region south of Quebec City). Gradually, "*Québécois*" has evolved to be used in a wider geographical, broader political and, in some cases, specific ethnic context, although the last is far more subtle. Some Quebec nationalists argue that "*Québécois*" are Quebec residents of French origin only, distinct from English-speaking Quebecers and ethnics/immigrants, as well as from francophones residing outside Quebec—they are a majority within the territory of Quebec rather than a minority within Canada. This terminology gradually emerged during the Quiet Revolution as many within the francophone community have sought to demonstrate their specificity and a greater self-confidence. This is uniquely the case among separatists—they exclusively employ the term *Québécois*, avoiding at all cost "French Canadian" or any other term that uses the word "Canadian."

A more inclusive interpretation of *Québécois* is that anyone residing in Quebec is a Québécois, that is, the term has a territorial but not necessarily an ethnic or linguistic meaning. This usage avoids accusations of ethnocentrism and allays fears of sensitive immigrants and anglophones that they are unwelcome and/or are being relegated to second class citizenship in their home province.

To many non-francophones, however, this new *Québécois* identity is grounded in ethnic factors that go beyond French language capability and residency in Quebec. Non-francophones—even native-born anglophones whose roots in Quebec go back several generations—have difficulty accepting a partial and certainly an exclusive designation as *Québécois* people. Irrespective of social class and ethnic backgrounds, they identify themselves as Canadians as well as or even rather than *Québécois*. Many francophone Quebecers, on the other hand, consider themselves *Québécois* first and Canadians second.

The term *Canadien* in the traditional sense is now an anachronism in Quebec (except for hockey teams) and will likely disappear when the older generation passes away. Also, "French Canadian" is being used less frequently in Canada as people seek to be identified within a specific ethnic or provincial context. Terms such as "Franco-Ontarian," "Franco-Manitoban," and "Acadian" are now commonly used to describe people of French origin in various areas outside the province of Quebec.

in which to locate or expand a business that present fewer "complications." In an attempt to keep in step with the rest of the continent, and under pressure from international lenders, recent Quebec governments since the early 1990s have attempted to downsize. This has involved the government divesting itself of or substantially cutting back some government-owned businesses, reducing bloated bureaucracies, containing annual expenditures—all under the watchful and anxious eyes of New York bankers and other financiers poised to downgrade Quebec's still-enormous debt in the absence of radical financial surgery.

Quebecers, of course, like most Canadians, have become accustomed to many free services, from sidewalk snow-plowing to major medical operations. However, the harsh reality now is that the government has no other choice than to reduce the number of facilities and workers, and thus the benefits of a heretofore very generous welfare state. Compounding the situation, the federal government has reduced the size of the "grants" it annually transfers to Quebec. Throughout all of this, it is important to note that Quebec labor unions, especially those representing the civil service, retain considerable economic clout and political influence, and will only begrudgingly relinquish any ground they have gained in the past decades. Politicians who tamper with the status quo will likely pay a heavy price.

While Quebecers can justifiably take pride in the success of such multinational, Quebec-based corporations as Bombardier and the dynamism of its numerous small entrepreneurs, there are clouds on Quebec's economic and political horizon as it approaches the twenty-first century.

THE KEY ROLE OF DEMOGRAPHY IN HISTORY AND THE FUTURE

All of Quebec's economic and political issues are inherently linked to the province's diversity in population. The great debates of the 1970s and 1980s often pitted anglophones (citizens of English heritage) and allophones (citizens of national origins other than English and French) against francophone nationalists. While there was by no means solidarity within the anglophone community, the overwhelming majority agreed that they wanted to remain part of Canada. Except for a few noted exceptions, the allophones, too, were solidly federalist. This was not the case in the francophone community. A majority of high school and university students, university professors, high school teachers, and government bureaucrats supported the idea of some form of sovereignty or independence. The majority of workers, however, and a significant majority of the business elites and federal government employees (including the military) favored remaining within the Canadian Confederation, albeit modified.

An important perennial issue for francophones has been the survival of the French language and French Quebec society in light of the overwhelming majority of anglophones and the pervasiveness of American culture. An open and free choice educational system was seen as a threat to survival because the vast majority of allophone and anglophone students, or even some francophones, would gravitate to the Protestant (English) school system because fluency in English would give them the flexibility to move freely to another part of Canada or to the ultimate destination, the United States. When several prominent demographers, using data that some researchers have contested, predicted that within one or two generations francophones would become a minority in Quebec, it was suggested that unless drastic measures were taken, traditional Quebec society was doomed. Nationalists argued that the inducement program designed to attract students to the Catholic (French) system was not enough and that constraints and even prohibitions needed to be placed on the Protestant system. Once in power (from 1976 on), the separatist Parti Québécois succeeded in getting passed the highly controversial Law 101, with the implications discussed above.

With these developments, many anglophones and allophones began to feel that they were not wanted in Quebec and were uncomfortable at best and angry and bitter at worst. They progressively lost control of their historical institutions and some language rights, and have been leaving Quebec in ever-increasing numbers. For generations, significant numbers of anglophones, especially the English, have left the province for other parts of North America. This process has been accelerating since the beginning of the Quiet Revolution. A combination of factors has contributed to this exodus— the general movement of the economic center of Canada westward to Toronto and even to Calgary, Edmonton, and Vancouver; the lure of the United States; the general malaise of the Quebec economy; the heavy tax burden in Quebec compared with other areas of North America; the significantly reduced political and economic influence of the English-speaking community; and the negative manifestations of laws and policies to make Quebec more French.

While this population shift may delight some Nationalists, who see these departures as resulting in fewer "no" votes in the next referendum, more forward-thinking observers recognize the enormous amount of expertise, money, experience, and creativity being lost to the province. In fact, an important characteristic, even a legacy, of the English-speaking minority is its institutions. The cultural environment in North America and the better-than-average economic opportunities available to native-born, English-speaking inhabitants facilitated the creation and development of their own network of prestigious educational and other social institutions. As well, English-speaking Quebecers have their own radio and television stations, libraries, newspapers, bookstores, etc. The Museum of Fine Arts and other prestigious institutions were created, funded, and staffed primarily by members of this community. And they have used their own financial resources to create health and social welfare institutions and services of high quality. Many of the historical museums scattered throughout rural Quebec— some now operated by francophones—were established and have endured thanks to anglophone philanthropy, creativity, and volunteerism.

Yet, as the power and influence of the anglophone community in Quebec have diminished, these Quebecers are viewed by the ultranationalists now as less of a "threat" to francophone society. Moreover, the actual number of French-speaking people and the proportion of unilingual francophones have been increasing, and more and more recent immigrants, thanks to Law 101, are integrating into the francophone community. "Integration" is an important word because, to some nationalists, anything less than "assimilation" is unacceptable. Some of these same nationalists are also concerned that these young "néo-Québécois," as they are sometimes called, retain strong ties to English Canada, having voted heavily "no" in the referendum, and do not accept the Nationalist vision of a homogeneous Quebec society. Consequently, senior government officials and cultural leaders have lately made a series of intemperate remarks that have been mildly racist and anti-ethnic or at least have been interpreted as such by the people involved.[6] Anti-anglophone graffiti still found in some parts of Montreal are gradually being replaced by a few anti-ethnic or even anti-Semitic slogans. Some callers to French-language radio talk shows have complained that there are too many "ethnics" in Quebec. Of course, with a high unemployment rate (among the highest in North America), scapegoats are inevitably sought for the economic malaise.

It is true that the composition and character of the non-French population of Quebec has never been more ethnically diverse. Today, people of British descent are not even the most numerous (see Table 7-1).

Ethnic and religious diversity has always been more characteristic of the anglophone minority than of the francophones, and even in the past, such upwardly mobile groups as Jews and Irish Catholics have reached pinnacles of prominence and economic power once the exclusive preserve of the English. The English-speaking "community" has traditionally had a much greater capacity for and success in attracting and assimilating immigrants. This has been primarily due to the very active, and often dominant, role that they have played in certain major sectors of the provincial economy. But it has also been due to the pervasiveness of the English language worldwide and in the rest of Canada, as well as the fact that, until the 1970s, the French-speaking community did not always seek or even welcome immigrants in their midst.

But the number and proportion of the total population of non-French, non-English ethnics in Quebec have changed significantly during the past several decades. Older ethnic communities, such as Jews, Germans, Poles, and Ukrainians, had largely integrated into the anglophone community by 1960 and have noticeably declined in number since. Being "marketable" throughout North America and sharing the anxieties of the ethnic English, they have joined the general anglophone exodus in substantial numbers. This trend does not bode well for the anglophone community in Quebec in the long run, especially in areas outside the region of Montreal where numbers have declined precipitously of late.

Postwar immigrants, such as the Portuguese, Italians, and Greeks, are for the most part still allophones and have not yet fully integrated into either of the two principal linguistic groups. Together they form a significant minority. Quebec has recently attracted more Italians and many other ethnic communities such as Haitians, Vietnamese, and Chileans. Further, the provision of Law 101 requiring children of all immigrants to attend French schools has effectively stopped the replenishment of the anglophone community—greatly reduced by departing anglophones—by anglicized allophones, or by the immigration of English speakers. The children of those not already francophone are, because of Law 101, now assimilating into the majority francophone community.

French Quebec will survive and develop more readily than French-speaking communities outside the province—that is clear. However, it is too early to tell whether the French-speaking Québécois mainstream will be able successfully to incorporate the highly diverse ethnic, racial, and religious character of its recent immigrants, let alone its anglophone minority. In a sense, the vertically segmented social structure that existed in Quebec prior to the 1960s, where anglophones represented and bore the "burden" of pluralism (in their schools, hospitals, etc.), must now be projected to characterize the francophone society of the future primarily because of Law 101. The policy of francization of immigrants will add substantial numbers to the francophone proportion of the population, and result in far greater interaction with the host francophone Québécois society.

In addition, the non-French Canadian ethnic francophones, who are already competing for jobs that are increasingly hard to find in a relatively weak economy, represent values, attitudes, religions, beliefs, and even diets different from those of their hosts. Certainly most French-speaking politicians and opinion leaders are making every effort to create the institutional support for and a climate of opinion favorable to their successful "assimilation." Nevertheless, these leaders do not necessarily speak for the francophone population as a whole which, for example, continues to support the maintenance of a denominational rather than a language-based, nondenominational school system. Such a preference works at cross purposes with the assimilationist goals of the leaders. Overall, as the next millennium approaches, Quebec society is still sadly divided.

Notes

1. Beginning sections of this chapter draw from "French Canada," a chapter authored by Richard Beach and Martin Lubin in William W. Joyce, ed., *Canada in the Classroom* (Washington, D.C.: National Council for the Social Studies, 1985): 89-110; and Richard Beach, "A Travers les Frontiers," *Journal of Cultural Geography*, 8, no. 2 (1988): 81-94.

2. Since the 1950s, the usage of the term "francophone" for French speakers and "anglophone" for English speakers has become common. Immigrants whose language of daily use is neither English nor French are referred to as "allophones," or more recently as "ethnics."

3. See the section on pp. 116-117 on "Who and What are Canadians of French-speaking Ancestry" for the historical development of terms used to describe Canada's two founding peoples.

4. Though the majority of the population retained a relatively insular view of life and work, some Quebecers sustained and strengthened family ties with the northeastern United States. Again, the Catholic Church played a coordinating and often dominating role. It met many needs of first- and second-generation Franco-Americans by establishing churches, schools, seminaries, newspapers, social organizations and hospitals locally, and by helping them retain ties to their religion, language and heritage. These relationships continued through the first half of the century. New England for the first time also became a destination for some tourists from Quebec.

5. "Let's talk about us (French speaking Quebecers). Sixty percent of us have voted in favor . . . It's true we have been defeated, but basically by what? By money and the ethnic vote . . . In the long run, finally, we will have our own revenge and we will have our own country." Excerpts from Premier Parizeau's Referendum night speech (translation provided by author).

6. The following public statement which was made by Pierre Bourgault, prominent Quebec nationalist and former adviser to Parti Québécois Premier Jacques Parizeau, soon after the referendum, elicited a very negative reaction from non-native francophones. "It is the Jews, the Italians and the Greeks who cast an ethnic vote. It is they who are racist, not us. They have only one objective, to block (sovereignty). To win, we will have to do like them: an ethnic vote!"

Sources

Gagnon, Alain-G. *Quebec Beyond the Quiet Revolution.* Toronto: Nelson Canada, 1990.

McRoberts, Kenneth. *Quebec: Social Change and Political Crisis.* Toronto: McClelland and Stewart, 1994.

McRoberts, Kenneth. *Misconceiving Canada: The Struggle for National Unity.* New York: Oxford University Press, 1997.

Scowen, Reed. *A Different Vision.* Toronto: Maxwell MacMillan Canada, 1991.

Young, Brian, and John Dickinson. *A Short History of Quebec.* Toronto: Copp Clark Pitman, 1993.

Chapter 8
Canada Within the Social Studies
William W. Joyce

This chapter explores Canada's position within the social studies curriculum. It begins with a rationale for educating Americans in general and students in particular about this immense nation to our north. Then, it analyzes problems associated with the use of middle school social studies textbooks on Canada in U.S. schools. Next, it explores subject matter on Canada that can be taught in grades five through twelve and in college. Finally, it closes with a discussion of the many sources of assistance available to educators.

RATIONALE FOR STUDYING CANADA

A basic premise underlying this publication is that for a variety of historical, geographical, cultural, economic, and political reasons, Canada merits a prominent position in U.S. social studies curricula at the upper elementary, secondary, and college levels. In their introduction to the precursor to this volume, William Joyce and Macel Ezell noted that Americans' profound ignorance of Canada, its people, and its institutions is especially disturbing when one acknowledges that the two nations are the world's best friends and by far each other's most important trading partner. Over the years, the two have maintained compatible views on a broad spectrum of international issues; they cooperate in mutual defense and peacekeeping efforts; they cherish and nurture family and cultural ties; they share democratic values; and, of course, they are bound by geography and history.[1]

Donald H. Bragaw, a former president of National Council for the Social Studies, asserted that the Canada-U.S. relationship, "unique in world affairs, allows the two nations to search for solutions to common problems affecting their shared future. Students should be given an opportunity to study this special relationship."[2] Consider these realities cited by Christopher Sands of the Center for Strategic and International Studies:

- An estimated 90 percent of Canadians live within one hundred miles of the U.S. border.
- Canada and the United States maintain the largest trade relationship in the world, amounting to nearly $1 billion dollars a day.
- The Canadian market for U.S. goods and services is double the size of the United States' next largest trading partners, Japan and Mexico.
- More than 100 million border crossings were recorded in 1996.
- Though Canada is a major agricultural competitor with the United States in world markets for grains, it is a major customer for U.S. winter vegetable and citrus growers.

- Annually, U.S. and Canadian armed services personnel train together under the auspices of NATO and NORAD and engage in special deployments such as those to Bosnia and Haiti.
- Canada works side-by-side with the United States in the North American Free Trade Agreement, the Organization of American States, the United Nations and its agencies, the Group of Seven industrialized nations, and Asia-Pacific organizations.
- The United States maintains $100 billion in direct investment in Canada and about an equal amount in portfolios.[3]

Charles Doran and Joel Sokolsky argue that this unique relationship conveys to Canada advantages over other nations in its dealings with the U.S. president and Congress. These advantages result from Canada-U.S. linkages via automotive industries on both sides of the border; regional, especially north-south, linkages between U.S. states and provinces (for example, Canadian-U.S. management of the Great Lakes); strong, positive bureaucratic ties between U.S. and Canadian government officials; and the prevalent U.S. perception of Canadians as friendly, nonthreatening neighbors.[4] Sands, in addition, says that the common bonds between the two nations, the physical proximity of Canadians and Americans, and the high degree of interaction between them create "local" foreign policy, but that this relationship and the perceptions it creates shift U.S. Congressional attention away from Canadian issues and toward issues and events elsewhere in the world where a greater sense of crisis is perceived.[5] One significant consequence is that Americans can become lulled into taking our close relationship with Canada for granted.

Perhaps no Canadian event in recent history jogged U.S. complacency more than the evening of October 30, 1995, when the results of the latest Quebec referendum were announced: 49.4 percent of the electorate voted for independence, and 50.6 percent against. U.S. media coverage—especially post-referendum conjecturing about the future of Canada and its relations with the United States—was extensive. But, after registering shock and dismay over this event for several weeks, the U.S. media returned to its previous policy of limiting Canadian coverage to the bare essentials.

THE PROBLEM WITH TEXTBOOKS

A consequence of this all-or-nothing approach to coverage of Canadian events by our domestic media is that Americans learn very little about that country on a day-to-day basis. When U.S. middle school students study "our neighbor to the north," they receive the majority of their information from mostly slanted, dated, inaccurate textbooks. Over the years, these books are rarely changed: revisions consist of updated demographic data, but few significant textual alterations.

Two studies document the inadequacies of social studies textbooks on Canada. In their study of twelve commonly used grade 6/7 social studies texts, Marion Salinger and Donald Wilson reported "great variation and degree of intensity in the treatment of ideas considered significant by informed Canadians and Americans." These researchers' profiles of individual texts revealed a pronounced dearth of coverage of Canada's relations with the United States and other nations, as well as of the diverse people and issues of Canada. Moreover, the study revealed a strong bias in texts toward explaining contemporary phenomena in terms of environmental determinism and creating the impression that "Canadians are just like us."[6]

The tendency of textbooks to depict Canada, its people, and institutions in such simplistic, superficial terms was underscored in a later study by Michael Yocum. He found that the four most widely used U.S. middle school social studies textbooks failed to give students accurate, understandable contexts for studying Canada, perspectives on Canadian issues and concerns, and balanced analyses of relations between Canada and the United States.[7]

Yocum believes that problems of context, perspective, and balance and the biased political messages students receive from textbooks can be countered by teachers who are willing to expend the requisite effort. He advocates intensiveness over extensiveness of content coverage by zeroing in on a few significant topics for in-depth investigation, probably best done within small groups. A second method advanced by Yocum is to use passages from the textbook as a springboard for group and individual discussion. For example, a teacher might present seemingly contradictory, slanted, or incorrect passages to students, then ask them to generate research questions and eventually hypotheses. This approach can encourage students to read more critically and thus be less susceptible to the influence of implied political messages. It also enables teachers to add vitally needed Canadian perspectives.

The movement toward independence in Quebec provides meaningful opportunities for students to go beyond textbooks as they investigate significant issues that greatly affect Canadian-U.S. relations, while avoiding the pitfalls cited by Yocum. Students in upper elementary and middle school social studies classes can study the reasons why the independence movement has grown in Quebec. Examples of questions worthy of investigation include the following: Why do the people of Quebec regard themselves as different from those in the rest of Canada? What special status do Quebecers possess vis-à-vis other Canadians? How will Quebec's relations with the rest of Canada and the United States be affected by independence? High school students can examine secessionist rhetoric in detail: What promises are made by Quebec's leaders? How did factions in Quebec and elsewhere in Canada react to the close vote in the 1995 referendum? What was the official U.S. response? What scenarios are likely in the event of secession by Quebec?

Joyce recommends in his report, "American Responses to the 1995 Quebec Referendum," that at a more advanced level students can also explore these issues: the potential impact of Quebec's secession on U.S. trade with the rest of Canada and on Quebec's and Canada's immense debt (most of which is held by U.S. institutions); Quebec's potential role as a successor state; its possible membership in the North American Free Trade Agreement; changes in Canada's military status; possible changes in Quebec's boundaries; and implications of Quebec independence as perceived by other potential independence-minded parts of Canada.[8]

Over the course of such investigations, teachers would encourage students to utilize a wide variety of resources, including the Internet, CD-ROMs, books, news magazines, newspapers, videos, films, and other materials. Information on such resources is provided by the chapters in this volume by Yvon and by Smith and Preston.

Social studies textbooks produced by U.S. publishers have not improved significantly over the years. A notable exception is *0 Canada*, a lavishly illustrated, accurate, highly motivating textbook for upper elementary and middle school students. Written by George Sherman and published by the Center for the Study of Canada at SUNY Plattsburgh in Plattsburgh, New York, *0 Canada* is augmented by a useful teacher's guide and selections from notable trade books on Canada for children.[9]

CANADA'S POSITION IN THE CURRICULUM

Experts on teaching Canada in U.S. schools argue that it should be taught at all levels of the social studies curricula—elementary, middle school, high school, and college. New York, North Carolina, Maine, and Washington mandate the study of Canada at various levels, while Michigan and other states recommend such instruction. Typically when Canada is taught, instruction occurs in upper elementary and middle school social studies classes. To some extent in high schools and to a greater extent in colleges, Canada is taught within courses on geographic regions (North America, for example), literature, government, and world history. At the college level, courses on Canadian history, geography, politics, and culture and a variety of courses on Quebec are offered. Some universities offer interdisciplinary courses with significant Canadian content in such areas as resource development, fisheries and wildlife, the environment, marketing, labor and industrial relations, and the fine arts.

Helen Nugent advocates promoting learning about Canada through family visits in addition to formal education. At the preschool level, children can learn to recognize Canada's flag and national anthem, while children in the primary grades can learn when and how Canada celebrates its national independence, Thanksgiving, Remembrance Day (comparable to U.S. Veteran's Day), and Labor Day. Further, she recommends that upper elementary and middle school students learn to compare geographical regions of Canada with those of the United States (for instance, Atlantic Canada to New England; Central Canada to Mid-Atlantic/Old Northwest; Prairie Canada to Midwestern wheat belt; Cordillera to Northwest/Alaska). The folklore of each region can be explored in an effort to discern cultural differences and similarities.[10]

A decade ago, a team of educators meeting at the Quail Roost Conference Center in North Carolina prepared a document entitled *New Ways of Teaching Canada Within the Social Studies Curriculum* that suggested entry points for Canadian content in U.S. social studies curricula.[11] Examples from this publication are:

- Canadian topics in *geography* –predicated on geographic locations, place, relationships within places, movement, and regions– can function as effective vehicles for adding Canadian content. Illustrative topics include northern and western settlement and recent immigration from Asia and eastern Europe.
- *History* topics stress the presence of two founding peoples, the French and British, the role of conflict and compromise in the growth of democratic principles, the long-term evolution of the Canada population from native people to a multiethnic society, and Canada's transformation from an agrarian to an urban-industrial society.
- *Political* topics focus on Canada's evolution into an independent, representative government which subscribes to important, familiar political processes such as federalism, political parties, devolution of national government to the provinces, privatization of services, and protection of individual rights, as well as Canada's parliamentary form of government.
- Topics in *economics* stress Canada's important position in world affairs as well as its great wealth (as determined by its massive size, natural resources, foreign trade, capital investment, and trade relations) and its progressive economic relationship with the United States. Examples of other topics are Canada's difficulty in developing its natural resources and its strong regional diversity. Canada's leadership in the 1990s in extending NAFTA membership in Latin America might be added to this list.
- Cultural *development* topics center on the arts, humanities, and entertainment and have bilingual and multicultural manifestations. Examples include the powerful, pervasive influence of U.S. media; the infusion of new art and architecture introduced by Asian immigrants to Canada; the remnants of European roots (especially family connections); shared interests with U.S. citizens in music, sports, and literature; U.S. threats to Canada's evolving entertainment and publishing industries; and this nation's diverse cultural mosaic vis-à-vis perennial concern over its national identity.

Alleman's article in this volume describes a wide variety of activities for students who are engaged in the study of many of these and other Canadian topics. These activities are presented within the context of the National Council for the Social Studies' *Expectations of Excellence: Curriculum Standards for Social Studies.*[12]

CONCLUSIONS

A basic premise of this publication is that Canada merits a prominent position in the social studies curricula of our schools and colleges. The close and unique relationship between the United States and Canada and Canada's important role in world affairs support this premise. Unfortunately, the U.S. media and school programs do not accord Canada the attention it deserves. This is probably more a testimony to Americans' tendency to take Canada for granted than a reflection of Canada's perceived unimportance to the United States. Evidence of such neglect, benign as it may be, surfaces when one examines social studies curricula of the nation's schools. A cursory examination of courses of study and other curriculum documents quickly reveals that, when Canada is systematically taught, instruction only occurs in grades 6 or 7.[13] Rarely does Canadian content consume a total high school course.[14] Usually students learn about Canada through courses in such areas as the geography of North America, U.S. history, world history, and English literature, all of which typically accord Canada incidental status.

These realities, coupled with the low quality of textbooks conventionally used in teaching Canada, present formidable challenges to those teachers who are eager to teach Canada within the social studies. Fortunately, there are many social studies topics that can serve as contact points. Representative of these are common elements in the history and geography of the United States and Canada, the close family and cultural ties of these nations, and the high degree of integration that exists in their economies as well as their mainte-nance of the world's largest trade relationship.

Fortunately, many sources for relevant, low-cost instructional materials are available to help teachers at all levels build Canadian content into their teaching. Preeminent in this regard are college-based Canadian Studies centers located at the University of Maine, Michigan State University, the State University of New York at Plattsburgh, the University of Vermont, the University of Washington, and Western Washington University. These Canadian Studies centers offer up-to-date information, referrals, instructional materials, and support in planning curricula and instructional activities. Fax, e-mail, and mailing addresses of these centers can be found elsewhere in this volume. Still another source of assistance is the Special Interest Group on Teaching Canada of National Council for the Social Studies. Its members remain in contact via e-mail throughout the year and meet at the NCSS Annual Conference.

Notes

1. William W. Joyce and Macel D. Ezell, "Adding a New Canadian Dimension to Social Studies," in William W. Joyce, ed., *Canada in the Classroom: Content and Strategies for the Social Studies* (Washington, D.C.: National Council for the Social Studies, 1985), pp. 1-2.

2. Donald H. Bragaw, "Section I. Rationale for Studying Canada," in *New Ways of Teaching Canada Within the Social Studies Curriculum* (Durham, N.C.: The Consortium for Teaching Canada, 1988), p. 3.

3. Christopher Sands, "Canada: A Case of Local Foreign Policy," Policy Paper on the Americas, Vol. 8, Study 1 (Washington, D.C.: Center for Strategic and International Studies, 1996).

4. Charles F. Doran and Joel Sokolsky, *Canada and Progress: Lobbying in Washington* (Halifax: Nova Scotia Centre for Foreign Policy Studies, Dalhousie University, 1985).

5. Sands, "Canada."

6. Marion Salinger and Donald Wilson, "Canada in American Schools: A Janus Look," Report on a National Study on the Teaching of Canada in American Schools. (Durham, N.C.: Center for International Studies, Duke University, 1984).

7. Michael Yocum, *Political Messages in Middle School Social Studies Textbooks on Canada Educational Outreach Series.* Education Outreach Series, Paper I (East Lansing, Mich.: Canadian Studies Centre, Michigan State University, 1991).

8. William W. Joyce, "American Responses to the 1995 Quebec Referendum." Paper presented at the annual meeting of the British Association for Canadian Studies, Swansea, Wales, March 1997.

9. George Sherman, *O Canada: Its Geography, History, and the People Who Call It Home* (Plattsburgh, N.Y.: Center for the Study of Canada, State University of New York, Plattsburgh, 1995).

10. Helen M. Nugent, *Teaching About Canada,* ERIC Digest 44 (Bloomington, Ind.: Clearinghouse for Social Studies/Social Science Education, Indiana University, 1987).

11. "New Ways of Teaching Canada Within the Social Studies Curriculum," pamphlet written by social studies educators (Durham, N.C.: The Consortium for Teaching Canada, 1988).

12. National Council for the Social Studies, *Expectations of Excellence: Curriculum Standards for Social Studies* (Washington, D.C.: NCSS, 1994).

13. Dean June, of the Attica, New York, Middle School and a frequent presenter at NCSS national meetings, teaches an outstanding course on Canada within his social studies curriculum.

14. Notable exceptions are extremely successful multidisciplinary courses on Canadian cultures designed and taught by high school teachers Ruth Writer in Buchanan, Michigan, and Richard Boulrice in Peru, New York.

Chapter 9
Instructional Activities

Janet Alleman

General ideas about teaching for conceptual understanding and about teaching social studies for social understanding and civic efficacy have influenced Jere Brophy's and my position on learning activities. These ideas were gleaned from the works of John Dewey, Hilda Taba, Ralph Tyler, and other curricular theorists, as well as the works of more recent authors influenced by them.[1]

Our position is rooted in certain assumptions about key features of ideal curricula, even though those features are seldom reflected in the instructional materials used in today's schools.[2] We think that the principles for selecting, designing, implementing, and evaluating instructional activities that we have formulated are especially pertinent for teachers who will be both designers of curricula, undoubtedly drawing from a range of sources, and key stakeholders in implementing courses or units of study about Canada.

All courses and units focusing on Canada (or any topic, for that matter) should be driven by major long-term goals, not content coverage lists. (An example of a long-term goal regarding Canada might be to help students develop an in-depth understanding and appreciation for what it means to be "Our Neighbor to the North.") Thus, teaching activities designed or selected to achieve this or other goals should be included because educators view them as means to help students learn important capabilities and attitudes, not just to acquire cultural literacy construed in a narrow "trivial pursuit" sense.

Content should be organized into networks structured around important ideas, and these ideas should be taught for understanding and application. These assumptions about curricular goals and content are fundamental to the planning or selection of activities because content provides the cognitive base for activities. If goal-oriented planning has produced a curriculum featuring coherent Canadian content structured around powerful ideas about the country, it will be natural and easy to use such content as a basis for activities that call for students to use it in applications involving inquiry, invention, problem-solving, or decision making. (An example might be having students collect daily newspapers for two to three weeks and study references to Canada. Are they positive or negative? How do they relate to political or cultural aspects of Canada? If you were the U.S. ambassador to Canada, what would be your priorities and why?) However, if planning about Canada is merely guided by coverage lists and produces a parade-of-facts curriculum, the effect will be to restrict teachers and students to a reading, recitation, and seatwork approach to pedagogy. Activities likewise will involve isolated recall and be mostly low-level and uninteresting.

Activities should not be self-justifying ends in themselves, but instead means for helping students accomplish major curriculum goals. Activities can be designed to fulfill this function by providing structured opportunities for students to interact with content, preferably by processing it actively, developing personal ownership and appreciation of it, and applying it to their lives outside of school. Utilizing local citizens or local experts in the field, students in other classes, or volunteer mentors can enhance interest in and authenticity to the activity.

We assume that the knowledge and skills aspects of the curriculum focusing on Canada will be integrated in ways that are consistent with the previous requirements and that the skills included will be the ones most naturally suited to applications of the content of the course or unit. Critical-thinking skills and attitudes about Canada can be developed most naturally through assignments addressing value or policy issues that arise when studying particular content and that connect to what is presented in the media.

We also assume that sets of activities will be embedded within the curriculum unit or course of study that teachers create for teaching about Canada, that different activities will serve different functions, and that these functions will evolve as teachers develop their plans. When introducing new content about Canada, for example, you might emphasize activities designed to stimulate interest, establish an anticipatory learning set, or link the new learning to prior learning. (Examples might be providing students with opportunities to compare and contrast Quebec with the other provinces or making such predictions as how Quebec's secession from Canada could affect Canadian–U.S. relations in the future.) When developing content, teachers should stress activities that allow students to extend and apply their learning. (For instance, students might submit editorials on relevant topics to the local newspaper.) When concluding subparts of the course or unit as a whole, you might plan activities that help students appreciate the connections among the many facets of Canada (its economy, government, history, etc.) and provide them with opportunities to synthesize their learning.

Activities should be assessed with an eye toward their costs as well as their benefits. All activities should serve as a means of accomplishing the unit or course goals, and they should be reviewed in terms of their time and trouble. Some activities entail other costs as well, such as financial expense (e.g., a field trip of several days for an entire class). These costs need to be identified and assessed at the initial planning stage.

The key to the effectiveness of an activity is its cognitive and affective engagement potential—the degree to which it gets students thinking actively about and applying content. This thought process should preferably occur in conjunction with students' awareness of curricular goals and of their role as socially conscious citizens with current and future connections to Canada. If the desired learning experiences are to occur, student involvement must include cognitive and affective engagement with important ideas, not just physical activity or time on task.

The success of any activity—one you design, one you select from activities included here, or one you draw from another source—depends not only on the activity itself, but on the teacher's planning and teacher-student discourse before, during, and after the activity. Activities are likely to have maximum impact when the teacher: 1) introduces them in ways that clarify their purposes and engages students in seeking to accomplish those purposes; 2) scaffolds, monitors, and provides appropriate feedback concerning students' work on the activity; and 3) leads the students through appropriate post-activity reflection on and sharing of insights that have been developed. Consistent with the assumptions that we have described and based on our curricular analyses and research, we suggest these primary principles for designing or selecting activities: goal relevance, appropriate level of difficulty, feasibility, and cost effectiveness.[3]

We encourage classroom teachers crafting their own courses or units about Canada to read each of the chapters in this bulletin (each addresses a particular aspect of studying Canada), and then to ferret out the major understandings, establishing how they match the goals of their unit. The activities that follow are driven by the goals and major understandings that we have identified; we expect that teachers will make modifications based on their students. The major point is to be sure that any activity used is goals-driven, feasible, cost-effective and is at an appropriate level of difficulty.

The instructional activities included here have been designed in accordance with the principles developed by Brophy and Alleman, are aligned with the NCSS position regarding Powerful Teaching and Learning, and incorporate the ten themes that serve as organizing strands for the NCSS social studies curriculum standards.[4] These strands are:

- **I** **CULTURE**
- **II** **TIME, CONTINUITY, AND CHANGE**
- **III** **PEOPLE, PLACES, AND ENVIRONMENTS**
- **IV** **INDIVIDUAL DEVELOPMENT AND IDENTITY**
- **V** **INDIVIDUALS, GROUPS, AND INSTITUTIONS**
- **VI** **POWER, AUTHORITY, AND GOVERNANCE**
- **VII** **PRODUCTION, DISTRIBUTION, AND CONSUMPTION**
- **VIII** **SCIENCE, TECHNOLOGY, AND SOCIETY**
- **IX** **GLOBAL CONNECTIONS**
- **X** **CIVIC IDEALS AND PRACTICES**

Although, with appropriate adaptation, each activity may be used with students at any grade level, each as it is written may be best suited for either the elementary, middle school, or secondary school years. As at least an initial guide, the initials "E" for elementary, "M" for middle, and "S" for secondary appear parenthetically with each activity.

CHAPTER 1: AN INTRODUCTION TO THE HISTORY OF CANADA
NCSS Strand: ❶ TIME, CONTINUITY, AND CHANGE
Goals

▶ Develop an understanding of and appreciation for the major events that have shaped the "story" of Canada during the past 500 years.

▶ Develop an understanding of and appreciation for the major conflicts that the people of Canada have experienced over time, as well as a sense about how these conflicts have influenced the country's development.

Student Activities

1. *Which have been the most significant events?*
   Have students select what they consider to be the seven most significant events in Canada's history. Plot them on a timeline. Have students write a short statement for each choice and explain why they think it is one of the most important events. Each student should be prepared to share his or her choices and reasons with the whole class. A large-group discussion should ensue. (M)

2. *Which leader in Canada's history has had the greatest impact and why?*
   Preparing for a debate is an excellent way to sort through the issues and get clearer about what participants really think. After reviewing the chapter focusing on the history of Canada and gathering additional data about Canada's leaders, have students prepare a brief debate involving a select group of Canadian leaders. Identify on a timeline years that each leader was in office. This activity could be carried out in a group format, with each group responsible for gathering data on a specified leader. A spokesperson would offer the arguments in support of the individual. A large-group discussion would follow the debate.
   Key points to keep in mind in preparing and presenting a debate include:
   - Adequate class time should be allotted for exploration of the issue, gathering the appropriate information, and preparing for the formal presentation.
   - Time allotments for the speakers should be reinforced.
   - Speakers should not be interrupted, but open discussion can follow immediately after all positions have been expressed.
   - Usually one class period is adequate for the debate.
   - A debate issue should be stated clearly, specifically, and pointedly.
   - Each debater should thoughtfully and with adequate documentation prepare his or her position. Debating tactics should remain secondary to clear and forthright presentations of points of view and substantiation of facts. (S)

"From the Immigrant"

Bleak, barren spot, ah!, Why should I
 forsake
A fertile land to threat thy worthless
brate?
Labor alone they fertile land surveys,
Breathes the dull round, or prematurely
pays
A hard won pittance, through distress and
toil.
Still doomed again to lavish on they soil;
O land! that's slothful, miserable spot,
Ungracious sandbank! May it be my lot
Remoote to dwell 'mong happier kind
abodes
And leave to grasshoppers a land of toads!
Thou barren waste; unprofitable strand,
Where hemlocks broad in unproductive
land,
Whose frozen air on one bleak winter's
night
Can metamorphose dark brown hares to
white!
Whose roads are rivers, o'er your
fountains
See icebergs form your shining mountains
And drifted snow, from arctic regions.
Gives sheer employment to Canadians,
Here roads ne'er known for many a
summer.
And now past o'er by each new comer.
All wrought one night, nor made of stone
or gravel,
Complete withal and next day fit to travel.
Here forests crowd, unprofitable lumber,
O'er fruitless lands indefinite as number.

3. *Which decade in Canada's history do you consider to have had the most impact and why?*
   Have students form cooperative groups of five. Designate a facilitator, recorder, and spokesperson. Allow some class time for preparation (with the understanding that out-of-class time will be necessary) and approximately one class period for presentation and large-group discussion. Guidelines for cooperative groups include:
   - Make sure that the goal and tasks are clear.
   - Each member of the group should have a designated role.
   - Both individual and group accountability should be built into the assignment.
   - See NCSS Bulletin 87 for more guidelines.
   Using a range of resources, have each group decide which decade in Canada's history has had the most impact and why. Encourage each group to find concrete examples to support its position. (S)

4. *Nationalistic or globalistic?*
   Have each student imagine he or she is a Canadian teenager. Have students review the content focusing on Canada's history, then write short essays explaining why they are proud of their national or global perspective. The student should cite reasons for his or her perspective and include specific examples. After all of the students have completed their essays, they can work in groups to share their responses. Conclude with a whole-class discussion. (M, S)

5. *How did it feel to be an immigrant to Canada in the early twentieth century?*

Have students review the section of the history chapter that describes the period when Canada experienced the major influx of immigrants and its consequences. Then have each student prepare a short paper responding to the question: "What were the costs and benefits associated with immigration?" Most immigrants came to stay in the new world, but when Standish O'Grady arrived in 1836, he looked around, saw what was to follow, and returned to Ireland. Have the students read the poem[5] he wrote and be prepared to discuss it.

Suggested questions for discussion:
- Why do you think Standish returned to Ireland?
- What do you think would have been the "typical" immigrant's reaction? Why?
- What were the three impressions Standish had of Canada? Do you think they were valid? Why or why not? (M)

CHAPTER 2: THE GEOGRAPHY OF CANADA
NCSS Strand: ⓘ PEOPLE, PLACES, AND ENVIRONMENTS
Goals
- To develop an understanding of and appreciation for Canada's geography—how its multiplicity of land forms have shaped its regional identities and economic patterns.
- To develop an understanding of and appreciation for the distinctions between the hinterland and the heartland of Canada.
- To develop an understanding of and appreciation for the statement "Many people think Canada has too much geography."
- To develop an understanding of and appreciation for Canada's physical and cultural patterns and their interactions, such as land use, settlement patterns, cultural transmission of customs and ideas, and ecosystem changes.

NCSS Strand: ⓥⓘⓘⓘ SCIENCE, TECHNOLOGY, AND SOCIETY
Goals
- To develop an understanding of and appreciation for how science and technology can transform the physical world.

Student Activities
1. *Life in Canada as a teenager.*
   Have students imagine that they are Canadian teenagers. Have each student select the hinterland or heartland as his or her home and write a letter to a U.S. teenage pen pal (selected from the class) describing life in Canada. Encourage students to provide lots of specifics and frame their letters from teenagers' interests. Have the pen pals exchange letters and critique each other's work. Select letters for large-group sharing. (M, S)

2. *Hinterland or heartland?*
   Have students imagine that they have decided to become Canadian citizens and live and work in the place of their choice for the next ten years. Have them create photo essays explaining their choice and why. Detailed explanations about their careers and leisure activities enacted in the area of their choice are expected. Encourage them to share and discuss their responses with the class. Which were the most convincing and why? (M, S)

3. *Is it regionalism or nationalism?*
   Canada is often described as a country of paradoxes. One example is
   the conflict between regional and national views of Canadians. Encourage students to use as many sources as they can for analyzing
   this paradox. Ask students to cite their sources for each example and
   be ready to discuss their findings. A three-to-five-page paper should
   be prepared by each student as evidence of his or her investigation
   and application. (S)

4. *How has Canada's geography had an impact on its economy?*
   Have students work in threes for the purpose of discussing Canada's
   geography and how it has influenced its economy. Ask each group to
   create a graphic that depicts the connections. Then have each discuss
   the peoples' roles in acknowledging and addressing the geographic
   phenomena. Have Canadians utilized their geography to the fullest? If
   so, how? If not, why not? Graphics and explanations should be the
   stimulus for a large-group discussion. (M, S)

5. *You are the developer.*
   Have students imagine that they are encouraging a major change in
   land use or a shift in settlement pattern in Canada. Where would they
   launch their initiative and why? Encourage them to work in pairs and
   prepare a presentation using maps, facts, and figures to support their
   position. (S)

6. *You are the tour guide for the geographers' annual meeting.*
   Divide the class into groups of seven. Each group is to assume the role
   of the planning committee for the geographers' tour through Canada.
   The geographers have allocated five days for the experience. Remind
   students as they are planning their tours that the geographers want to
   focus on Canada's geography. Encourage students to plan carefully
   and to collect visuals to heighten interest. Invite geography majors
   from a nearby college or university, if possible, or other interested
   individuals, to serve as the panel for selecting the tour that the geographers will take. (M)

7. *My future as an environmentalist.*
   Have students review the geographic conditions that characterize
   Canada and the human influences that have changed their initial
   "faces." Then ask each student to write a one-page response to the
   question, "Would I, as an environmentalist, find a bright professional
   future in Canada?" Why or why not? If possible, invite local people who
   are environmental experts or share an interest in the topic to serve as
   the panel for providing feedback to students regarding their ideas. (S)

8. *Scientific and technological challenges.*
   After students have examined the content focusing on Canada's heartland and hinterland, have them work in pairs to discuss which area will
   be more affected by science and technology in the future and why. Then

have each pair speculate about the nature of potential scientific break-throughs that would most dramatically affect these areas and assess their costs and benefits. (S)

CHAPTER 3: CANADIAN GOVERNMENT AND POLITICS
NCSS Strand: ⑩ POWER, AUTHORITY, AND GOVERNANCE
Goals

- Develop an understanding of and appreciation for the contemporary political scene in Canada and a sense of how it has evolved to where it is today.
- Develop an understanding of and appreciation for Canada's political system and how it contrasts with the U.S. system.
- Develop an understanding of the Constitutional Act of 1982 and its impact on Canada's political system.
- Develop an understanding of and appreciation for the Meech Lake Accord.
- Develop an understanding of and appreciation for the challenge in governing Canada.
- Develop an understanding of and appreciation for multiparty parliaments and the potential challenges such a system will have on Canada's future

NCSS Strand: ⑤ INDIVIDUALS, GROUPS, AND INSTITUTIONS
Goals

- Develop an understanding of and appreciation for group and institutional influences and their impact on people, events, and elements of culture.

Student Activities

1. *The evolution of Canada's political scene.*
   Have students work in small groups to identify five to seven political events that have had the most impact on the current situation. Encourage the groups to use graphics containing detailed explanations of the selected events, along with their rationale for their significance. Then have each group prepare a one-page description of the current political situation accompanied by pictures or a cartoon to dramatize the present-day government in Canada. Each group should have an opportunity to share its work with the class.
   Due to the high interest level of the Canadians regarding these political matters, members of the community could be invited to the class and participate in a class discussion. If so, follow-up questions for open discussion might be: Where do we go from here? What can we, as future voters, contribute to Canada's political future? (S)
2. *Comparing and contrasting Canada's political system with that of the United States.*
   Have students, working in groups of five to seven, determine the likenesses and differences between the two political systems. Encourage

the groups to create graphics to depict these likenesses and differences. Each group should be prepared to explain the likenesses and differences and decide if they strengthen or weaken the political systems. (M, S)

3. *What about the Constitutional Act of 1982?*

    Have each student write a one-to-two-page essay explaining the Constitutional Act of 1982 and how he or she thinks it has influenced Canada's political system. Arrange for a political figure or mentor to critique the essays, paying particular attention to clarity of explanations and thoughtful reasoning. Invite the political figure or mentor to visit the class and share the patterns that emerged in the essays, commenting where appropriate. Follow up with a class discussion. (S)

4. *Creating a cartoon about the Meech Lake Accord.*

    Have students review the Sherman chapter and, if possible, additional references to develop an in-depth understanding of and appreciation for the Meech Lake Accord. Then have them, individually or in pairs, design a cartoon to illustrate its impact. Key points to remember in designing a cartoon include:

    - Most cartoons of social significance deal with political themes, although some are related to economic or other social matters.
    - The value of cartoons used in social studies classes lies in the ideas represented rather than the symbols.
    - A cartoon represents a particular viewpoint or interpretation and contains persuasive or propagandistic material.

    Have students share their cartoons in class. Then display all of them on the bulletin board. Discuss with students: How are they alike? How are they different? (S)

5. *Governing Canada: A challenge fit for King Solomon.*

    Have each student do a "fast write" (ten-minute time allocation) expressing what this phrase means to him or her. Then have students work in triads sharing their responses. Have each triad take ten minutes for planning role plays that reveal their views. Randomly select triads to enact their plans. Questions for the debriefing might include: What elements of geographic and/or cultural diversity were expressed in the role plays? Do you view these as particularly challenging? Why? Why not? What other elements (geography, cultural, or other) were brought to mind as you witnessed the role plays? Do you think that the French Canadians were overreacting? Why? Why not? Are Canadians in other provinces overreacting? Why? Why not? (S)

6. *Multi-Party Parliaments: What are their track records?*

    Have students use computer data as well as library hard-copy references to learn more about multiparty parliaments and their impact on countries where they have existed. The research could be done in groups with a designated scribe/reporter for taking notes. After an allocated time for researching the topic, a large-group discussion should be facilitated. A graphic could be created on white board or flipchart paper capturing the salient points about multiparty parliaments. What groups of people seem to be having the most impact on multi-parliament initiatives? How would you characterize them? How do they become influential? Then, challenge students to think about this model for Canada's future. Advantages? Disadvantages? Challenges? (S)

7. *You be the judge: Is Canada geographically ridiculous and politically impossible?*

   Divide the class into teams with half taking the affirmative position and half taking the negative position. Time should be spent examining the issues and seeking concrete examples to illustrate key points. During one class period, have representatives of each side serve as the debate teams and share their positions. Invite local government officials or other individuals interested in the topic as the audience. An alternative to a full-class debate could be a paired activity in which students work in twos to examine both sides of the question followed by a class discussion. (M, S)

CHAPTER 4: CANADA AND THE WORLD
NCSS Strand: ⊗ GLOBAL CONNECTIONS
Goals

- Develop an understanding of and appreciation for the impact that conflict, cooperation, and interdependence has had on Canada and its people—and an understanding and appreciation for how Canada's position has had an impact on other parts of the world.
- Develop an understanding of and appreciation for the causes, consequences, and possible solutions to persistent, contemporary, and emerging global issues such as pollution, environmental protection, etc.
- Develop an understanding of and appreciation for the effects of technologies on the global community.

NCSS Strand: ⊗ CIVIC IDEALS AND PRACTICES
Goals

- Develop an understanding of and an appreciation for what it means to be a responsible citizen.

Student Activities

1. *Survival or good will?*

   Arrange the students into cooperative groups. Have each group select a facilitator, spokesperson, and recorder. The task for the groups is to review the content of the course that has focused on Canada's global initiatives and to select what they consider Canada's five most important global activities. Then, they should decide which of them have occurred out of survival and which have occurred out of good will. Students should be prepared to give reasons for their responses and cite examples to illustrate. For example, recently Canada sent troops and aid to Zaire and Rwanda. If a group selects this global initiative as one of the most significant, it would have to decide if Canada did this to protect its own survival or because of its value of good will. Students should be encouraged to use outside sources—people, newspaper and magazine articles, supplemental books, Internet data, etc. After completing this segment of the activity, the class should discuss what it means to be a responsible citizen—and what, if anything, the citizens of Canada should be doing to promote good will. A subsequent conversation could follow regarding citizens of the United States. (M, S)

2. *Global peacekeeping.*
Have students write essays that defend or refute the statement that Canada has played a vital role in the world as peacekeeper. Encourage them to use a variety of sources as evidence. The essays should contain examples in support of the position selected. If possible, invite students from another class or interested citizens from the community to critique the essays (based on criteria about peacekeeping). What, if anything, should individuals as responsible citizens do to promote global peacekeeping? (S)

3. *Where/how is Canada visible?*
Each student should be provided with a world map and asked to locate five to ten sites where Canada has created a presence. Students should plot the sites and write a paragraph for each, describing the Canadian influence. Have them share their responses.
This activity might be extended to include speculations regarding Canada's global future. The discussion should center on rationales for these possibilities. Students could be assigned to groups with each group preparing an editorial to the local newspaper addressing Canada's future global presence—and how it might affect local areas. (M)

4. *An enlightened attitude toward multiculturalism.*
Canada has long been characterized as a nation with an enlightened attitude toward multiculturalism. Have students use a variety of supplemental resources to substantiate this claim. Then divide the class into groups, and have each plan and present a skit that illustrates a specific example of this multicultural attitude. After debriefing students who participated in the skits, ask then what evidence is there that this multicultural attitude exists in their own community. Ask students to gather evidence and bring it to class for a large-group discussion. Encourage informal surveys, interviews, photos, newspaper clippings, etc. as evidence. (M, S)

5. *Economic connections around the world.*
Display a large world map with the caption "What are Canada's economic connections around the world?" Arrange the students into groups in order to respond to this question. After they do the necessary

research to acquire examples, have groups use pictures, symbols, drawings, words, etc. to depict Canada's economic picture from a world perspective. As a class, decide how you would describe this picture—is it optimistic or pessimistic? Why? (S)

6. *Promoting tourism becomes globalism.*
   Divide the class into groups of five. Have each group pretend it is a travel agency charged with promoting Canada's tourist attractions to people around the world. Have each group create a "travel" package illustrating Canada's greatest attractions. Each group should identify and be prepared to explain what part of the world would be the most likely market for the tour package and why. Role plays could be conducted as a means of creatively sharing the research and decision making. (E, M, S)

7. *Canada and its changing position vis-à-vis the United States.*
   Have pairs of students prepare photo essays that describe Canada's changing face on the world scene as the result of its near neighbor to the south. Have students share their essays with the entire class. A follow-up discussion should address the current and potential consequences of these changes. The class should speculate about the typical Canadian attitude toward the United States as the result of these changes. If possible, invite interested community citizens to the class to critique the essays. Some should be asked to represent Canadians and some should represent U.S. citizens. They could be given specific roles such as businessperson, retiree, researcher, etc. A follow-up conversation could be held focusing on the individual's role in promoting positive relationships across the border. What is the responsibility of people concerned about his or her country and its people? (M, S)

CHAPTER 5: THE CANADIAN ECONOMY
NCSS Strand: ⑦ PRODUCTION, DISTRIBUTION, AND CONSUMPTION
Goals
- Develop a better understanding of and appreciation for the American economy and the solid links it has with Canada—its largest trading partner.
- Develop an understanding of and appreciation for the staple thesis and its impact on Canada's development and growth.
- Develop an understanding of and appreciation for Canada's governmental influence on the country's economy.
- Acquire a sensitivity to Canada's current economic conditions and future prospects.

Student Activities
1. *Economic snapshots show the resemblances.*
   Divide the class into two groups. One will represent Canada and the other will represent the United States. Have each group gather pictures,

facts, and figures (using texts, election data bases, etc.) that can demonstrate the economic story of the two countries. Designate two bulletin board areas for the displays. For organizational purposes and for discussion, subdivide each team into groups of five to seven. Each subteam facilitator should encourage members to examine the data and pictures to ensure that the display presents a big idea about the economy (i.e., the GDP of Canada was $18,598 in 1994; the living standard in Canada is high as evidenced by its infant mortality rate). After the subgroup discussions have concluded (with the bulletin board displays as evidence of their findings), conduct a large-group discussion using the pictorial information as the stimulus. Conclude the discussion by asking "Do you think Canada and the United States economies are more alike or different? Why?" (S)

2. *What do you make of the staple thesis?*

The "staple thesis" proposes that a nation's economic growth and development are based on the export of staples—raw materials or primary resources for which it has a comparative advantage. Have students work in pairs and create editorials that express their reactions to this theory. Encourage them to use specific examples to illustrate the economic linkages or disconnects that support their position. Have students submit their editorials to the local newspaper for publication. (S)

3. *Which staple has been most important across time?*

Canada's economy has been based upon four great staples: fish, fur, lumber, and wheat. Have each student select one of the four staples and trace its historical development and economic "payoff." The "product" should result in a short essay with facts and figures. Select students across groups to share their findings. As a total class, decide which staple has been most important and why. (M, S)

4. *Changing structure of the Canadian economy.*

Arrange the students in groups of three. Each group is to decide what its position would be if it were asked to give advice to a Canadian high school senior regarding his or her future, based on the changing structure of the Canadian economy. Use Table 9-1 as source of data. Allocate fifteen minutes for the triad discussions. Then conduct a large-group discussion. Encourage groups to share their rationale. (S)

5. *So what is the government's role?*

The importance of government participation in the economy is enormous, although often it is difficult to measure. Encourage students to think about the special interest groups in Canada and the range of views they would hold regarding government involvement in the country's economy. Then divide students into groups of three to five, and have each design a cartoon depicting one of these views. Key points in designing a cartoon include:

Table 9–1. Changing structure of the Canadian economy

Output by Sector as Percent of Total Production

Industry	1870	1926	1970	1994
Agriculture	34.3	18.1	3.3	2.5
Forestry	9.9	1.3	0.8	0.6
Fishing/Trapping	1.1	0.8	0.2	0.1
Minerals and Petroleum	0.9	3.2	4.0	5.1
Manufacturing		21.7	23.3	21.6
Construction		4.1	6.3	6.1
Transportation and Communications	22.6	9.6	8.9	5.2
Electric Power, gas and water		2.8	2.9	2.8
Wholesale and retail trade		11.6	12.4	15.1
Finance, real estate, insurance	31.2	10.0	11.6	19.2
Public administration		3.4	6.9	7.5
Service		12.9	13.5	14.1

Source: About Canada, *Center for Canadian Studies, Mount Allison University, from M. C. Urquart. R.H.A. Buckley, Historical Statistics Canada, 1995.*

- The value of cartoons used in social studies classes lies in the ideas represented rather than the symbols.
- A cartoon represents a particular viewpoint or interpretation and contains persuasive or propagandistic material. (S)

6. *What are the pros and cons concerning high protective trade barriers?* Have students imagine that they are employed as governmental officials charged with doing in-depth research regarding Canada's trade barrier history. In triads, have students gather and analyze data and be prepared to share their positions, including rationales, with the class. Invite local government officials to the class to critique the students' work and to participate in the discussion regarding the high protective trade barriers. (S)

7. *What does trade mean to Canada?* After students have had an opportunity to review the content focusing on Canada's economy, ask each to do a "fast write" on the question "what does trade mean to Canada?" After the timed activity (teacher and students collaboratively determine time limit), have students share with each other in pairs. If bulletin board space is available, students could be encouraged to bring pictures to depict what trade means to Canada. If time permits, have students speculate about the future of Canada's trade position. Encourage students to seek input from local citizens and share the responses with the class. (M, S)

CHAPTER 6: CANADIAN CULTURE IN THE LATE 1990s
NCSS Strand: ❶ CULTURE

Goals

- Develop an understanding of and an appreciation for the meaning of culture.
- Develop an understanding of and appreciation for the likenesses and differences between "Canadian" and "American" culture.

Student Activities

1. *How are we alike and different?*

   Have students review the chapter "Canadian Culture in the Late 1990s." Select one major difference between the two cultures. Have the students explain in writing what he or she views as the major difference and why. Then visually depict the contrasts. Students should be prepared to share their written and visual responses with their peers.

   After completing the activity that addresses differences, have students review the chapter again. The use of additional resources would be helpful. This time, focus on the cultural likenesses between the United States and Canada. Students should explain in writing what they view as the major likenesses and why. Then, have them visually depict the likenesses. They should be prepared to share their written and visual responses.

   An alternative to this approach is to divide the class so that half focuses on cultural differences and half focuses on likenesses. Then, have groups share the results in a large group. Discuss the value in examining both likenesses and differences. (M)

2. *"Culture is the way we live."*

   Ask students to imagine that they are photographers whose assignment is to create photo journals that explain the statement "Culture is the way we live" from a Canadian perspective. Use this assignment as a stimulus for encouraging students to seek pen pals from Canada. Encourage students to request photos from pen pals for their journals. Have students share the results with their peers. If possible, ask pen pals to evaluate the accuracy of the photo journals. (M)

3. *You be the judge!*

   Have students study the list of cultural differences on the handout. After each statement, have the students write whether they agree or disagree. Have them provide a documented example to support their response. After they complete the assignment and engage in a large-group discussion, ask each student to do a "fast write." Allocate ten minutes for this activity. Pose this question: "Should we focus on the differences if indeed we want to become more tolerant and appreciative of others? Why or why not?" After ten minutes of individual responding, have students share their ideas in pairs followed by a class discussion addressing this question. (S)

4. *Casual relationships.*

Divide the class into groups. Have each group select a facilitator, recorder, and spokesperson. Provide maps, photos, and books to stimulate thinking about these connections. The task is for the group to figure out how Canada's history and geography have influenced its culture. Each group should take an overall position and then seek many examples to support it. Students will have a designated time period to share their positions with the class. (M, S)

CHAPTER 7: QUEBEC: PAST AND PRESENT
NCSS Strand: ❶ CULTURE
Goals

- Develop an understanding of and appreciation for the meaning of culture and be able to compare similarities and differences in the ways Canadians in Quebec and in other parts of Canada meet human needs and concerns.
- Develop an understanding of and appreciation for individual and group differences regarding their responses to physical and social environments and changes to them on the basis of shared assumptions, values, and beliefs.

NCSS Strand: ❷ TIME, CONTINUITY, AND CHANGE
Goals

- Develop an understanding of and appreciation for time, chronology, change, conflict, and complexity as a means of "telling the story" of Quebec.

NCSS Strand: ❸ PEOPLE, PLACES, ENVIRONMENTS
Goals

- Develop an understanding of and appreciation for the ways people create places that reflect culture, human needs, government policy, and current values and ideals.

NCSS Strand: ❹ PRODUCTION, DISTRIBUTION, AND CONSUMPTION
Goals

- Develop an understanding of and appreciation for the influence of value and beliefs in economic decisions.

Student Activities

1. *What is different?*

Secure the English and French versions of the Canadian National Anthem. Have students study them carefully. How are they alike? Have student construct a chart like the one below depicting the likenesses and differences with explanations. Then, discuss how the anthem reflects Canada's history and its people. (M)

English and French Versions of the National Anthem

Likenesses	Differences	Explanations

2. *What are the most significant events in shaping French Canada?*
   Ask students what they see as the ten most significant events in the development of French Canada. Using a variety of library resources, have students identify the fifteen to twenty key events that have played a major role in molding French Canada into what it is today. Then, using their best judgment with documentation, narrow the list down to ten. Have students place these ten events on a timeline. Each student should be able to defend each chronologically and in terms of its significance in French Canada's development. Next, working with a partner, each should share his or her individual timeline and try to convince the other that the events he or she selected are the most significant. (Underscore the importance of having adequate documentation.)
   The challenge for each pair is to reach consensus. If the pair can, the next task is to construct a new timeline. Regardless of the outcome, however, each pair should be prepared to present the results to the class. If time permits, a class discussion should ensue, focusing on the most significant events and why. (M, S)

3. *Check out the economic situation in Quebec.*
   According to Beach's chapter in this book, the Quebec economy continues to exhibit an overdependence on traditional, obsolete, and labor-intensive manufacture of textiles, clothing, footwear, leather goods, and furniture. What does this mean? The following words are associated with economics:
   Domestic demand
   Foreign demand
   Consumer spending
   Service expenditures
   Spending for durable goods
   Spending for nondurable goods
   Unemployment
   Construction expenditures
   Business
   Residential
   Imports
   Exports
   Inflationary trends

Handout for Activity 3, "You be the judge." (Chapter 6)

Cultural Comparison	Agree or Disagree?	Documented Example

1. Canadians are socially and emotionally colder than Americans.

2. Canadians show more deference to authority and to hierarchical elites than Americans.

3. Canadians have much more direct governmental action— and for the most part, these are acceptable (i.e., national health care system, the Wheat Board, etc.)

4. Canadians are more law abiding than Americans.

5. Canadians have a more pervasive feminine quality to their literature than the Americans.

6. Canadians are less involved in their political parties at the grassroots levels than Americans, and political activity at these levels is less dynamic.

7. Canadians are more tolerant and supportive of ethnic differences than are the Americans.

8. Canadians are more tied to their regional identities than Americans.

* *Students should be encouraged to add to the list.*

Have students locate data for each of these words and concepts. You might use cooperative learning techniques for making assignments. Encourage students to use a variety of library and computer resources as well as resource people to assist in the assignment. After the group assignments have been completed, conduct a class discussion focusing on the data with the overarching question, "On the basis of the information gathered, how does Quebec benefit or lose by being one province out of ten in Canada?" Have students defend their positions. (S)

4. *What does art tell you about a place?*

Probably the most powerful influences on Canadian painting have been the land and the people. Geographical features have always fascinated painters, while Native peoples, frontier people, trappers, and others have provided fresh material as well. The early painters tended to see the new land and its people through European eyes and, because they were educated in Europe, these artists often imposed European techniques on Canadian subject matter.

Have students study paintings by Cornelius Krieghoff. Ask them to list their observations and questions. Encourage students to examine the painting for European influences and discuss their observations. Then ask students, individually or in pairs, to do some research to learn more about the artist and be prepared to share their insights with their peers.

If students in your class are particularly interested in art or if your curriculum encourages integration with art, provide students with a list of famous Canadian artists of the nineteenth and twentieth centuries and ask them to research an artist and his or her work and then prepare a one-page position statement explaining how his or her work was or was not influenced by the land and/or people. Some famous artists include:

Robert Bateman
Emily Carr
Maurice Cullen
Lawren S. Harris
A. Y. Jackson
Paul Kane
Cornelius Krieghoff
William Kurelek
J. E. H. Macdonald
Norval Morrisseau
Tom Thomson (M, S)

5. *What does it mean?*

When students enter the classroom, direct their attention to a large sign that you have prepared. It reads, "French Canadians residing outside Canada are both hostages to and beneficiaries of a strong

Quebec that continues to remain a part of Canada." Note: This activity should occur near the end of the study of French Canada so that students will have the knowledge to respond appropriately.

Have students take a designated period to write their responses (e.g., fifteen minutes). Then ask students to work in triads, sharing and discussing their responses. The activity should culminate with a class discussion about similarities and differences and reasons to support the responses. (S)

6. *Interviewing historical characters*

This technique can make history more interesting by creating a living process in your classroom. It can be implemented in a variety of ways. A volunteer resource from the community, another teacher, you, or students in the class can assume the identity of historical figures. Those individuals willing to learn about the characters will be interviewed by the class.

Prior to beginning, the class should review basic techniques for interviewing and agree on several key questions. To make the experience more meaningful, every student could assume a role as a historical figure, with guests serving as reporters. During the interview, students should raise their hands just as reporters do at an actual news conference. The individual(s) playing the role(s) of the historical character(s) should attempt to imitate the types of responses the actual character would give. When the interview(s) conclude, each student (or pair) should be asked to write a newspaper article covering the event. The articles should be shared with the class. Select some for submission to the school or community newspaper. (E, M, S)

7. *Should (could) the province of Quebec survive as an independent entity?*

Divide the class into groups of five. Have each group consider the question and collect related resources. Allocate time for group discussion and preparation. Then, randomly select one group to serve as a panel for the class. Remind the panelists that they need to think clearly about their views and prepare adequately so that the presentation will be objective. During the panel's preparation time, the other groups can prepare for the panel and write a one-page summary of their views. While each panelist can specialize in gathering data on a particular aspect of the topic, the presentations should be interrelated to facilitate an exchange of ideas. One student should serve as the chairperson and another as the recorder. Time should be allotted for each panelist's presentation and for questions and discussion. Make sure that the role of the audience has been clearly identified. For example, should members of the audience ask questions during the panel discussion? Should they be responsible for notetaking?

Invite local community members to participate in the activity either as additional panelists or as observers willing to respond to the panel at the conclusion of its presentation. (S)

Notes

1. R. Zais, *Curriculum: Principles and Foundations* (New York: Harper and Row, 1976) and Jack Fraenkel, *Helping Students Think and Value: Strategies for the Social Studies,* 2nd ed. (Englewood Cliffs, NJ: Prentice-Hall, 1980).

2. Jere Brophy and Janet Alleman, "Activities as Instructional Tools: A Framework for Instructional Analysis and Evaluation," *Educational Researcher* 20 (1991): pp. 9-23.

3. For more details, see: Janet Alleman and Jere Brophy, "Taking Advantage of Out-Of-School Learning Opportunities for Meaningful Social Studies Learning," *The Social Studies* 6 (1994): pp. 262-67; Jere Brophy and Janet Alleman, "Activities as Instructional Tools"; Jere Brophy and Janet Alleman, "Planning and Managing Learning Activities: Basic Principles," in A*dvances in Research on Teaching: Vol. 3. Planning and Managing Learning Tasks and Activities*, ed. Jere Brophy (Greenwich, Conn.: JAI Press, 1992), pp. 1-45; and Jere Brophy and Janet Alleman, *Powerful Social Studies for Elementary Students* (Fort Worth, Tex.: Harcourt Brace, 1996). These same references provide secondary principles that apply to selecting and implementing sets of activities.

5. Originally published in 1842, this poem is reprinted in Victor Howard's *A Canadian Vocabulary* (East Lansing, Mich.: Michigan State University, 1981), pp. 41-42.

Chapter 10
Resources for Learning and Teaching about Canada
Gail F. Curry Yvon

A wide variety of resources are available to educators to help bring Canadian studies alive for their students. This chapter describes materials in many different categories, ending with contact addresses.

COMPLIMENTARY AND LOW-COST RESOURCES

Because "free" and "inexpensive" are key words in most teachers' vocabularies, educators who are teaching about Canada are fortunate to have the services of organizations in both the United States and Canada that offer complimentary and low-cost materials and assistance.

In the United States, the National Consortium for Teaching Canada, whose members have written this book, offers curriculum materials, workshops and seminars, films and videos, and program consulting. Their Canadian studies centers across the United States provide easy access for educators at all levels from coast to coast.

In addition to the Canadian Embassy in Washington, D.C., and consulates in several cities around the country, the provincial governments of British Columbia, Nova Scotia, Quebec and Saskatchewan also have U.S. offices. Teachers will find resources in print and electronic format at these offices as well as those of the Canadian Tourism Commission; their addresses are listed at the end of this chapter.

KEEPING CURRENT ON CANADA

One concern often expressed by teachers is "How do I find out what is happening in Canada today? I know where to find good background information, but my students need current topics." A variety of periodical publications ranging from up-to-the-minute Canadian news summaries on the Internet to free newsletters produced several times a year will answer this need.

Look for comprehensive World Wide Web Canadian news sites such as *CANOE* (**Can**adian **o**nline **e**xplorer) and the Southam News page. Try *Canadiana: The Canadian Resource Page* for a wide range of Canadian topics. Find Canada's national newspaper, *The Globe and Mail* and access *NEWSCAN,* a weekly compilation of newspaper coverage across Canada, at the site of the

---

World Wide Web Sites on Canada

CANOE
www.canoe.ca

Southam News page
www.southam.com/nmc

Canadiana: The Canadian Resource Page
www.cs.cmu.edu/unofficial/Canadiana

The Globe and Mail
www.globeandmail.ca

Canadian Embassy-Washington, D.C.
www.cdnemb-washdc.org/index-e.html

Matinternet
www.matin.qc.ca./1.htm

LaToile du Quebec
www.toile.qc.ca

Canadian Education on the Web
www.oise.on.ca/~mpress/eduweb.html

Maclean's
www.canoe.ca/macleans

Canadian Embassy in Washington, D.C. Discover news and more *en français* from Quebec sites, *Matinternet*, and *LaToile du Quebec*.

As educators interested in Canada, you will find everything relating to Canada and education at *Canadian Education on the Web*. This site will direct you to the provincial departments of education, educational networks, teachers' organizations, and elementary and secondary schools across Canada.

Another way to use Canadian newspapers is to participate in the Newspapers In Education (NIE) program "Target Date," which enables students to collect newspapers published on a specific date for a comparison study. Contact your newspaper's NIE coordinator for a program description and list of participating newspapers in Canada, Australia, and the United States.

Try *Maclean's*, Canada's weekly magazine published by Maclean Hunter Publishing Limited in Toronto, Ontario, on the Internet at www.canoe.ca/ macleans, for a comparison with U.S. news magazines and/or an in-class school program. Colleagues teaching French will want to consult *Actualité*, *Maclean's* semimonthly French language counterpart.

Your school or university librarian will lead you to useful magazines or journals beginning with the word "Canadian," such as *Canadian Geographic* and *Canadian Forum* (politics and the arts). But would you think to look under Beaver or Quill or Saturday Night? You'll find *The Beaver: Exploring Canada's History*, *Quill and Quire* (book news and reviews), and *Saturday Night* (multi-topic monthly).

And be sure to get on the mailing lists for complimentary newsletters such as *Teaching Canada* from SUNY Plattsburgh and the University of Vermont's *Canada!* (both aimed at teachers), general newsletters from other National Consortium for Teaching Canada members, and the government of Quebec's *Update* and *Rencontre*, a publication covering aboriginal topics.

MAPS, ENCYCLOPEDIAS, ATLASES, AND TEXTS

Many teachers say that their school libraries need better reference materials about Canada. Good Canadian encyclopedias come in both print and electronic form. For example, McClelland and Stewart's reasonably priced *Junior Encyclopedia of Canada* offers five volumes of succinct entries with color illustrations on most pages. Their *Canadian Encyclopedia Plus* on CD-ROM combines dictionary, thesaurus, and encyclopedic information with several thousand multimedia items. A most comprehensive reference is the annual *Canadian Almanac and Directory* distributed by Gale Research in Detroit, Michigan. Categories like education, government, and tourism are indexed in a quick reference format. The 1995 edition of *Acadia of the Maritimes: Thematic Studies from the Beginning to the Present*, edited by Jean Daigle, Université de Moncton, is the key reference on Canada's "other" French peoples.

If special library gift funds are available in your school district, the handsome University of Toronto Press *Historical Atlas of Canada* series, said by its editors to be the largest cartographic project ever undertaken in

Canada, could become the core of your system's geographic resources. Another contribution of cartographer Geoffrey Matthews is the school-level *Nelson Canadian Atlas*, produced by Nelson Canada of Scarborough, Ontario. Teachers desiring a broader, continental reference will find reproducible materials such as the atlas *North America Today*, from World Eagle Publishers in Littleton, Massachusetts. A one-volume gift possibility is *The National Atlas of Canada* by Macmillan Company with the Department of Energy, Mines, and Resources/Information Canada. This department has also produced a very useful, inexpensive set of maps entitled *Canada Then and Now: Maps of the Nation's Growth 1867-1982*. The three maps depict the early geography of Canada and the progressive evolution of provincial and territorial boundaries, culminating with Canada in the 1980s.

The Symbols of Canada, a kit for Young Canadians from the Canadian Heritage Department, is an excellent source of federal and provincial emblems, with map references and historical information. These and other products are available from Canada Communication Group Publishing, the official publisher for the Government of Canada, Ottawa, Ontario, Canada, K1A 0S9 (819-956-4800). A recent addition to geography materials for middle school students is Ted Scott Henson's *Discovering Canada Using the Five Themes of Geography* from Frank Schaffer Publications (1-800-421-5533).

Canadian maps are available from several other sources at reasonable cost. See the Canadian offerings in *Maplink: Maps for the Entire World*, Santa Barbara, CA (fax 1-800-627-7768). Map and book offerings of the National Geographic Society and the Canadian Geographic Society are well known to educators. Road atlases such as Hildebrand's separate Eastern and Western Canada editions provide the current data needed for travel-related study. Teachers should ask regional map dealers how to obtain Canadian topographic maps, the realistic shaded relief map of Canada, and the dramatic raised relief satellite image from WorldSat International.

Are you ready for the changes that will affect Canada's map in 1999? As the new territory of Nunavut is created from the eastern portion of the Northwest Territories, both the shape of Canada's northern regions and the names of many arctic communities will be different. U.S. students can get a head start on this important topic via the Internet site [www.arcticpersp.org] for Arctic Perspectives, an organization whose mission is to help build an awareness and understanding of the interrelated aspects of the Arctic region. Outstanding examples combining traditional Inuit culture with modern technology range from a 1996 dogsled expedition to Arctic school home pages.

One standard text about Canada is obviously not enough for any U.S. classroom. Both Canadian and U.S. publishers have produced texts that offer students a comparison. Some examples at middle level are: SUNY Plattsburgh's vibrant, colorful, *O CANADA*; Key Porter Books' beautifully illustrated *The Story of Canada*; Grolier's recent *Discover Canada* specific provincial titles; and Fitzhenry and Whiteside's updated *Canada: Growth of a*

Nation and *Canada: The Twentieth Century*, with special Art Gallery and chapter Advance Organizers. Teachers and upper-level students can find background information in Wayne Thompson's annual *Canada 199-*, part of Stryker-Post's World Today Series; John Saywell's revised *Canada: Pathways to the Present* from Stoddart Publishers; and the 1996 *ACSUS Papers Series* of ten introductory paperbacks published by Michigan State University Press in conjunction with the Association for Canadian Studies in the United States.

LEARNING ABOUT OUR LARGEST TRADING PARTNER

Social studies educators responsible for Canadian economic and trade topics will find help from the Canadian Foundation for Economic Education, the Brown University Choices Project, and Statistics Canada. CFEE in Toronto, Ontario, has produced the Canada/U.S. Border Project Teaching Resource Kit for secondary level, plus other print and CD-ROM products for schools. Lessons contain reproducible material focusing on the Canada-U.S. economic relationship with a goal of increasing awareness among young people in both nations. An optional final lesson is based on the television show "Jeopardy!"

The CHOICES for the 21st Century Education Project at Brown University is familiar to many teachers for its curricular units on current foreign policy issues. The topic of trade with Canada is a feature of the 1995 unit, *U.S. Trade Policy: Competing in a Global Economy,* which includes a condensed description of the trilateral North America Free Trade Agreement. The comprehensive *Statistics Canada Catalogue* is published every other year with between-year supplements (1-800-263-1136 for information).

Teachers can obtain daily information releases by fax or on the Internet, weekly highlights, the quarterly *Canadian Social Trends* with its Educator's Notebook page of classroom suggestions, plus maps and electronic products. Schools with CD-ROM capability may want to investigate E-STAT, Statistics Canada's electronic learning package developed from both census and socio-economic information databases. It offers graphing and mapping capabilities and lesson plans for grades 7-12.

The ACSUS-Plattsburgh web site provides a wealth of information about Canadian Studies and resources for students and educators, as well as links to other University centers and useful Canadian sites.
http://canada-acsus.plattsburgh.edu/

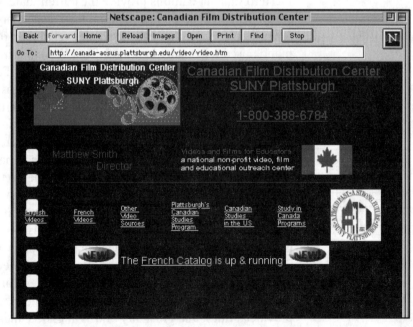

FINDING AND INTEGRATING CANADIAN LITERATURE FOR YOUNG PEOPLE

An exciting development for social studies teachers looking to integrate their work with other curricular areas is the growth of quality Canadian literature for young people. Many outstanding fiction and nonfiction examples with Canadian characters and settings are now available internationally. From the powerful language and realistic teen experiences of Newfoundland's Kevin Major to the sensitive portrayals of difficult lives by Ontarian Jean Little, U.S. students will enjoy the literature approach to understanding Canada.

The Canadian government web site is a mother lode of information about Canada.
http://www.gc.ca

Good starting points are listings of noteworthy and award-winning books in Canadian literature prize categories and such organizations as the Canadian Children's Book Centre and the National Library of Canada. The Book Centre (416-975-0010) offers a yearly catalogue of reasonably priced materials such as Book Week Kits, multicultural and classics suggestions, the annual Our Choice guide to the best new books and videos, bookstore contacts, and a twice-yearly comprehensive list of over fifteen different book awards.

The Vicky Metcalf Award, presented annually since 1963 by the Canadian Authors Association to a writer for a body of work "inspirational to Canadian youth," is of particular value in acquainting U.S. educators with major Canadian authors of literature for young people. Past winners are:

    1997 - Tim Wynne-Jones
    1996 - Margaret Buffie
    1995 - Sarah Ellis
    1994 - Welwyn Wilton Katz
    1993 - Phoebe Gilman
    1992 - Kevin Major
    1991 - Brian Doyle
    1990 - Bernice Thurman Hunter
    1989 - Stéphane Poulin
    1988 - Barbara Smucker
    1987 - Robert Munsch

1986 - Dennis Lee
1985 - Edith Fowke
1984 - Bill Freeman
1983 - Claire Mackay
1982 - Janet Lunn
1981 - Monica Hughes
1980 - John Craig
1979 - Cliff Faulknor
1978 - Lyn Cook
1977 - James Houston
1976 - Suzanne Martel
1975 - Lyn Harrington
1974 - Jean Little
1973 - Christie Harris
1972 - William Toye
1971 - Kay Hill
1970 - Farley Mowat
1969 - Audrey McKim
1968 - Lorraine McLaughlin
1967 - John Patrick Gillese
1966 - Fred Savage
1965 - Roderick Haig-Brown
1964 - John F. Hayes
1963 - Kerry Wood

From the National Library of Canada (613-996-7774) or at the comprehensive web site [www.nlc-bnc.ca/publications/ruoi/eruoi.htm], teachers may obtain the bilingual Read Up On It kit with bookmarks and poster as well as award-winning titles and noteworthy recommendations on a specific yearly theme. The Children's Literature Web Guide site of David K. Brown, University of Calgary [www.ucalgary.ca/~dkbrown/] provides not only all updated Canadian Children's Literature Awards, but also author, publisher, and bookseller information, resources for teachers, discussion groups, and more.

In the United States, most members of the National Consortium for Teaching Canada offer bibliographies of Canadian books for young people. For example, SUNY Plattsburgh published *Selected Bibliography of Canadian Children's Literature* by librarian Emily Castine in 1995. And the University of Maine has compiled *The ABCs of Canadian Literature for Young People: Awards, Bibliographies and Choice Articles.*

Teachers seeking periodicals for their school libraries will find journals published in different regions of Canada. Canadian Children's Literature/ Litterature Canadienne Pour La Jeunesse is published quarterly at the University of Guelph in Ontario. *Canadian Content: Resources for Teachers and Librarians from Gabriola, British Columbia,* provides quarterly information on books and other materials in a thematic newspaper format. Reviews and free resources are also available online at [schoolnet2.carleton.ca/english/virtprod/cdncont/main.htm]. Your local bookseller may be familiar with the growing selection of Canadian publications for school level. If not, bookstores across Canada are able to serve U.S. customers. Examples include Woozle's in Halifax, Nova Scotia; The Double Hook Bookshop, Inc., in Montreal, Quebec; The Children's Book Store in Toronto, Ontario; and Vancouver Kidsbooks in Vancouver, British Columbia.

Social studies educators will find a variety of relevant literature categories to share with colleagues:

1. Canadian historical fiction often parallels wartime periods in the United States and is thus particularly valuable for providing new perspectives on familiar events. These books are excellent ways to open students' eyes to the expulsion of the Acadians, the Loyalist experiences in Revolutionary times, the Civil War flight to freedom in Canada, the Japanese-Canadian internment of World War II, and other experiences of Canadian young people. For example, help them understand the Canadian connection to the Civil War with Barbara Smucker's vivid depiction of slavery in *Underground to Canada* and the dangerous world of the 1860s in Janet Lunn's R*oot Cellar.*

2. Stories set in Canada's distinct geographic regions not only illustrate life in the Maritimes, Central Canada, the Prairies, the Mountain West, and the North, but provide a basis for a north-south comparison with U.S. geography. The beautiful "children's books as works of art" by Tundra Books, now available from McClelland & Stewart, are standouts in this category. Let the works of James Houston help students "feel" life in the Arctic, and show them rural Quebec in the 1600s through the eyes of an eighteen-year-old orphan in Suzanne Martel's *The King's Daughter.*

3. Canada's mosaic of cultural groups—from Inuit and Indian peoples to British and French explorers and settlers to more recent arrivals from around the world—is brought to life in both fiction and nonfiction. *Let's Celebrate* from Kids Can Press in Toronto provides a full calendar year of celebrations and activities. Authenticity regarding works by and about Native Peoples can be verified through the resources of the Canadian Alliance in Solidarity with the Native Peoples (CASNP), P.O. Box 574, Stn. P, Toronto, Ontario M5S 2T1.

4. Collections of folktales, poetry, and biographies illuminate Canadian experiences of today and yesterday. *Share a Tale: Canadian Stories to Tell Children and Young Adults* is Irene Aubrey and Louise McDiarmid's Canadian Library Association collection of seven types of stories gathered over more than two years. There is poetry for everyone's ear and eye in the collections by David Booth, the humor of Dennis Lee, and the revised anthology of Mary Alice Downie and Barbara Robertson, *The*

New Wind Has Wings. Fitzhenry and Whiteside's *Canadian Lives* cover past and present in well-illustrated softcover for middle-level readers. *Her Story: Women from Canada's Past* (Volumes I and II), published by Vanwell Publishing Limited, is Susan Merritt's celebration of the lives of thirty-two women from many cultural groups who made significant contributions to Canada's history. Many Canadian publishers offer series of biographies, and encyclopedias at all levels include hundreds of shorter biographies of Canadians.

This attempt to help U.S. social studies educators locate and integrate Canadian literature for young people is only the tip of the iceberg. One way to extend our knowledge and to recognize professional contributions in this field is to follow the work of Professor Wendy Sutton and her colleagues at the University of British Columbia. It was Professor Sutton's chapter, "Using Canadian Literature to Understand Canada," in the 1985 NCSS publication, *Canada in the Classroom: Content and Strategies for the Social Studies,* that convinced this writer of the importance of the literature component in helping our students learn about Canada. Teachers and school librarians will be pleased to learn of the following sources by Professor Sutton and her colleagues Ronald Jobe and Paula Hart:

- Sutton and Jobe's "Beyond Munsch: Canadian literature for children and young people," in T*he Reading Teacher,* Vol. 45, No. 8 (April 1992). This periodical is published by the International Reading Association, Newark, Delaware.
- Jobe and Hart's "Reading the World: Canada, Parts I and II," in *Book Links,* September and November, 1993. This periodical is published by the American Library Association, Chicago, Illinois. The article is adapted from their 1993 book, *Canadian Connections: Experiencing Literature with Children,* from Pembroke Publishers, ISBN 0-921217-70-61.

BETWEEN PRINT AND CYBERSPACE:
CANADA IN AUDIO, VIDEO, AND COMPUTER SOFTWARE

Music that truly reflects Canada's people and regions has moved from original recordings to audiocassettes and compact discs. Thanks to the Smithsonian Folkways Recordings Collection of the Smithsonian Institution's Office of Folklife Programs in Washington, D.C. (202-287-3262), Canadian music in English and French is readily available. Teachers who ask at local music stores will also be able to order songs that relate to their regions. For example, northeasterners will find Atlantic Canada artists Rita MacNeil, Stan Rogers, and Denis Ryan all on "Songs of the Sea" (SMPC-1006). French-speaking students will learn that before Céline Dion and Roch Voisine came Felix LeClerc, Gilles Vigneault, and Edith Butler. History was recorded in Gordon Lightfoot's "Canadian Railroad Trilogy" and "The Wreck of the Edmund Fitzgerald."

Video programs enhance the study and appreciation of Canada at all levels from elementary to college. U.S. educators are fortunate to have access to the Canadian Government Educational Collection and Quebec Government Video Collection entrusted to the Canadian Film Distribution Center at the State University of New York (SUNY) Plattsburgh (1-800-388-6784). The center offers a comprehensive, bilingual catalog indexed by broad subject categories and title, along with professional assistance in selecting videos appropriate for specific school purposes. The National Film Board of Canada also has a U.S. office in New York (514-283-9441). In addition to providing its highly regarded film collection, NFB representatives seek input from educators in updating earlier videos. An excellent source of innovative learning materials is the CRB (Charles Rosner Bronfman) Foundation Heritage Project based in Montreal, Quebec (514-878-5250). The Heritage Minutes video series of mini-movies about notable Canadians and events with teaching ideas, the Canadian Broadcasting Corporation television specials on video, and the related internet site (www.heritage.excite.sfu.ca] and colorful, complimentary Heritage Post newsletter and are valuable to both Canadian and U.S. young people.

CD-ROMs are finding their place in school-level Canadian studies. As noted earlier, McClelland & Stewart's *Canadian Encyclopedia Plus* combines complete text with several thousand multimedia items. *Adventure Canada,* a media award winner, allows students to click on to Canada's natural or political regions and provides a comprehensive teacher's guide. *Fortress of Louisbourg* takes viewers to eighteenth-century Nova Scotia to experience the French-British conflict and life in the fortress town. Contact the SUNY Plattsburgh Film Distribution Center (1-800-388-6784) and Virtual Reality Systems Inc./Didatech Software Ltd. in Blaine, Washington (604-303-1200) for more information about these and additional Canadian media resources.

CD-ROMs can also bring newspaper stories to your students. The Herald OnLINE Services (902-426-3384) will provide the Halifax Herald Ltd.–Online Catalogue of dozens of topics available on CD-ROM from its Nova Scotia newspapers at reasonable cost. Each student will be able to cover a different story about the Acadians, NAFTA, Quebec and Canadian unity, even the Toronto Blue Jays and the first-ever bridge to Prince Edward Island.

Teachers seeking interactive software will want to contact MECC of Minneapolis, Minnesota (1-800-685-MECC, ext. 529), for information about their Canada-related offerings. For example, Canada Geograph II lets students discover many facets of Canada with its "living map" and interactive databases. The National Geographic Society offers its award-winning *Zip Zap Map*! Canada software game for grades four to adult learners (1-800-368-2728). The challenge of putting major geographic features on the map of Canada before they fall off the computer screen serves different students by varying the level of difficulty and speed. Middle-level students can experience Canada's geography as they simulate driving an 18-wheel truck and making decisions in Cross*country Canada* from Virtual Reality/Didatech.

Finally, how do U.S. educators find and evaluate the growing body of Canadian learning resources from print to media? The journal *Resource Links: Connecting Classrooms, Libraries, & Canadian Learning Resources* (604-925-0266 or e-mail cclr@rockland.com), provides this assistance in six issues per year. The members of the National Consortium for Teaching Canada welcome this journal to our collective expertise as we dedicate ourselves to the teaching of Canada in the United States and pledge to be at your service/à votre service!

RESOURCE ADDRESSES

National Consortium for Teaching Canada

Institutional Members

Bowling Green State University
Canadian Studies Center
Bowling Green, OH 43403-0260
Telephone: 419-372-2457
Fax: 419-372-2875

Bridgewater State College
Canadian Studies Program
Bridgewater, MA 02325
Telephone: 508-697-1387
Fax: 508-697-1707

University of Maine
Canadian-American Center
154 College Avenue
Orono, ME 04473
Telephone: 207-581-4220
Fax: 207-581-4223

Michigan State University
Canadian Studies Center
International Center
East Lansing, MI 48824-1035
Telephone: 517-355-2350
Fax 517-353-7254/6393

SUNY Plattsburgh
Center for the Study of Canada
133 Court Street
Plattsburgh, NY 12901
Telephone: 518-564-2086
Fax: 518-564-2112

University of Vermont
Canadian Studies Center
589 Main Street
Burlington, VT 05401
Telephone: 802-656-3062
Fax: 802-656-8518

University of Washington
Canadian Studies Center
Henry M. Jackson School of International Studies
Box 353650
Seattle, WA 98195-3650
Telephone 206-543-6269
Fax 206-685-0668

Western Washington University
Center for Canadian-American Studies
Bellingham, WA 98225-9110
Telephone: 360-650-3728
Fax: 360-650-3995

Associate Members

Boise State University
Canadian Studies Program
Room C-213
1910 University Drive
Boise, ID 83725
Telephone: 208-385-3427

Brigham Young University
Canadian Studies Program
774 SWKT
Provo, UT 84602
Telephone: 810-378-2453
Fax: 801-378-5730

Duke University
Canadian Studies Center
Box 90422
Durham, NC 27708-0422
Telephone: 919-684-4260
Fax: 919-681-7882

Franklin College
Canadian Studies Program
Department of Journalism
Shirk Hall
Franklin, IN 46131
Telephone: 317-738-8196
Fax: 317-738-8234

University of Central Florida
Canadian Studies Program/
Florida-Canada Institute
Orlando, FL 32816-1356
Telephone: 407-823-2079
Fax: 407-823-0051

Provincial and Territorial Tourism Offices

British Columbia
Tourism British Columbia
Parliament Buildings
Victoria, British Columbia
CANADA V8V 1X4
Telephone: 1-800-663-6000
Fax: 604-801-5710
www.tbc.gov.bc.ca/tourism/tourismhome.html

Alberta
Travel Alberta
Box 2500
Edmonton, Alberta
CANADA T5J 4G8
Telephone: 1-800-661-8888
Fax: 403-427-0867

Saskatchewan
Saskatchewan Tourism Authority
Dept. 962 CTC, Suite 500
1900 Albert Street
Regina, Saskatchewan
CANADA S4P 4L9
Telephone: 1-800-667-7191, ext. 963
Fax: 306-787-5744
www.sasktourism.sk.ca

Manitoba
Travel Manitoba
7th Floor, 155 Carlton Street
Winnipeg, Manitoba
CANADA R3C 3H8
Telephone: 1-800-665-0040, ext. CG6
Fax: 204-948-2517
www.gov.mb.ca/itt/travel/explore/index.html

Ontario
Ontario Travel
Queen's Park
Toronto, Ontario
CANADA M7A 2R9
Telephone: 1-800-668-2746
Fax: 416-443-6818

Quebec
Tourisme Québec
P.O. Box 979
Montreal, Quebec
CANADA H3C 2W3
Telephone: 1-800-363-7777, Operator 110
Fax: 514-864-3838
www.gouv.qc.ca

Newfoundland and Labrador
Tourism Newfoundland and Labrador
P.O. Box 8700
St. John's, Newfoundland
CANADA A1B 4K2
Telephone: 1-800-563-6353, Operator CTC
Fax: 709-729-0057
www.gov.nf.ca/itt/business/tourism.html

New Brunswick
Tourism New Brunswick
P.O. Box 6000
Fredericton, New Brunswick
CANADA E3B 5C3
Telephone: 1-800-561-0123
Fax: 506-789-2044
www.gov.nb.ca/tourism/

Nova Scotia
Tourism Nova Scotia
P.O. Box 456
Halifax, Nova Scotia
CANADA B3J 2M7
Telephone: 1-800-565-0000
Fax: 902-453-8401
explore.gov.ns.ca/virtualns

Prince Edward Island
Department of Tourism
P.O. Box 940
Charlottetown, Prince Edward Island
CANADA C1A 7M5
Telephone: 1-800-463-4734
Fax: 902-629-2428
www.gov.pe.ca/info/

Yukon
Yukon Tourism
P.O. Box 2703
Whitehorse, Yukon
CANADA Y1A 2C9
Telephone: 867-667-5340
Fax: 867-667-3546
www.touryukon.com

Northwest Territories
Northwest Territories Tourism
P.O. Box 1320
Yellowknife, Northwest Territories
CANADA X1A 2L9
Telephone: 1-800-661-0788
Fax: 867-873-0163
www.edt.gov.nt.ca

PROVINCIAL OFFICES IN THE UNITED STATES

British Columbia
BC Trade and Investment Centre
Suite 930-720 Olive Way
Seattle, WA 98101
Telephone: 206-628-3024
Fax: 206-628-3023

Nova Scotia
Office of Nova Scotia in New England
4 Copley Place, Suite 110
Boston, MA 02116
Telephone: 617-262-7677
Fax: 617-262-7689

Tourism Nova Scotia
136 Commercial St.
Portland, ME 04101
Telephone: 207-772-0017

Quebec
Délégation Générale du Québec
One Rockefeller Plaza, 26th Floor
New York, NY 10020
Telephone: 212-397-0200
Fax: 212-757-4753

Saskatchewan
Saskatchewan Provincial Government Office
630 5th Avenue, Suite 2107
New York, NY 10111
Telephone: 212-269-9100

CANADIAN CONSULATES IN THE UNITED STATES

Washington, DC
Canadian Embassy
501 Pennsylvania Avenue, NW
Washington, DC 20001
Telephone: 202-682-1740

Atlanta
Canadian Consulate General
1175 Peachtree Street, NE
100 Colony Square, Suite 1700
Atlanta, GA 30361-6205
Telephone: 404-532-2000

Boston
Canadian Consulate General
Suite 400, 3 Copley Place
Boston, MA 02116-3795
Telephone: 617-262-3760

Buffalo
Canadian Consulate General
Suite 3000, 1 Marine Midland Center
Buffalo, NY 14203-2884
Telephone: 716-858-9581

Chicago
Canadian Consulate General
Suite 2400, 2 Prudential Plaza
180 North Stetson Avenue
Chicago, IL 60601
Telephone: 312-616-1860

Dallas
Canadian Consulate General
St. Paul Tower, Suite 1700
750 North St. Paul Street
Dallas, TX 75201-3051
Telephone: 214-922-9806

Detroit
Canadian Consulate General
Suite 1100, 600 Renaissance Center
Detroit, MI 48243-1704
Telephone: 313-567-2208

Los Angeles
Canadian Consulate General
9th Floor, 550 South Hope Street
Los Angeles, CA 90071-2627
Telephone: 213-346-2773

Miami
Canadian Consulate
Suite 1600, 200 South Biscayne Blvd.
Miami, FL 33131
Telephone: 305-579-1600

Minneapolis
Canadian Consulate General
Suite 900, 701 Fourth Avenue South
Minneapolis, MN 55415-1899
Telephone: 612-332-7486

New York
Canadian Consulate General
16th Floor, Exxon Building
1251 Avenue of the Americas
New York, NY 10020-1175
Telephone: 212-596-1691

Seattle
Canadian Consulate General
412 Plaza 600
Sixth and Stewart
Seattle, WA 98101-1286
Telephone: 206-443-0336

Chapter 11
Technology in the Classroom
Matthew Smith and John Preston

Including technology in our lesson plans is no longer an option, but a necessity. The pace of change in information, which has a shorter "shelf life" than ever before, and the capacity of images to convey information to students of varying abilities, are only two of the many advantages of employing technology in education. The use of technology to assist teaching about Canada exemplifies the efficiency and cost-effectiveness of such tools as educational videos, CD-ROMs and the World Wide Web.

Furthermore, it should be our goal to expose our students to the various options and opportunities within their educational environment. In essence, we want to utilize the technology in two ways: education for a stronger foundation; and the development of strong workforce skills that will prepare students for the job market.

VIDEO RESOURCES

The best educational video materials on Canada come from two sources: the National Film Board of Canada (NFB); and the Canadian Broadcasting Corporation (CBC). Both the NFB and the CBC are funded by the Government of Canada, but operate independently, and have worldwide reputations for quality and the integrity of their productions. Recently, private production companies have begun to produce excellent educational videos, many of which have found their way into the major video collections of Canadian Studies programs at U.S. colleges.

There are several Canadian video collections in the United States that feature educational material. The largest and most comprehensive video library in the country, perhaps the largest collection outside Canada, is located at SUNY Plattsburgh's Canadian Film Distribution Center (CFDC). The CFDC has over 2,000 educational videos and films which cover every aspect of Canada, including Geography, History, Politics and Government, Social Studies , and much more. There are also sizable collections at the University of Vermont's Canadian Studies Program and the University of Washington's Canadian Studies Center (addresses provided below). In fact, a good place to begin your search for Canadian educational videos is at a Canadian Studies center at a college near you. A list of colleges and universities which have a Canadian Studies program is available on the World Wide Web at: http://canada-acsus.plattsburgh.edu/programs/orgprog.htm

This list is updated frequently, as are most web pages, so check back from time to time to see the most recent list. The Association for Canadian Studies in the United States (ACSUS) at (202) 393-2580 can also provide this information.

The following videos are in the Canadian Film Distribution Center's collection, and many of them can be found in the University of Vermont and the University of Washington's collections as well. They are all suited to teaching Canada in K-12 educational institutions, and will effectively show Canada to your students.

Oh Canada
This is an excellent general interest video on Canada, good for all ages. Features include a spectacularly photographed overview of the Canadian landscape, and good basic information about Canada and Canadians. (26 minutes)

Canadian Parliamentary Video
A dynamic and concise look at the inner workings of the Canadian Parliamentary system with appropriate comparisons to the U.S. system. Explains Canada's system of government in a manner geared toward middle school-high school level social studies classes. (30 minutes)

The Sweater
An animated version of a short story by Quebec author Roch Carrier, set in the rural Quebec of his boyhood. Carrier recalls the passion for playing hockey, which he shared with the other boys of his community. It was the time of Rocket Richard, the Canadiens' greatest star. A funny, poignant story animated in a style that evokes the period of the late 1940s. Also available in French as *Le Chandail*. (10 minutes)

The Stories of Tuktu
This series is an excellent set of short (14 minute) documentaries on the traditional lifestyle and activities of the Inuit (sometimes called Eskimo) peoples of Canada's north. These live-action videos will give your class a sense of what life was like for these resourceful people. They show hunting, fishing, crafts, family life, building an Igloo, games and much more. Here are the individual titles in the series, which can be appreciated by students at all levels:

Tuktu and His Animal Friends
Tuktu and His Eskimo Dogs
Tuktu and His Nice New Clothes
Tuktu and the Big Kayak
Tuktu and the Big Seal
Tuktu and the Caribou Hunt
Tuktu and the Clever Hands
Tuktu and the Indoor Games
Tuktu and the Magic Bow
Tuktu and the Magic Spear
Tuktu and the Snow Palace

Tuktu and the Ten Thousand Fishes
Tuktu and the Trials of Strength

The World Turned Upside Down

In the early 1780s, just following the American Revolution, about half of the hundred thousand United Empire Loyalists who wished to remain aligned with England fled northward to resettle in British North America, now Canada. This historical drama, based on the account of Hannah Ingraham, 11 years old at the time of her family's flight to Canada, was filmed entirely on location at the King's Landing Historical Settlement near Fredericton, New Brunswick. The film vividly recreates the persecution and hardships the Loyalists faced as they built a new life in the sparsely populated wilderness. Valuable for Canadian Studies, history and social studies. (24 minutes)

First Journey, Fort William

Set in 1815, this is the dramatic story of a child of the fur trade, son of a native mother and a Scottish-Canadian fur trader. John Mackenzie's father is a wintering partner of the Montreal-based North West Company, which was for decades the wealthiest merchant enterprise in North America. To mark his entry into adulthood, 12-year-old John is traveling for the first time to Fort William, the Company's lavish winter headquarters by Lake Superior. In following his journey, the film reveals the complex network of people— Scottish, French and native Canadian—who made up fur trading society and gave a unique flavor to the opening up of Canada's northwest. Meticulously recreated from historical record and shot on location at the restored Fort William. (24 minutes)

The Voyageurs

A film about the men who drove big freighter canoes into the wilderness in the days when the fur trade was Canada's biggest business. The film recreates scenes of a century ago on the 5,000 km river trade route to the Athabasca: canoeing, portages, camping, cooking and singing. A good companion video to *First Journey, Fort William*, which shows a typical fur trading post to which the canoes might have been heading. (19 minutes)

Crac

Born in a country of love, in a plentiful Québécois forest, a rocking chair is brought back, after a very full life, to a museum of modern art. That night, it remembers the rhythms of parties long ago and carries the paintings of abstract painters in her new environment, along with it. A veracious story of Quebec yesterday and today, a masterpiece of humor and tenderness by Frederick Back. Includes traditional fiddle music and dancing. Animated. (15 minutes)

Montreal, Quebec City, Toronto, Ottawa, Vancouver Tourist Videos

If your class is planning a trip to one of Canada's major cities, these videos are great introductions to its sights and points of interest. Watching the video before you go will present the information to your students, which will then be reinforced by the trip and your comments. These videos are valuable tools for teaching about Canada and Canadians even if you're not planning a trip, as they show cultural events, geographical features, economic information and the people in each of the cities. (30-40 minutes)

Rand McNally's Canada

This high quality travel video covers the entire country: dog-sledding in the Yukon; following Polar Bears in the Arctic; Vancouver's Stanley Park and Victoria's Butchart Gardens in British Columbia; dinosaur hunting in Alberta; a ride with the Royal Canadian Mounted Police in Saskatchewan; a viewing of the architectural treasures in Old Montreal and Old Quebec City (including the Winter Carnival); and finally fishing in New Brunswick's Mirimachi River. Excellent photography. (38 minutes)

The following videos are available through the University of Vermont.

First Nations: The Circle Unbroken

A thirteen part series (4 videos) about the relations between the First Nations and the Canadian government. Each segment is about twenty minutes in length and covers a myriad of issues such as cultural identity, land claims, hydropower, education of children, and the First Nations ways of life. Produced by the National Film Board of Canada for use in elementary and secondary schools. The series comes with a teacher's guide which provides further background on issues, ideas for activities, and more.

Explorers Of Canada

A wonderful compilation of films about Samuel de Champlain, David Thompson, and Wilhjalmur Stefansson. These pieces provide an excellent background in the European founding and mapping of Canada. A wise choice for integrating geography and history in three lessons. The time allotted to each explorer is : Champlain, 14:43 minutes; Thompson, 28:00 minutes; Stefansson, 15:56 minutes.

The View From Here

This is a great resource for those who are teaching Canada from an interdisciplinary approach. This 28-minute video provides an overview of the major Canadian pieces from the painting, sculpture, print, and photographic collection at the National Gallery of Art in Ottawa.

MAJOR CANADIAN VIDEO COLLECTIONS IN THE UNITED STATES

Canadian Film Distribution Center
SUNY Plattsburgh
2 Draper Ave.
Plattsburgh, NY 12901
1-800-388-6784
http://canada-acsus.plattsburgh.edu/video.htm
e-mail: canada-acsus@plattsburgh.edu

University of Vermont
Canadian Studies Program
589 Main St.
Burlington, VT 05401
802-656-3062
http://www.uvm.edu/~canada/film.htm
e-mail: canada@zoo.uvm.edu

University of Washington
Canadian Studies Center
Thomson Hall, Box 353650
Seattle, WA 98195-3650
http://weber.u.washington.edu/~canada/
e-mail: canstud@u.washington.edu

CD-ROM

The CD-ROM is an excellent teaching tool which has yet to be fully exploited. CD-ROMs offer an audio/visual treatment of Canada, which can be used by an individual student, or by a group (through networked computers) in a directed activity, or as a research or reference tool. Some advantages that CD-ROMs offer over the World Wide Web are:

1 *Stability*—once purchased, they are always instantly available and unchanging, unlike WWW sites which open, close, move, and change material with alarming frequency and without advance notice.
2 *Control*—the teacher has control over the material the student is using. It's easy to go astray on the WWW and look up the latest hockey scores instead of concentrating on that map of Canada.
3 *They operate independently*—unlike a World Wide Web resource, CD-ROMs don't require Internet access and can be accessed through any computer equipped with a CD-ROM player in any room in your school, which frees students from doing research, quizzes, or reference work during the precious lab time in the electronic classrooms many schools now have.
4 *They have a fixed cost*—CD-ROMs cost between $30 and $100 and

require no connection fees, Internet service, Ethernet cards, modems, or phone lines. CD-ROMs don't require Internet access, and can be accessed through a computer equipped with a CD-ROM player in any room in a school, which frees students from doing research, quizzes or reference work during the precious "lab time" in the electronic classrooms that many schools now have.

CD-ROMs also offer a focus in that they provide a single, "authoritative" source of information for younger students, who may be confused by the varied, conflicting and incomplete sources of data on a given subject which would be found on the Internet. Many CD-ROMs contain audio and video, clips of Canada and famous Canadians, illustrations and photographs, biographies, and hypertext "hotlinks" to related articles, similar to World Wide Web links. The following CD-ROMS are especially interesting and effective:

The 1997 Canadian Encyclopedia Plus (McClelland and Stewart)

This CD is updated yearly and costs about $100. It includes a search function that quickly locates the resources you are seeking, and has about 100,000 hot links between articles. Features include: 50,000 articles, 3,500 illustrations, 70 QuickTime movies, 75 wildlife audio clips and audio clips of readings by famous Canadian authors. There is also a Canadiana Quiz, a dictionary of Canadian English, and an encyclopedia of all things Canadian and prominent Canadians.

The Fortress of Louisbourg (Fitzgerald Studio)

This CD-ROM about the recently reconstructed Fortress of Louisbourg, an 18th century French fortress on Cape Breton Island, Nova Scotia, is sure to attract the attention of your students. They can look at 500 photographs, 40 minutes of video and 400 pages of printable text on the founding, battles, lifestyle and reconstruction of the Fortress. There are also animated versions of the battles between the English and the French and a 3-D model of the town.

With Flying Colours: A Classroom Kit On Canadian Symbols

Truly a wonderful multimedia kit for K-12 educators! The video, CD-ROM, and audio tape provide a wealth of information on Canada's symbols and provide an excellent background for further study on Canadian identity. The kit is produced by Heritage Canada. A teacher's guide is included.

Canadian Geographic Explorer: An Interactive Journey Around Canada

This CD-ROM/Multimedia Kit is spectacular! It is loaded with 3-D satellite images, a flight simulator, a geographic archive, photos, video clips, and over 500,000 map combinations. It will excite students and teachers for hours. The cost is around $50.00.

INTERNET RESOURCES

World Wide Web

Note: World Wide Web addresses change frequently and without notice. Addresses were valid at the time of publication.

It is as important to teach our students how to find pertinent information on a given subject, as it is to have them read it. Finding information about Canada on the World Wide Web will give them skills they can use in any subject area. The provincial governments of Canada, which have jurisdiction over education, have set up a number of websites devoted to education which can provide you, the teacher, with valuable information, as well as almost unlimited data for your students.

One of the best organized Canadian educational websites is Canada's *SchoolNet*, which is at: http://www.schoolnet.ca/ The first links on the home page are to the home pages for the Departments of Education at the 10 provincial and 2 territorial governments. These links contain resources such as individual schools' home pages (great for finding e-mail pals—we used to call them pen pals before the computer era) and discussion groups, pedagogy sites, student activities, and links to other Canadian educational websites, most of which are geared toward you, the teacher.

Scroll down a bit, past the links to the provincial Education Ministries home pages, to the menu which lists academic disciplines. There are excellent resources for Social Studies teachers on the Humanities page, with subheadings for Languages, History, Geography, Law, Media, and Other Social Sciences, and a link to *SchoolNet*'s First Peoples homepage, which has information on Canada's Native peoples. All the links featuring a Canadian flag are, obviously, mostly Canadian in their content. The others may be mainly U.S. based, or have mixed content.

History

The history section currently has 2 quizzes on the War of 1812 and on Acadia (mainly about the expulsion of the French inhabitants in 1755 from this territory by the British). There is also a link to Canadian Women in History, which features interesting stories and anecdotes on the roles women played in Canada's history.

Geography

The geography section features a quiz (under the heading National Atlas of Canada) which can be adjusted to your students' level. There are several quiz categories: Canada's land; its people; shapes of Canada; and Canada—a land of superlatives. Users can choose the level of difficulty and number of questions, and even assign a time limit if desired. There are links to a Canadian Arctic page and the Nunavut Implementation Commission's homepage. If your students haven't heard of Nunavut, have them look up the details of setting up Canada's newest territory, now part of the Northwest Territories.

Law

Canada's laws on Hate Crimes should be a lively topic for discussion, as Canada's concept of free speech greatly differs from that of the U.S. Click on "The Law Room" and scroll down a bit to see the Legal Briefs section. One of the links located there is about Internet Hate Crimes and is geared toward students in grades 10-12.

Media Room

The Media Awareness link on this page has activities in media literacy for K-12.

First Peoples

This page has hundreds of links to websites by and about North America's original inhabitants. There are lists of both Canadian and U.S. based First Nations, as well as information on Treaties, Culture, Projects and News. Naturally, if you click on any page, there are many further links to be explored.

Many of these linked pages have histories of the Native Peoples, legends, stories, and explanations of their language (some include a short vocabulary) and data on current Native land claims, which include vast areas, especially in Western Canada.

The *Culture* home page contains photos, museum listings and information about events like the powwow and the potlach. The *Elders* page has traditional stories, legends, creation stories and myths of Native peoples from across the continent. The *Schools* page has dozens of links to Native schools' websites, in almost every province. You can look at what their kids are studying, maybe even get an online conversation going with their class!

OTHER POPULAR SITES AND IDEAS FOR LESSON PLANS

The Canadian Kids Homepage:

This is an excellent site with over 300 links to WORLD WIDE WEB sites which are sorted by topic. Among the many sites listed are: First Nations (Indians) sites; The Book Nook (a site for young readers); The Canadian Teachers Librarian Home page; and the Young Canadian Inventors home site. The site address is: http://www.onramp.ca/~lowens/107kids.htm

The Aboriginal Youth Network

Produced by aboriginal youth, this site is an excellent place for youth to "hang out" and get to know people from around the world. It provides viewers a place to chat, get news updates, find out more about aboriginal events, and learn more about literature. A "must see" for those teaching about Native peoples. The website address is: http://ayn-0.ayn.ca

Canadadisk: Lesson Plans From the Canadadisk Website

There are many lesson plans on line for teachers. Stop by the Canadadisk site for a ready-made list of lessons on diverse topics such as: oral history;

Canadian Unity Conference; cruise the news; exploring our roots; Great Lakes and the St. Lawrence River; immigrant ancestors and many others. The web site address is: http://schoolnet.carleton.ca/cdisk/LessonPlans/ LessonPlans.html

Well Known People Who Happen to Be Canadian
This is an excellent site that provides information and links to actors, businesspeople, entertainers, musicians, scientists, journalists, sports heroes, and many other popular characters who happen to be Canadian. A possible activity for school aged children might be a mini-biography report or project. The site address is: http://alvin.cbc.gov/terning/Canadians.html

Symbols of Canada
The Beaver, the Flag, national anthem, origin of the name Canada, the maple tree, the maple leaf, the Arms of Canada, and official colors are all high-lighted on this site at: http://www.pch.gc.ca/main/ceremon/symb_e.htm

The Museum of Civilization and National Gallery of Canada Web Sites
These are two of the nation's finest museums on Canadian Culture. These sites provide a wealth of information in a very colorful and picturesque manner. Both are excellent sites for educators and students alike. The National Gallery of Canada site at http://national.gallery.ca/eindex.html provides a wonderful tour and lots of information about Canadian Art and the exhibits at the Gallery. The Museum of Civilization is a place where Canadi-ans can truly explore their roots and culture in depth. The web site address is: http://www.cmcc.muse.digital.ca/cmcchome.html

The Canadian Politics Site
This site is filled with web links and information on everything that is political and tied to government. Viewers have the opportunity to find information on political parties and their views to conducting research on the Canadian Constitution. So, if you are conducting research or have an affinity for politics, government, and current affairs this site will excite your senses. The site address is: http://www.library.ubc.ca/poli/cpweb.htm

NEWSPAPERS
One classroom activity which is sure to stir discussion is reading Canadian newspapers. From the local issues to the Canadian perspective on interna-tional stories, your students will find no end of fascinating current events. The most extensive list of Canadian newspapers on the Internet can be found at: http://canada-acsus.plattsburgh.edu/papers.htm Also listed at this site are news services, Government news sources and some Canadian magazines.

Newspaper Activity On The Net:

Using online newspapers and magazines can be an excellent way to gain insight from people at various locations throughout Canada. You can start this activity by selecting a topic for the students to explore (i.e., Quebec Separation). The next step is to assign newspapers to students in the class. Each student will get a newspaper from a different region or area. Students may read for 20 minutes and then freewrite about what they have read in the editorials or news pieces. The next day select a different newspaper (in this case select a newspaper that is likely to provide opposing views or other viewpoints) and again give students time to read and freewrite.

As a homework assignment after the second paper is read, students then are given the task of writing a one or two page response to what they have read. What are the thoughts of the students? Before, During, After? How did their thinking on the chosen issue evolve over time? Activities like these give students the opportunity to gather information, interpret the data, judge, compare and contrast the issues at hand. Debates also help develop the higher order thinking skills like interpreting, judging, comparing, contrasting, inquiry, theory, organizing, and evaluating.

Two activities that work well when teaching about Canada are the Travel Brochure of Canada; and the Mini-book of Canada/Region of Canada. These two activities are interdisciplinary in their approach and will definitely interest your students.

Travel Brochure of Canada

The goal of this activity is to create a brochure or travel magazine about Canada with photos, collages, drawings, paintings, symbols, and other resources provided by the teacher. The main purpose of this piece is to entice people to come to Canada to visit or to live.

Students would gather information about Canada using encyclopedias, magazines, newspaper clippings, books, and electronic resources. The travel guide/brochure can include such items as: history, geography, maps, pictures, information about laws, schools, things people can do, job opportunities, environment, entertainment and other cultural activities. Students can do this as an individual project or as a group activity. This activity helps students to learn more about Canada and helps them to develop marketing skills, learn more about the power of persuasion, and give them the opportunity to promote their ideas and thoughts.

Note: Resources and materials for this and other similar projects can be either downloaded from the Internet or obtained from local colleges, consulates, embassies, and Canadian Studies centers.

Mini-Book Of Canada Activity

This activity can be a week long unit or a three week unit, the sky is the limit. This activity really works well with groups of three or four. Dividing your students into groups with varying degrees of ability and interests can be a challenging and rewarding experience. The goal is to have students use their creativity to design a mini-book, complete with cover jacket, that is original, attractive in appearance, and shows organization in thought, and a document that can be used by others to learn.

Students begin by creating an introduction to the mini-book, followed by a dedication, table of contents, and then content, and conclusion. Possible chapters might include, but are not limited to geography, history, native peoples, immigration, politics, culture, sports, entertainment, business, arts, education, science, and current affairs.

Each chapter can be 1-3 pages or more in length. You may choose to assign topics/chapters to specific students or allow them to choose which ones they will research and write. These projects truly cross all the disciplines and therefore most groups when chosen by the teacher tend to really excel and create fine pieces of work. Each student really can develop their abilities to organize, create, visualize, conceptualize, devise, and write while enjoying the activity. Note: these mini-books on Canada can also be adapted to be mini-books on the provinces and territories of Canada.

CONCLUSION

As we can plainly see, there is an abundance of Canada-oriented educational media available, most of it at a nominal cost.

Resources as varied as daily newspapers, photographs of Canadian wildlife, historical records and recreations, maps, interviews and others too numerous to mention, are readily available as moving, talking, clickable, downloadable, colorful, attention-getting, up-to-date, educational materials that will hold the interest of your students. One "bonus" feature of using technology to teach Canada, is that it helps students develop research skills that will easily transfer to other classes, skills which are necessary to function in the wired society in which our students will one day find themselves.

About the Authors

Editors

William W. Joyce is director of the Canadian Studies Centre at Michigan State University. His publications include *Canada in the Classroom*, textbooks on Canada for middle school students, professional books in social studies education, and a chapter in the *Handbook of Research in Social Studies Teaching and Learning*. A founder of the new NCSS Special Interest Group, Teaching Canada, Joyce's research interests include the Quebec secession movement and the treatment of Canada in the U.S. press.

Richard Beach is a Distinguished Service Professor of the State University of New York (SUNY). He has directed SUNY Plattsburgh's Center for the Study of Canada for more than 20 years. Beach is the author, editor and managing editor of many books, atlases, articles, reports and reviews, and was the recipient of the Donner Medal in Canadian Studies in 1995. He served for 10 years on the executive committee of the Association for Canadian Studies in the U.S., and from 1985-87 as elected President. He currently is President of the American Council for Quebec Studies.

Contributors

Janet Alleman is a professor of teacher education and school administration at Michigan State University. A contributor to *Canada in the Classroom*, which preceded this publication, she is actively engaged in outreach activities of the MSU Canadian Studies Centre and in the NCSS Special Interest Group, Teaching Canada, and the NCSS Task Force for Advanced Teacher Certification. Her most recent publications include *Powerful Social Studies Teaching and Learning* (with Jere Brophy) and a chapter in the *Handbook of Classroom Assessment: Learning Achievement and Adjustment.*

Donald K. Alper is professor of political science and director of the Center for Canadian-American Studies at Western Washington University in Bellingham. For nearly 20 years he has been actively involved in developing educational materials on Canada for American teachers. During this time he has conducted teacher workshops in California, Oregon and Washington state. He has authored articles, chapters and papers on Canadian politics and Canada-U.S. issues. Alper's current research focuses on transboundary issues involving the Pacific Northwest states and Western Canada.

Michael S. Bittner is pursuing a doctorate in education at the University of Washington. He has served as Associate Director, Canadian Studies Center, University of Washington, and as Chair of the National Consortium for Teaching Canada and President of the Canada-America Society. He is also the former editor of *Canadian Accents/Accents/Les Accents Canadiens* and *News Scholars - New Visions in Canadian Studies.*

Michael Broadway is Professor and Head of the Geography department at Northern Michigan University, Marquette, Michigan. He has taught courses on the geography of Canada at the State University of New York at Geneseo and Plattsburgh. He has led geography field trips to all of Canada's provinces. Broadway's research has focused on changes in the social and economic composition of Canadian inner cities and rural industrialization in Alberta. His work has been published in *The Canadian Geographer, The Canadian Journal of Urban Research, Prairie Forum,* and *The American Review of Canadian Studies.*

Anthony Cicerone is coordinator of the Canadian Studies Program at Bridgewater State College in Bridgewater, Massachusetts. Cicerone's teaching and research interests focus on the Canada-U.S. trade relationship with specific reference to Atlantic Canada and New England. He conducts numerous seminars designed to promote U.S.-Canadian trade and business and advises U.S. businesses with Canadian interests.

Victor Howard served for nearly a quarter century as director of the Canadian Studies Centre at Michigan State University. A co-founder of the Association for Canadian Studies in the United States and a recipient of the Donner Medal for his contributions to Canadian Studies and numerous research grants, he has published extensively in this field. Currently, he is editor of the Canada Series of books for the MSU Press.

Mark J. Kasoff came to Bowling Green State University in 1991 as Director of Canadian Studies and Professor of Economics. His prior position was chair of the economics department at the State University of New York at Potsdam, located close to the Canadian border in upstate New York. From 1968-82, he served on the faculty of Antioch College in Yellow Springs, Ohio. Kasoff's research interests include Canadian direct investment in the U.S., Canada-U.S. trade flows and NAFTA, and comparative business costs between Canada and the U.S.

Jeanne Kissner is Director of International Projects at the Center for the Study of Canada, SUNY-Plattsburgh. She is a founding member of the NCTC and has been involved in outreach work of the Center for 20 years. Dr. Kissner has been awarded the Medal of the *Ordre des Francophones en Amérique*, the *Prix du Québec*, and the Donner Medal in Canadian Studies.

William Metcalfe, born in Toronto, directed the Canadian Studies Program at the University of Vermont for over a decade. During his thirty-five years at this university he chaired the History and Music Departments. A founding member of the Association for Canadian Studies in the United States, he served for sixteen years as Editor of the *American Review of Canadian Studies* and in 1993 received the Donner Medal for his contributions to Canadian Studies.

John Preston is outreach coordinator of Canadian Studies at the University of Vermont and serves as chair of the National Consortium for Teaching Canada. A former elementary and high school teacher, he has designed world wide web sites for educators and gives presentations on bringing technology to the classroom.

Marion Salinger formerly served as Coordinator for International Studies at Duke University. She has led workshops in both Canada and the United States. Her publications include *The International Traveler: A Teacher's Guide*; *The Year of the Maple Leaf: A Minitext for Teaching Canada*; and (with Donald C. Wilson) *The Portrayal of Canada in American Textbooks*.

George Sherman is a secondary social studies teacher and Associate for School Outreach at the Center for the Study of Canada, SUNY Plattsburgh, where he has been co-editor of the semi-annual magazine, *Teaching Canada*, for 15 years. He is the author of *The Canada Connection in American History*; *Teaching About the Canadian Parliamentary System*; *The Canadian Parliamentary Video* and the student textbook, *O Canada, its Geography, History, and the People Who Call it Home*.

Matthew Smith is the Director of the Canadian Film Distribution Center, a national nonprofit education film and video service, at the State University of New York at Plattsburgh, and is Webmaster for the Canadian Studies in the U.S. World Wide Web site. Mr. Smith teaches Canadian Cinema at SUNY Plattsburgh and is a candidate for the Ph.D. in Communication in the joint doctoral program at Concordia University, Université de Montréal and Université du Québec à Montréal, specializing in the social and cultural aspects of technology.

Matthew Sparke is an assistant professor of Geography and International Studies at the University of Washington. He has published articles on topics relating to gender, capitalism, and post-coloniality. His forthcoming book *Negotiating Nation-States: North American Geographies of Culture and Capitalism* concerns the way in which economic and cultural processes have come together in the contemporary renegotiation of Canadian and US national identities. His new research centers on the reconfiguration of borders in transnational regions.

Gail Yvon has served as Outreach Coordinator for the University of Maine Canadian-American Center since 1987. She has often answered the question, "I teach *X* grade. Can you help me find good material on Canada?" Gail entered Canadian Studies after earning her M.Ed. from the University of Maine in 1983. She has compiled and literally "carried" resources to teachers and librarians at all levels and has directed numerous workshops for teachers. This chapter fulfills Gail's wish to offer her best suggestions in one significant publication.

Index

Y

Z